KATHLEEN KENNEDY

Books by Lynne McTaggart

THE BABY BROKERS

KATHLEEN KENNEDY

Kathleen Kennedy

Her Life and Times

by LYNNE McTAGGART

THE DIAL PRESS
Doubleday & Company, Inc., Garden City, New York
1983

Library of Congress Cataloging in Publication Data

McTaggart, Lynne.
  Kathleen Kennedy, her life and times.

  1. Kennedy, Kathleen, d. 1948.   2. Presidents—United States—Brothers
and sisters—Biography.   3. Kennedy family.   I. Title.
E843.K45M37   1983   973.922′092′4 [B]
ISBN 0-385-27415-7
Library of Congress Catalog Card Number 83-1979

For Jack

ACKNOWLEDGMENTS

This book was the brainchild of Juris Jurjevics, the former editor-in-chief of The Dial Press. While editing a biography of Jack Kennedy, Juris realized what no one else had in almost forty years—that Kathleen Kennedy's life and death was a good story.

I was the lucky writer asked to dig up that story.

Because Kathleen has been a closed subject in the Kennedy family and the little that has been written about her is inaccurate, the information in *Kathleen Kennedy: Her Life and Times* came from original source material, primarily personal interviews. I spoke with virtually all the close friends and relatives of the principal characters in this book. Most of Kathleen's aristocratic British friends—including her in-laws—were extremely forthcoming and candid. Many of those I interviewed gave hours of their time, sharing memories, diaries, letters, scrapbooks, and photograph albums with me. In fact, a good number of the photographs that appear inside were taken from private collections. All the controversial material concerning Kathleen's marriage, her involvements with men, and her relations with her family is based on numerous exhaustive interviews with her in-laws and closest friends. Two extraordinarily detailed accident reports and the recollections of British and French eyewitnesses made it possible to reconstruct her final airplane trip. Dinah Bridge, Patsy Carter, Lady Elizabeth Cavendish, Jane Compton, the Duke of Devonshire, Countess Fitzwilliam, Baron Harlech, Charlotte Harris, Lady Angela Laycock, and Harry Sporborg were among those who supplied information about Kathleen's affair with Fitzwilliam and her subsequent estrangement from her family.

I wish to thank the following people for contributing their recollections and documents: Baron Adeane, Mother Allpress, Elizabeth Dunn Anderson, Margaret, Duchess of Argyll ("the Whigham"), Patter Ashcraft, the Hon. Chiquita Astor, the Hon. John Jacob Astor, Philippa, Viscountess Astor, Baron and Lady Astor of Hever, Joan Auten, the Hon. Sarah Baring, Alice Bastien, Sister Dorothy Bell, Katharine "Tatty" Spaatz Bell, Mother Binney, the Countess of Birkenhead, Thomas Bilodeau, Dolly Bostwick, Baron Brabourne, Christopher and Dinah Bridge, Godfrey Broadhead, Lady Elizabeth Cavendish, Patsy White Carter, Blair Clark, Howard Clark, Nancy Tenney Coleman, Jane Compton, Henri Coste, Major James Cowley, Eleanor Hoguet DeGive, the Dowager Duchess of Devonshire, the Duke of Devonshire, Luella Hennessy Donovan, William Douglas-Home, the Earl of Dudley, Father Duffy, Thomas Egerton, Mary Ewing, Major Frank Farnhill, Paul "Red" Fay, the Countess of Feversham, Dennis Fisher, the Countess Fitzwilliam, Lady Virginia Ford, Alastair Forbes, Lady Edith Foxwell, Sir Hugh Fraser, Charles Garabedian, Lady Elizabeth Glendevon, Peter Grace, Kay Halle, Baron Harlech, Charlotte McDonnell Harris, William Randolph Hearst, Jr., Nancy Hoguet Helmer, Peter Hoguet, Lord and Lady Holderness, Henry James, Jr., Anne McDonnell Johnson, the Hon. Janet Kidd, Thomas Killefer, Harvey Klemmer, Lady Angela Laycock, Patricia Laycock, Lady Lloyd, Laurie Macdonald, Sir Fitzroy and the Hon. Veronica Maclean, Laura, Duchess of Marlborough, Edward McLaughlin, Doreen Butler Millbank, Bishop Paul Moore, Jack Munson, Cam and Reddie Newberry, Sancy and Larry Newman, Murrough O'Brien, Tony and Sue Pelly, Paul Petit, Jack Pierrepont, Major Jack Pringle, Eben Pyne, James Reed, Jewel Reed, Admiral James Reedy, Ted Reardon, Derek Richardson, Michael Richey, George "Barney" Ross, James Rousmaniere, the Duke of Rutland,

Stewart Scheftel, Josephine Sippy Schwaebe, Joe Simpson, Ilona Solymossy, Charles Spalding, Harry Sporborg, the Hon. Richard Stanley, Charles Sweeny, Robert Sweeny, Sir Tatton Sykes, Jack Thursby, Lady Anne Tree, Father Tracy, Frank Waldrop, Olive Cawley Watson, Page Huidekoper Wilson, and John B. White.

Eunice Shriver generously consented to a long interview and kindly allowed me to meet that still formidable matriarch, Rose Kennedy. Although the Kennedy family cooperated with me, this is not an authorized biography.

Thanks are due to the following for assisting me in background and period research: Rudolf Clemen, Jr., of the American Red Cross National Headquarters; Paul Sargeant of the London Imperial War Museum; Dave Powers, Alan Goodrich, William Johnson, and the rest of the staff of the John F. Kennedy Library; the library staff of the London *Daily Telegraph;* employees of Chatsworth and Wentworth Woodhouse; Chris Garrett of *The Tatler;* Suzanne Van Langenburg of *Harper's* and *Queen;* Sergeant-Major Clive Candlin of the Coldstream Guards; the library of the *Boston Herald;* and Charles Kidd of Debrett's, who introduced me to what became my bible on this project, *Debrett's Peerage.*

I am deeply grateful to Laura Vaughan for so ably performing crucial eleventh-hour research, and to Adam Gavzer and Stephen Pushkin for photographing old photographs in private albums and magazines. Louise Kramer of Channel 13 kindly allowed me to view the Granada television dramatization of Evelyn Waugh's *Brideshead Revisited,* and the BBC set up a special screening of producer Anne Head's film of Antonia White's *Frost in May.* I am indebted to Julien Antoine, an official in Privas, who unearthed an invaluable French accident report, and to Lindy Shaw, Brigitte Sassot, Patrice Benefice, Anne Schombourger, Cathy Harrison and Ib and Sylvie Bellew for their help with translation.

Hank Searls and Herbert Parmet, two authors of Kennedy books, shared with me their insights on Kennedy family members. Lynne and Leonard Krumer generously recounted their own memories of wartime.

I owe a special thanks to Norman Lonsdale, Arthur Gavshon, George Jatania, Nilina Parker, and Robin Harris, all of whom, in some way, helped me to get started.

Hundreds of books in England and America contributed background information on the Kennedys, the forties, and the war, but I consulted most frequently with the following: *Times to Remember* by Rose Kennedy (Garden City: Doubleday & Co., Inc., 1974); *The Founding Father: The Story of Joseph P. Kennedy* by Richard J. Whalen (New York: New American Library, 1964); *The Lost Prince: Young Joe, the Forgotten Kennedy* by Hank Searls (Cleveland: The World Publishing Company, 1969); *Aphrodite: Desperate Mission* by Jack Olsen (New York: G.P. Putnam's Sons, 1970); *The Search for J.F.K.* by Joan and Clay Blair, Jr. (New York: Berkley Publishing Corporation, 1976); *Jack: The Struggles of John F. Kennedy* by Herbert S. Parmet (New York: The Dial Press, 1980); *The House: A Portrait of Chatsworth* by the Duchess of Devonshire (London: Macmillan, 1982); and *Bombers and Mash* by Raynes Minns (London: Virago Ltd., 1980).

For all sorts of editorial assistance I'm grateful to Mindy Werner, Allen Peacock, and Caroline Shookhoff. As always Gerry Toner offered wise legal counsel. Cary Ryan did the most magnificent copy-editing job I've ever had and kindly offered critical last-minute assistance. Marianne Velmans and the staff of Doubleday's London office helped to expedite our trans-Atlantic communications.

This book owes an enormous debt to the awesome talents and dedication of my editor at The Dial Press, Joyce Johnson.

Bernie Gavzer, Dee Palmer, Gail Kramer, and Cynthia Harrison gave me hours of sympathetic listening when I most needed it.

My dear agent and daily booster, Gloria Safier, was the best friend anyone could ever have.

Finally I must thank Jack Straw, for living through every word of this book and for helping me to understand why Kathleen loved the British.

"There was nothing extraordinary about her. She was like all the rest of us back then, who thought of nothing—nothing but ourselves."

Nancy Tenney Coleman

KATHLEEN KENNEDY

Prologue

The departure of his family to England was everything that Joseph P. Kennedy, the newly appointed ambassador to the Court of St. James's, could have wished for. On March 9, 1938, their embarkation to join him was covered as front-page news.

Aboard the *Washington* reporters and photographers mobbed Mrs. Kennedy and the children. Pathé News cameras rolled while they each said a few awkward words into a cluster of microphones. As the ship pulled out of the dock Teddy, a chubby six-year-old in short pants and knee socks, slipped off his little camel wool cap and waved it to the crowd.

The ambassador was the first Irish Catholic to be sent to the English court, and the family had not yet become accustomed to being in the limelight. Newspapers now sought out every last detail about the nine Kennedy children, all of whom had inherited their father's direct stare and flashing smile. The ambassador was secretly delighted that his children were upstaging him. He had far-reaching ambitions for them, and the publicity, like the appointment itself, fit into his master plan.

Even in the midst of all the excitement eighteen-year-old Kathleen Kennedy wasn't sure that she wanted to leave America. She looked forward to mingling with English aristocrats and dining with important heads of state, but there was so much that she was leaving behind. She and her steady boyfriend would be separated for a year or more, and she would miss all the debutante balls of her friends. Until very recently she had attended a convent school so strict she had not been let out a single night. But now that she had graduated, her parents were finally allowing her to go on dates. Before her father's appointment she had looked forward to glamorous nights at the Stork Club or the Manhattan Room of the Hotel Pennsylvania. Mr. Kennedy's ambassadorship was ruining the best year of her life.

Almost from the moment she arrived in England, all Kathleen's misgivings vanished. "Kick," as she was called, took immediately to British ways and the extravagance of aristocratic life. Before long she seemed more at home with the British upper class than with her own clannish family. In 1938 Kathleen Kennedy dazzled English society as no American has before or since. During the bleak days of 1943, when she returned to Britain, one young aristocrat called her "the best thing that America ever sent us."

As time went on Kathleen's one perfect season in England before the war became more and more difficult to hold on to. She turned twenty-one the year that Japan bombed Pearl Harbor; she died three years after America bombed Hiroshima. Once the war began, it seemed to her that nothing in her life before 1941 had ever really occurred. That might have been why Kathleen went back to London, hoping to find everything as it had been before.

One

As soon as he heard that Robert Worth Bingham, the incumbent occupant of the post, was ill and going to resign, Joseph Kennedy set his sights on becoming ambassador to Britain. All through the fall of 1937 he courted Jimmy Roosevelt, President Franklin D. Roosevelt's son, dropping hints about the appointment.

When Jimmy finally relayed the request to his father, Roosevelt laughed so hard he almost tipped over his wheelchair. The thought of redheaded, profane, Irish-Catholic Joe Kennedy in a position traditionally reserved for dignitaries from old moneyed Episcopalian families was a great joke, the greatest joke in the world.

It was one joke, however, that the President took seriously. Roosevelt had a political debt to pay off. During his 1932 and 1936 campaigns Joe Kennedy had worked for him tirelessly and contributed huge donations. Although FDR had appointed Kennedy in 1934 as the first chairman of the Securities and Exchange Commission and then, in 1936, as chairman of the Maritime Commission, the Irishman was evidently after bigger stakes. He had been bitterly disappointed when Roosevelt had not given him a Cabinet position as secretary of the Treasury and had made it known that he would not accept the alternative appointment he was offered—secretary of Commerce. But FDR had considered Kennedy too independent-minded to head the Treasury, believing that he would work at cross purposes with the administration's New Deal policies.

Apart from his ethnic background Kennedy had much to recommend him for the ambassadorship. He was refreshingly blunt. His tough negotiating abilities could be put to good use in trade agreements. He was also fabulously wealthy, an important attribute, since the meager ambassadorial salary could not begin to cover the costs of entertaining on the lavish scale to which British dignitaries were accustomed. But Roosevelt had another, less lofty reason for sending Kennedy to England. Although he had worked very hard in the last election, he was often publicly critical of the President. At times FDR even considered Kennedy "dangerous" and thought it might be politically wise to get him out of Washington.

He decided to give Kennedy the appointment, but not without making him grovel for it. One day in the late fall of 1937 he invited Kennedy into the Oval Room. He greeted him, then said with a straight face, "Joe, would you mind taking your pants down?"

After Kennedy sheepishly complied, Roosevelt surveyed his bare knees in mock alarm. "Joe, just look at your legs!" he exclaimed. "You are just about the most bowlegged man I have ever seen." He reminded Kennedy that the ambassador to the Court of St. James's would have to go through a presentation ceremony in which he wore knee breeches and silk stockings. "Can you imagine how you'll look?" he asked. "When photos of our new ambassador appear all over the world, we'll be a laughingstock."

Kennedy, who had taken every word seriously, begged to be allowed a chance to get special exemption from the British government on dress protocol. Several days later he produced a letter, which he had obtained through the British embassy, granting him special permission to substitute a cutaway coat and striped pants for the knee breeches in court appearances. Roosevelt had pretended to vacillate a little. In early December, Kennedy finally received word that he had gotten the job.

The ambassadorship would put the final stamp of respectability on the son of an Irish-Catholic saloonkeeper who had grown up in Boston. Although Joe Kennedy's father had been unusually affluent and influential in local ward politics, Kennedy had discovered as a youth that Irish Catholics had virtually no chance of penetrating the Yankee-dominated bastions of social and political power in Boston. Joe Kennedy had chafed more than most boys at his second-class citizenship, even though Patrick Kennedy, his father, had tried to set young Joe apart from the sons of his Irish-Catholic neighbors by sending him to Boston Latin and Harvard, both traditionally the exclusive domains of the sons of prominent Protestant Back Bay families. As he grew up Kennedy had single-mindedly pursued social advancement among his WASP counterparts far more than academic achievement. Tirelessly he cultivated his most popular and influential classmates at Harvard and made unsuccessful bids for the "best" clubs.

At twenty-five he had become a bank president, but his social status in Boston did not really improve until he married the mayor's daughter, the catch of the town for an Irish Catholic with ambition. Rose Fitzgerald, voted the prettiest girl at Dorchester High School, had succumbed to Kennedy's persuasive charms over the objections of her father, John F. "Honey Fitz" Fitzgerald, who didn't think Kennedy good enough for her.

After their marriage Kennedy had embarked upon a series of staggering financial conquests. Before becoming a banker his experience in managing a brokerage house had given him an education in the essentials of stock-market manipulation. In the midst of the booming twenties he struck out on his own as a lone wolf operator in a highly speculative market. In rapid succession he invested in a shipyard, bought a chain of movie theaters, speculated in real estate, and took over a movie company that cranked out B westerns and soap operas. He formed a company, Gloria Productions, which produced the first talkie for the "Queen of Hollywood," Gloria Swanson. In equally rapid succession Rose Kennedy produced eight children, most of whom were born within a year or two of each other.

During the late twenties Kennedy became romantically involved with Swanson, maintaining her in a separate "hideaway" on Rodeo Drive in Beverly Hills. Their romance lasted for several years, until an innocent query of Swanson's led to her discovery that Kennedy's lavish presents and even the hideaway itself had been charged to her personal account. By that time, however, Kennedy had amassed some five million dollars from Hollywood and was ready to move on. In 1929 he survived the stock-market crash by pulling out his money early, then short-selling the deflated stocks. The end of his affair with Swanson apparently improved his relations with his wife for the time being. In 1932, after a four-year gap, he and Rose had their ninth baby.

Kennedy had been obsessed with accumulating wealth, but his real objective was a more elusive prize—social position and prestige for himself and his children. In 1925 he had set up a trust fund for each one of them that would eventually swell to ten million dollars apiece by the mid-1940s. The funds were set up to be released in stages to the children after specific birthdays. But for all his reputation as the "marvel of the Boston financial world," Kennedy's social standing with the Boston brahmin society did not improve enough to suit him. He realized that if he stayed in Boston, he would always be thought of as Honey Fitz's son-in-law. His daughters still couldn't hope to make their debuts in proper Boston society. In the mid-twenties, after he had been blackballed from a country club on the South Shore, where the family summered, Kennedy finally decided he had had enough. He packed up his growing family in a privately rented train and headed for New York.

After a year in Riverdale the family moved into a Georgian mansion on several acres of land in Bronxville, a wealthy community within easy commuting distance of New York. But while New York society was far more open than Boston society, even the moneyed New York Irish families viewed Kennedy disdainfully as a Wall Street operator and double-dealer who had made his fortune through profiteering and exploitation.

By the early thirties, when Roosevelt announced his candidacy, Kennedy had spent twenty years accumulating all the money he and his nine children would ever need. He didn't necessarily agree with much of Roosevelt's platform, but he recognized the candidate as an obvious winner to whose rising star it would be advantageous to attach himself. Once again a hunch of his proved correct: his alliance with Roosevelt launched him as a popular political figure in his own right. Rewarded for his backing of the President by government appointments, Kennedy won a reputation as a "two-fisted, hard-hitting executive" and growing support among the Catholic and the financial communities. It was known that FDR admired Kennedy's financial savvy, and Wall Street was grateful for what was considered to be Kennedy's tempering influence on the expansive President.

Kennedy had not left his growing reputation in governmental circles to chance. He demonstrated a remarkable knack for cultivating influential members of the Washington press corps. Reporters and editors received regular invitations to Marwood, Kennedy's rented mansion in the capital, built by a playboy for his chorus-girl wife and outfitted with gold-plated bathroom fixtures and a one-hundred-seat basement movie theater. When Kennedy was appointed SEC chairman, several of his friends at *The New York Times* had prevailed upon the influential *Times* correspondent Arthur Krock to write a glowing introductory column about him. Krock continued to make almost embarrassingly laudatory mention of Kennedy's every move.

The ambassadorship promised to provide Kennedy with a further boost to his image. Germany had recently reoccupied the Rhineland, and the new German leader, Adolf Hitler, had been making increasingly vociferous demands about the need to incorporate all peoples of German origin into the Fatherland. The treaties of the Great War of some twenty years earlier were collapsing, and there were those in Britain who were looking anxiously to America in anticipation of another crisis. With the political situation in Europe so troubled, the United States ambassador to England would be the most important American abroad.

This prospective role in shaping world events was less tantalizing to Kennedy, however, than the honor and prestige that went along with the job. British society was not only the most exclusive in the world but the one that was most off limits to an Irish Catholic. Like most of his fellow Irish Americans, Kennedy hated the British for their centuries-old domination of the mother country. As ambassador he would be thrust into that closed circle. The idea of having the English upper crust bowing and scraping to him was irresistible.

As official hostess of the American embassy Mrs. Kennedy, who had pushed her husband to request the ambassadorship, would have an important position in her own right. Rose Kennedy had had some previous experience at glad-handing, as Honey Fitz's illustrious daughter. On many occasions she had accompanied the unflaggingly energetic, spirited "John F." to public functions, often as a surrogate for her reticent mother. These skills, which had lain dormant for all the years that she had been preoccupied with the raising of her large family, could now be put to use. Mrs. Kennedy also realized the social implications of her position. She may have been written up in society columns as the mayor's daughter, but only in those reserved for Irish Catholics. Like her husband she pursued social acceptance with the fervor of someone mounting a personal crusade. "Tell me," she once said, turning to a twenty-year-old college friend of one of her sons from a prominent Massachusetts family, "when do you think the nice families of Boston are going to accept us?"

Kathleen was the fourth Kennedy child after Joe Jr., Jack, and Rosemary. Her middle name was Agnes, after her mother's younger sister. Nobody but Mrs. Kennedy, however, called Kathleen anything but Kick, although everybody had forgotten where the nickname came from. It could have started as a mispronunciation of "Kathleen" and then turned into "Kick" to differentiate her from Kico, or Kathryn Convoy, the Kennedys' Irish nurse. However Kathleen got her nickname, it seemed to suit her spunky, vivacious personality. She was brighter and quicker than any of the other children except her brother Jack. Jack had a keenly inquiring mind (he read everything he could get his hands on), but Kathleen was a better all-around student because she applied herself to her studies and never needed tutoring, as the other girls did. She favored Jack with her reddish-brown hair and blue-gray eyes and was small and dainty, like her mother. Friends of the Kennedys thought that the boys rather than the girls had been blessed with the refined good looks of the family. But Kick was so ebullient and sharp that no one ever thought of her as anything other than very pretty.

She had the status in the family of eldest daughter, since her older sister, Rosemary, was brain-damaged. At twenty Rose, as she was called, after her mother, had the mental capacity of a fourth-grader. Mrs. Kennedy, who was an extraordinarily devout Roman Catholic, believed Rosemary had been sent to her by God. Nevertheless, she and Mr. Kennedy were ashamed of their daughter's handicap and worried that it had been genetic, although it was probably the result of a bad delivery. They had had Rosemary examined by countless specialists and teachers, always hopeful that someone would provide a "cure." Taking a cue from the family, Kathleen's friends never spoke of Rosemary as "retarded" but merely as a little "different" or a little "funny" or, at worst, a little "silly."

Perhaps because of Rosemary's handicap Jack and Kick, the two children born before and after her, were always very close despite their three-year age difference. Jack had been a sickly child, born with an unstable back and prone to illnesses of every description, including scarlet fever, asthma, and bronchitis. He had grown up frail and introverted, often overpowered by his competitive older brother.

Dark-haired with a captivating smile, Joe Jr. was strong, healthy, and his father's favorite. Two years older than Jack, Joe took his position as eldest seriously. During Mr. Kennedy's frequent absences in Hollywood and Washington, Joe played surrogate father. At thirteen-year-old Joe's request the Kennedys had allowed him to be godparent to his youngest sister, Jean, born in

1928. In school he had shown himself to be a natural leader, a good athlete, and a diligent scholar, although academic study did not come easily to him.

Joe bullied his fragile younger brother. It was with Jack that his bad temper usually flared up. With particular ferocity Joe slammed footballs into Jack during touch football games on the two-acre bluff overlooking the water in front of the sprawling, green-shuttered, white clapboard house in HyannisPort that Mr. Kennedy had bought as a summer place after the family had moved to Bronxville. The competition continued through their years at Choate prep school and Harvard. Frequently compared by teachers to his model older brother, Jack made a poor showing at school and stopped trying to compete. By 1937, during his second year at Harvard, he became known as the likable, irreverent, unpurposeful Kennedy. The only area where Jack was able to best his brother was with the opposite sex, who found his easygoing nature, good looks, and offbeat sense of humor enormously attractive. Joe developed a habit of taking out Jack's girls, and no one was apparently off limits—not even Olive Cawley, a lovely seventeen-year-old from a good Protestant family whom Jack had dated steadily for several years. One evening, when Jack and another attractive date were at a New York club, Joe had him paged and left with the girl while Jack was busy trying to locate his elusive caller.

Over the years, as his competition with his brother intensified, Jack drew even closer to Kick. They had the same quick, self-deprecating humor (Joe Jr.'s was often biting and sarcastic), the same free-spiritedness and unharnessed energy. In their furious banter with each other they often reminded friends of Rosalind Russell and Cary Grant in *His Girl Friday*.

Kathleen and her brother Jack turned up together at all the little activities on the Cape—the barn dances in Osterville given by neighbors like Bunty Holbrook, the Saturday matinees at the Idle Hours movie theater in HyannisPort. After Jack got his license, the two would drive everywhere in his car. All the Kennedys were terrible drivers, but Jack burned rubber even pulling out of the Kennedy driveway.

At Mrs. Kennedy's insistence Rosemary was included in most social activities so that she would appear to be normal to outsiders. When she accompanied her brothers and sisters to dances at the Wianno Yacht Club, Mrs. Kennedy and the children's governess, Alice Cahill, would stand outside peering in the window to see if she was having a good time. When Rosemary was discovered at one dance sitting forlornly by herself, Mrs. Kennedy insisted that it was the boys' responsibility to keep their sister dancing, despite their protests that this cut into their own social life. Finally Alice Cahill came up with a scheme to invite Rosemary out for little trips or dream up special projects for her on those evenings when the others planned to go to the club.

Although very popular, Jack was shy and often looked to Kathleen to break the ice at parties. He deferred to his kid sister in many matters, particularly regarding girls. At sixteen, when Jack had first begun dating Olive Cawley, he had impressed upon her the importance of making a good impression on Kick.

Wherever she went, Kathleen made friends with the greatest ease. Even the constant uprooting of the family did not faze her, as it did her brothers and sisters, who were much more reluctant to move outside the close-knit family circle. The Kennedys moved three times a year—to Palm Beach, where they spent their Christmas and Easter holidays in the Spanish-style villa Mr. Kennedy had purchased; to HyannisPort for the summer; to Bronxville when school was in session.

When the Kennedys had first come to HyannisPort in 1929, Kathleen had promptly introduced herself to Nancy Tenney, another nine-year-old who lived in a house next door with a wrought-iron whale on the chimney. "Ken" and "Ten," as they called each other, soon became inseparable, even though the Tenneys, an old Boston banking family, regarded the Kennedys as shanty Irish. Another friend of Kathleen's was Mary Frances "Sancy" Falvey, the small blond daughter of the first Catholic family to settle in HyannisPort. Sancy lived in the house behind Kick's. On rainy days the three little girls played in the small room Sancy had to herself on the top of the Falvey garage. They worshiped movie stars and hung up photos of all their current favorites—Constance Bennett, Marlene Dietrich, and Gloria Swanson. There was a movie theater in the Kennedys' basement, and on many evenings the little girls got to see films there that had not yet been released. They knew Kathleen's father worked in Hollywood and had something to do with Gloria Swanson because one year Kathleen and the other Kennedy children received Christmas presents from her.

Nancy and Sancy had never met a family like the Kennedys. Mr. Kennedy was an awesome, terrifying figure. He would sit in his "bullpen," the terrace outside his second-floor bedroom, all day long and bark out deals. Even when they were swimming or sailing, they could often hear his voice carrying across the water. Visitors to the Kennedy house were astounded when he was called to the telephone to speak with a Hollywood mogul or the White House.

Everybody, particularly the Kennedy children themselves, feared his disapproval. Since Mr. Kennedy hated idleness, all the Kennedy children rushed into activity whenever he returned from a business trip. If he discovered the children lounging around or relaxing, he would shoo them off their seats with the command "Go do something."

Kathleen and her brothers and sisters lived by an exacting routine. Each day at exactly ten minutes to one Mr. and Mrs. Kennedy would march down the path to the beach from their house, take a short swim in the sound, dry off promptly, and head back inside. Immediately afterward lunch would be served, and the children were supposed to drop whatever they were doing and scramble to the table five minutes beforehand. Anyone late for the table would miss the first course. In the evening, after Mr. Kennedy retired, if the children were making too much noise downstairs, they would hear a single shoe drop with a terrific thud on the floor above. Instantly they would fall into a terrified silence. Nobody was more frightening than Mr. Kennedy when he was angry. A certain freezing stare from his steel-blue eyes over his wire-rim glasses was enough to make a child cower.

The adult members of the HyannisPort community soon realized they were not particularly welcome at the Kennedys'. The

Kennedys stocked no liquor and seldom invited neighbors in but instead centered their lives around their children. Mealtimes there reminded Kick's friends of school classroom sessions. Down would come the map kept rolled up on the dining-room wall. Mr. Kennedy would select a topic of conversation—current affairs, usually—and, after discussing it for most of the meal, grill Joe and Jack on their viewpoints. He would proceed to the other children, one by one. Invariably Joe Jr. agreed with his father. Many times Eunice, born a year after Kathleen, and Patricia, the fourth daughter, merely listened in, but Kick herself was often as vociferous and opinionated as her older brothers. When juvenile visitors were present at the evening meal, Mr. Kennedy made no attempt to disguise the fact that he was exclusively concerned with his own children. Their young guests were not often asked to participate in the discussion.

It was no secret that Mr. Kennedy had high hopes for his sons, particularly Joe Jr. As the firstborn, Joe bore all the weight of his father's political ambition. Even as a teenager he spoke with confident certainty of his plan to be the first Catholic President of the United States. Mrs. Kennedy had wanted the boys to attend Catholic schools and colleges, but Mr. Kennedy overruled her. To compete in the political world, his boys needed a superior education and the company of boys from prominent families. He insisted that they attend private prep schools and go on to his own alma mater, Harvard.

Although he concentrated his efforts on the boys, he expected each child to excel in some area. All his children were born to win. Joe would be the politician; Jack, perhaps a writer or college professor; and his third son, Bobby—who was as determined and ruthless as himself—the lawyer. Whenever he was away for long stretches on his business dealings, he corresponded regularly with his offspring and kept close watch on their academic progress. Even Rosemary received letters exhorting her to keep her weight down. Mr. Kennedy had no tolerance for tears and excuses. In letters home Jack regularly berated himself for his mediocre school performance.

The Kennedy girls did not receive the same educational opportunities as their brothers. As Mr. Kennedy took charge of the boys' education, so Mrs. Kennedy took charge of the girls'. She sent Kick and her four sisters to Catholic high schools so that they would have a strong religious background. She impressed on all the children the need to include religion as a part of daily life. She also encouraged them to make yearly weekend retreats. By 1938 Joe Jr. had been the head of the Catholic Club at Harvard, thirteen-year-old Bobby was an altar boy, and Eunice was displaying missionary zeal about converting their Protestant friends. "Listen, Ten," she would say to Nancy after she had accompanied the family to St. Francis Xavier, the little white clapboard church on Sea Street in HyannisPort, "don't you think you ought to become a Catholic?"

Mr. Kennedy also encouraged physical fitness and stamina. Every child except Rosemary had a sailboat and participated in sailing races. The Kennedys also had their own tennis court. The point, as Mr. Kennedy repeated emphatically, was not the game or how it was played or even good sportsmanship, but the prize. "We want no losers around here, only winners" was one of his typical admonitions. When the boys raced on Nantucket Sound, Kennedy trailed after them in his own boat, shouting out their mistakes. The dinner table provided a forum for an accounting and assessment of each child's daily activity, and any child who had slacked off had to eat his dinner in the kitchen. As Mr. Kennedy inquired about each child's performance in a daily sport, first or second place received automatic praise and anything less, automatic scorn. After every sailing race in HyannisPort the family station wagon would be dispatched to collect the batch of cups, bowls, plates, and other trophies. Joe Jr. and Eunice were the family's best sailors.

Eunice, who worshiped her older brothers, was the most athletic of the girls despite her poor constitution. Like Jack, she had a bad stomach and little stamina. As a teenager she grew so thin that everybody called her Puny Euny. At sixteen she was so nervous and high-strung that she slept with eye pads and ear plugs. When Kick's girl friends spent the night at the Kennedy house, they were warned not to flush the toilet for fear of waking her up.

Visitors to the Kennedys' were astonished by the fierce competition displayed by the children. "Which of us is the best-looking?" the guests were constantly asked. "Who has the best sense of humor?" Kick, everybody thought, was probably the nicest. She liked to win at tennis, but she was only an average athlete. Virtually all her allowance got spent on swing records and clothes. She liked nothing better than to have Alice Cahill accompany her to Saks Fifth Avenue and help her pick out skirt-and-sweater sets to wear with her saddle shoes.

The Kennedy children adored their father and talked of him constantly. When Mr. Kennedy came home, they crowded around the door in greeting. He was the parent they consulted when they had a problem. He was quick to forgive a failed attempt as long as the child agreed to try again. Little Teddy, the youngest son, actually thought his father's occupation was taking care of all of them.

They acted very differently with Mrs. Kennedy, whom they addressed politely as Mother. Forced to raise the nine children largely by herself in her husband's extended absences, Mrs. Kennedy had developed a host of regimens to cope with her large household. She treated motherhood as an organizational problem. Every Saturday night the children were weighed; every three weeks they had their braces tightened. Mrs. Kennedy was not given to physical demonstrations of affection. Holding babies was delegated to nurses while she tended to other areas of her children's upbringing. Every morning she would be seated at the breakfast table before the first child was awake and would remain there until the last one had staggered down, to make sure each of them ate the proper food and brushed his teeth. At night she would leave notes pinned to their pillows.

In her own quiet way she was a tight disciplinarian. Mrs. Kennedy did not believe that a child had a right to say no. If Kathleen was five minutes late in getting home from a dance in HyannisPort, Mrs. Kennedy would drive out looking for her. When Kick was younger, every night at exactly nine o'clock

Mrs. Kennedy would lean out the window and call "Kaaaathleen!" in that distinctive Boston drawl all the children imitated to summon her home from Nancy Tenney's.

Although she ruled the house in Mr. Kennedy's absences, once he came home, Mrs. Kennedy became invisible. At the dinner table she sat with the younger children and Rosemary, while Kathleen and her brothers gathered around their father, who would lead the lively conversation. When Mrs. Kennedy interrupted to ask one of the older children a question, she would often be ignored.

During Mr. Kennedy's long business trips former Boston Police Commissioner Joseph Timilty, one of her husband's cluster of loyal Irish Catholic companions, would occasionally escort Mrs. Kennedy to dances. Otherwise, she spent much of her time alone. She would read inside a little white prefabricated house on their private beach in HyannisPort or play daily golf games by herself. Mrs. Kennedy had been the youngest graduate in the history of Dorchester High School, but her children's friends, witnessing her withdrawn presence and long silences, often wondered if she weren't a little dull-witted.

With her friends Kathleen often giggled privately about her mother's incessant lessons in absolute trivia. "Now, Kathleen," Mrs. Kennedy had said purposefully after asking her into the house one sunny afternoon at HyannisPort, "I want you to learn how to arrange flowers."

"Arrange flowers?" Kick had asked.

"Yes, it's very important that you know how to arrange flowers," Mrs. Kennedy repeated. "I want you to take these scissors and the basket, and I want you to go out and pick flowers and arrange them." Kathleen had cut the flowers the wrong lengths, then put the basket down somewhere and forgotten about it. The flowers had all dried out and died in the hot sun. She had meant to do it correctly, but like so many things Mrs. Kennedy tried to teach her, it just didn't seem very important at the time.

Mrs. Kennedy recognized Kathleen's independent streak early on and made several attempts to harness it. In 1933, when Kick was thirteen, she decided her daughter was getting altogether too popular with boys. They were on the telephone with her for hours, inviting her to Saturday movie matinees and distracting her from schoolwork. Mrs. Kennedy's solution was to send her daughter to the same kind of convent school she herself had attended as a girl.

The Order of the Sacred Heart had been founded in France in the early nineteenth century and had tiny schools scattered all over Europe and America that accepted only girls from the best families. Sacred Heart girls were taught French literature, Christian doctrine, and needlepoint. Nuns were not sisters, but "Madame" or "Mother"; afternoon tea was *goûter* and holidays *congés*. The convent that Kathleen attended with some sixty other young ladies, ages thirteen through eighteen, was a former governor's mansion, situated on the tip of a ten-acre estate on Long Island Sound in Noroton, Connecticut. Classes were held in bedrooms with high ceilings and oak parquet floors. The opulent surroundings belied the austerity of the environment. More than most orders the ladies of the Sacred Heart glorified self-denial and obedience to authority. Girls attended Mass every morning before breakfast shrouded in black veils. They were taught to make a sweeping curtsy to the floor before the Reverend Mother. Silences were often imposed at meals; mail, even from families, was censored. Girls bathed twice a week and washed the rest of the time in a basin beside the bed. Cold water was considered an aid to purity; in order to wash in the winter the girls often had to break through a layer of ice. To discourage lesbianism, students were never permitted to go "two by two," as the mothers obliquely put it, and close friendships were promptly broken up. Boys could come by for tea on Sunday, but only if one of the mothers was present.

Although she complained to Nancy about the severity of the school, Kathleen adapted to her monastic routine. Many of her girl friends, even her Protestant ones, were attending similar boarding schools; Nancy herself didn't have much more freedom at Miss Pierce's School for Girls in Boston. Kathleen had also been taught that it was a sin for her not to attend parochial school, even though it was apparently all right for her brothers not to.

While at Noroton she met Charlotte McDonnell. Small, blond Charlotte, who resembled Kathleen, was every bit as headstrong. Not only had Charlotte fallen into disgrace for putting safety pins in her underwear, but she had been expelled for several days for carrying around a dirty joke book—the cover showed a man in a fur coat with a woman's legs dangling out of the bottom. Charlotte was one of fourteen children of a wealthy New York Irish-Catholic family. She invited Kick to stay at the McDonnells' enormous summer house in Southampton on weekends during the summer. Kathleen became her best friend, although her father did not approve of Mr. Kennedy and thought his children had terrible manners. The Kennedys always dropped their g's in speech—they were always "runnin', jumpin', goin'" —a quirk that Charlotte found infectious. Mr. McDonnell could tell that Charlotte had been to visit the Kennedys as soon as she opened her mouth.

Charlotte soon became aware of something peculiar about Kick's mother and father—the extent to which they led separate lives. The elder Kennedys stayed at separate hotels when they came to Manhattan—Mrs. Kennedy at the Plaza and Mr. Kennedy at the Waldorf. Mr. Kennedy had a terrible reputation as a womanizer. Even the teenagers Kick knew had heard rumors of his involvement with Gloria Swanson. Occasionally Mr. Kennedy even invited chorus girls from the Ritz to the house in HyannisPort when his wife was out of town. Some of Kathleen's young friends became reluctant to watch movies in the Kennedy basement. Mr. Kennedy would ask them to sit next to him and then proceed to pinch them during the feature. He kissed all female overnight guests on the lips—including girl friends of his sons.

When Charlotte was sixteen, she had once gone to call on Kick at Mr. Kennedy's apartment at the Waldorf. By mistake she had entered his suite. Mr. Kennedy, who was in the shower, called out that she should leave her coat on a chair and go to find Kick and Jack across the hall. Several minutes later he appeared in front of the three of them with a towel wrapped around him. "You'll never guess what happened," he said gleefully to Charlotte. "Will Hayes came in and saw your coat and turned around and walked away, thinking I had a girl in the bedroom."

Jack and Kick laughed along with Mr. Kennedy at the thought of the noted movie censor's embarrassment, but Charlotte was appalled. Her own father was very strict about what he said in front of his Catholic daughters. If he had said anything like that to a friend of hers, Charlotte thought she would have left home.

After Kathleen turned fifteen in 1935, Mrs. Kennedy sent her away for a year to the Holy Child Convent in Neuilly outside Paris to round out her Catholic education. Although the Parisian convent was as strict as Noroton, she was at least able to travel during her breaks. In late winter she had written in her pronounced backhand to Alice Cahill, who often acted as a mediator between the children and Mrs. Kennedy, "Do you think Mother will come over in March or April? Will you please write me exactly what you think 'cause I do not want to ask her to come if it is difficult, but would so much prefer her coming then as in end of June or July. If you're coming for a vacation why don't you take a hop over if Mother doesn't want to come?"

Kick had a date and it looked as though her mother's visit might interfere. At Gstaad over Christmas she had bumped into Derek Richardson, one of Charlotte's Southampton friends, who was studying at Cambridge. Derek had arranged to take her out in Paris several times and had once shown up with a Canadian boy as an escort for Kick's New York friend, Eleanor Hoguet, a Noroton student who was at the convent school with Kick. Some time later he invited her to May Week, the traditional June celebration at Cambridge. Kathleen had declined with the excuse that she didn't think she could get leave. She did not tell him that the Canadian boy had called to invite her and that she had already made plans to go.

When Mrs. Kennedy did not turn up during May Week, Kick headed off to Cambridge with Ellie Hoguet, who had also been asked to go. For four nights the two girls attended balls at the individual colleges. Ellie was amazed by the way the young Englishmen swarmed around Kathleen. At one point she seemed to have forty of them in tow. When she expressed some envy of Kathleen's spectacular popularity, her date tried to comfort her. "Ellie, Kick may get quantity, but you have quality."

In 1936, when Kathleen returned home and she really began dating, her amazing popularity continued. Nobody could quite figure out the key to it. Nancy Tenney often thought that it was Kick's aloofness; she never seemed to lose her head over anyone. Every friend Jack brought home from Harvard without exception fell in love with her.

When Kick returned to Noroton in 1936, she began dating Jack's roommate and best friend at Harvard, Torbert Macdonald, who was captain of the Harvard football team. Torby was absolutely nuts about her and kept her picture on top of his college bureau. But by the time Kathleen graduated in the spring of 1937, she had already moved on to Peter Grace, a twenty-three-year-old Yale graduate who was heir to the Grace Lines shipping fortune. She had met him one night when she accompanied Charlotte to a big dinner at the Grace home held by Peter's younger brother Michael for some friends from Notre Dame. When Peter had joined the guests, he was bowled over by seventeen-year-old Kathleen.

At the end of the meal his brother said to him tauntingly, "There's this guy here, a two-hundred-forty-pound fullback from Notre Dame, and we're going to give him the ball at one end of the hall. I bet you wouldn't dare tackle him." Peter was damned if he was going to show a yellow streak in front of Kathleen and her friends. "Give him the ball," Peter commanded. The fullback took the ball and began tearing down the hall. Peter was a terrific hockey and polo player who excelled at feigning plays. As they charged toward each other the fullback swerved right to avoid him, and Peter tackled him and broke his leg. "Now, if you don't want your friends to get hurt, don't bring them here," Peter coolly remarked to his brother.

When Peter and Kathleen began dating, she never let him forget the circumstances of their first meeting. "Pretty tough guy, aren't you?" she'd say with merciless regularity. Peter soon discovered that despite their six-year age difference, he had to be sharp as a tack to keep up with her.

It was not long before he was thinking of asking her to marry him. Although Mr. Kennedy had a poor reputation and no social standing, Peter was sure his family would give the union their blessing. His mother was Protestant, but his pious father, a daily communicant, would welcome a Catholic daughter-in-law into the family.

Peter was very devout himself, and Kathleen impressed him as a girl who feared the Lord. He approved of her modesty of dress and behavior, which was typical of the girls he knew from convent schools. Often he accompanied Kick and Charlotte to hear sermons by Father James Keller, a Maryknoll missionary, who sought out young people from wealthy Catholic families, impressing upon them their personal duty to society.

Until the news about Mr. Kennedy's ambassadorship Peter had counted on becoming engaged to Kathleen the following year. He immediately became somewhat less confident, although the greatest obstacle to his plans was not the year-long separation from Kathleen but the restless, vivacious energy of the prospective fiancée herself. Kathleen seemed incapable of looking very far ahead. He was her first real boyfriend, and at this point in her life she obviously wanted to play the field. She was a law unto herself.

In early February of 1938 Mrs. Kennedy suddenly developed appendicitis. After her operation the doctor insisted that she recuperate at least a month or two before leaving for England. Mr. Kennedy, who had already delayed his leave-taking, was eager to sail. He suggested that Kathleen accompany him and act as embassy hostess for a month until her mother and the smaller children could join them in late March.

Although at first she had been ambivalent about leaving, Kathleen was thrilled by the prospect of acting as hostess to important members of the British government. It was all so impressive. Her mother always talked about the old days when she was a mayor's daughter, but how much grander to be the daughter of an ambassador. Mr. Kennedy announced the change of plans and his daughter's new hostess duties to *The New York Times* and the Boston papers, which featured the story prominently. Peter even arranged for flowers to be waiting for her in London.

But as it turned out, Mr. Kennedy sailed by himself. Perhaps Mrs. Kennedy was unwilling to be overshadowed by her eighteen-year-old daughter. She had not been in the limelight since her own days as a Boston debutante.

The new ambassador received a farewell ribbing from Roosevelt ("You'll be a knockout in knee breeches," the President said during their last dinner). But FDR seemed to be the only one who didn't take his latest appointee altogether seriously. Mr. Kennedy landed at Southampton amidst a storm of flattering publicity. He was characterized by the British press as the freckle-faced redhead with "lots of go" who worked in his shirtsleeves with his feet propped up on the desk. During his first weeks in office he freely invited pressmen to the embassy, as he had in Washington, and charmed them with his candor. To the British reporter Kennedy embodied baseball, hot dogs, and Yankee slang. "You can't expect me to develop into a statesman overnight," he said engagingly during an early interview. One British newspaper referred to him as "one of the most dynamic men in the present day life of the United States," and another commented that Roosevelt had flattered Britain by sending one of his "closest advisers" as ambassador.

"It's a quarter past nine on Tuesday morning and I am sitting in a bathrobe at the Embassy and am supposed to dress in about an hour to get ready to be drawn to the Palace in a carriage with white horses to present my credentials to the King," Kennedy wrote giddily to a friend.

He further endeared himself to Fleet Street when he shot a one-hundred-twenty-eight-yard hole in one at a course in Buckinghamshire. The event, which made headlines all over Britain, was so well publicized that it ultimately became the subject of a verse competition in the *Sunday Observer*. Recognizing that one of his strongest suits with the British was the size of his family (one newspaper christened him the "U.S.A.'s Nine-Child Envoy"), Kennedy quipped, "I am much happier being the father of nine children and making a hole in one than I would be as the father of one child making a hole in nine." When the story made the American newspapers, Joe and Jack shot back a teasing telegram: "DUBIOUS ABOUT THE HOLE IN ONE."

In late March, several days before Kathleen was due to sail with her mother and the four youngest children, Peter Grace approached the publicist for his hockey team with a request. The team always scored heavily and never lost a game; consequently, as goalie, Peter never made the newspapers. But he wanted Kick, who was very impressionable, to leave the United States convinced of his superior athletic ability. "I want a real good headline before my girl goes to Europe next week," he said.

"Who's your girl?" the publicist asked.

"The new ambassador to England's daughter."

In the next game everybody on the team accommodated Peter. The coach moved him from goalie to wing, everybody passed him the puck, and he scored three goals. Just before Kathleen set sail, his name was finally in the headlines.

Kick was in the middle of the Atlantic when Peter's ploy backfired. Hearing through the hockey publicist that Kathleen was Peter's girl friend, a reporter from the *World-Telegram* telephoned Peter to confirm rumors that he and Kathleen were to be engaged. Peter panicked. "For goodness' sakes," he told the reporter. "It looks as though you are trying to stir up something. . . . Everybody will be saying that Mr. Kennedy gave my father shipping concessions in Colombia when he was Maritime Commissioner, or something. My father will be wild. Mr. Kennedy will be furious." The Maritime Commission had given a subsidy to the Grace Lines while Kennedy was chairman, but it had no connection with Kathleen and Peter's romance. Nevertheless, when the story broke, Peter's own injudicious remarks, which the reporter had duly quoted, implied that Kennedy had arranged for subsidies to be paid to the company of his future son-in-law.

The new ambassador was livid about the smear on his reputation.

Two

The moment they arrived in London, Mrs. Kennedy and the children were once again greeted by an army of reporters, but Kathleen was the one barraged with questions. Fleet Street had been primed with the *World-Telegram* story about Peter Grace and intended to capitalize on it. "I can't think how this started," Kathleen said falteringly, attempting to handle the press as she had seen her father do. "It's so silly. He's awfully nice. I like him a lot." As an afterthought she blurted out, "I do not know anything about him at all," possibly to avoid the appearance of taking a position—a tactic also adopted by her father on occasion. Exasperated, Joseph Kennedy also repudiated the rumors of an engagement—"She's only *eighteen!*" he exclaimed. Nevertheless, the following day a page 3 article in the *Daily Express* was headlined: KATHLEEN, AGED 18, IS IN LOVE.

Back in the United States, Kathleen's would-be fiancé worried that she was furious about the publicity, but he also secretly hoped that it would force her hand. Peter was astonished when he saw photographs of her arrival in London. *Boy, oh, boy,* he thought, *she looks just like a movie star.*

Mrs. Kennedy and the children moved into the palatial thirty-six-room embassy residence on Prince's Gate in fashionable

Knightsbridge. French double doors to the balcony opened on a view of the bridle paths of Rotten Row. Almost immediately the Kennedys became the object of endless fascination for the British public. Londoners smiled and waved at the family, as though they had become national property. Hardly a day passed without a photograph in the papers of little Teddy, taking a snapshot with his Brownie held upside down, or the five Kennedy children lined up on a train or bus. Columnists marveled at the slim, youthful appearance of the mother of nine. The ambassador continued to be solicited for peppery quotations. But in the society pages Kathleen was the star of the family. Before her arrival in London, *Queen,* a magazine devoted to the social life of royal and titled families, had prominently featured Kathleen in an article about the "buds" of the coming Season. The article pointed out—most likely because the ambassador had remarked that no daughter of his "gave five cents for this society stuff"—that Kathleen was "not especially interested in our social life."

Rosemary arrived with Eunice two months later, accompanied by Eddie Moore, the most trusted of Mr. Kennedy's coterie of Irish assistants and the man for whom his son Teddy had been named. Ostensibly he had come to England to work as the ambassador's right-hand man, but one of the chief duties that he shared with his wife was to look after Rosemary. On weekends, when she was let out of the special school she attended, she stayed with the Moores at the country home the ambassador had purchased in South Ascot. The Kennedys had decided that Rosemary would participate in all the social events of the Season with Kathleen, including a formal presentation at court, so that she wouldn't be compared to her spirited younger sister. The society pages were kind enough to include Rosemary in nearly every mention of Kick, referring to them both as "society favorites." But Kathleen was the one who received the attention and actual publicity, with Rosemary's condition quietly acknowledged.

Headlining Kick as "America's Most Important Debutante," the May 12 issue of *Queen* devoted a one-page spread to her. "I was impressed by her approximation to the best type of our own English girls of the same age," wrote the reporter. "She had none of that rather sophisticated air and ultra self confidence which is sometimes associated with youthful Americans." The interview ended when Kathleen had to leave for a pressing engagement. Mindful of her father's coaching on how to handle reporters, she had instructed the writer, "Don't forget to say how I like everything here in London and that I am having such a wonderful time."

Although delighted by Kick's success with the press, the ambassador supervised her image as strictly as he did those of his boys. He once scolded her soundly after hearing that on a shopping spree in Paris she had been spotted by a reporter chewing gum and wearing too much lipstick.

At one outing with several young women Kathleen was again chewing a giant wad of gum, probably an entire pack. Pointing to a horde of photographers coming toward them, one of her companions whispered loudly, "Look, Kick, the newspapermen. Get rid of the gum, swallow your gum!" But Kathleen shrugged off the warning and kept chewing even as cameras clicked.

Kathleen quickly became the most popular of the Kennedy children among the embassy staff, who found the other young Kennedys brusque. Before long she had struck up a friendship with Page Huidekoper, a resourceful nineteen-year-old who had managed to wangle a job in London as assistant to Joe Kennedy's press secretary. Page soon got the feeling that Kick was Joe Kennedy's pet, presumably because she appeared to be the one family member he couldn't push around. He was the kind of man, Page thought, who would only respect those he wasn't able to intimidate.

The Kennedys began receiving invitations from other foreign embassies as well as from members of the peerage. Mrs. Kennedy soon found herself discussing the idiosyncrasies of her children with the King of England. As wife of the American ambassador, with twenty-five servants at her disposal, she began to entertain in lavish style. Her day was largely taken up with the planning of menus and floral arrangements. Strawberries and moth orchids were flown in from Paris and shad roe from the States. Red, white, and blue peonies were planted in the embassy window boxes. In her diary Mrs. Kennedy began referring to her husband as "the ambassador." With the exception of Jack's presidency she would consider it the best time of her life.

It was soon apparent to British society that the American ambassador had his own ideas about how to entertain the aristocracy. During their first social endeavor, a dinner party to honor British Foreign Secretary Lord Halifax and his wife, the Kennedys showed a new Hollywood movie after the meal. It was an unorthodox precedent, which they would follow even in receptions for the Royal Family. Attending an embassy dinner in their honor, the king and queen would be treated to an uncut version of *Goodbye, Mr. Chips.*

Among politicians and reporters back home Joe Kennedy began promoting an image of himself as the most popular ambassador in the history of the post. He regularly fed Washington columnist Arthur Krock exclusives and planted duplicate versions of "confidential memos" with his old friends among the Washington and Boston press corps. Occasionally he bragged about his relations with key figures in British politics, particularly Prime Minister Neville Chamberlain, with whom he was soon on a first-name basis.

There were good reasons for many British cabinet members to cultivate the new American ambassador. Having annexed Austria, Germany now had her eye on the substantial German population in Czechoslovakia. Hitler claimed the Sudetenland had a right to become part of Grossdeutschland. The fate of highly industrialized Czechoslovakia was of great concern to the Western allies. With Britain allied to France, Russia, and Czechoslovakia through a network of treaties, the other countries looked anxiously to Neville Chamberlain for his guiding response to the German demands. The prime minister had up till then pursued a policy of "appeasement" toward Hitler—a pragmatic approach, since Britain was woefully ill prepared for any confrontation with a Germany that had stealthily rearmed after the Great War. Many British cabinet members, especially Halifax, were uneasy about what they saw as a wrongheaded and ultimately dishonorable course, and believed that another war was unavoidable. In such a crisis England would be dependent upon the United States for arms and supplies. It concerned them that Chamberlain, confident of his diplomatic course, had not pursued such an arrangement with America. With the European situation so volatile Ambassador Kennedy's contributions to British-American solidarity were thought to be crucial.

Franklin Roosevelt was quite amused by press reports about the entrée his Irish-Catholic envoy had gained to the most exclusive English drawing rooms. In truth, however, many among the aristocracy found the appointment of an Irish Catholic to the Court of St. James's to be in terrible taste—particularly the blunt, gum-chewing Mr. Kennedy. His bald announcement that he did not intend to wear the required silk stockings and knee breeches in formal court presentations was regarded as horribly bad form—as serious a violation of court protocol as his disclosure to reporters of the details of his first meeting with King George VI. Members of the oldest English families looked upon the Kennedys as brazen interlopers. Although one might occasionally enjoy them as vulgar novelties, the source of their wealth and their display of piety were the subjects of many pointed asides. Rumors flourished about the ambassador's sexual exploits. He delighted in his reputation as a ladies' man and actually encouraged gossip about supposed involvements with glamorous royal figures like the Duchess of Kent, the king's sister-in-law. Kennedy did have an ongoing affair with one wealthy woman in England and on several occasions used his office aides to arrange dates. Knowing, however, that any flagrant indiscretions would get back to Roosevelt, Kennedy cut down on his actual extramarital activities.

Kathleen and Rosemary's imminent presentation to society gave Mrs. Kennedy an excuse to mingle with many of England's best families. Protocol required Mrs. Kennedy to meet the mother of any debutante before Kathleen and Rosemary could attend her party. She was soon having teas with the likes of Lady Edwina Mountbatten, whose goddaughter, Sally Norton, was written up as one of the year's outstanding debs, and Lady Redesdale, the mother of Debo, the youngest of the Mitford girls.

Each week Rose Kennedy was supposed to meet with these aristocratic matrons in Mayfair to pore over lists of eligible titled sons to determine who would be suitable to be introduced to their daughters. Unless she arranged for a chaperone, Mrs. Kennedy herself would attend the Season's balls with Kick and Rosemary, chatting with other mothers while their debutante daughters ticked off the names of the young gentlemen listed on their programs. When Mrs. Kennedy herself could not be present, she often sent a newfound friend, Marie Bruce.

As Rose Kennedy soon discovered, a mother's participation in a debut into society was every bit as important as a daughter's. When the time came for Kathleen and Rosemary to be presented at court, it was she who actually received the invitation from the palace and who would have to go with them as their sponsor.

Right from the start Kathleen's life was dictated by the hectic activities of the London Season. Although the Season (it was always referred to in upper case) often began immediately after Easter, the official starting date was April 26, with the First Spring Meeting at Newmarket and the opening of the summer exhibit at the Royal Academy of Arts. Then came the major race meetings in June—the Derby and Royal Ascot, the most celebrated—and the tennis championships at Wimbledon. The Henley Rowing Regatta was held in early July, followed by racing during Goodwood Week and the Yachting Regatta at Cowes. The Royal Garden Party at Buckingham Palace at the end of July marked the official close of the Season, whereupon members of the peerage took to the country or spent September at Le Touquet (known as Mayfair Across the Channel). Those left behind in England in August headed north for the Glorious Twelfth, the start of grouse shooting, followed by the Scottish season and winter hunts.

Between April and August debutantes attended balls and dinner parties held in their honor nearly every night. There were numerous charity extravaganzas and theme balls, the most lavish of which was the Jewels of the Empire Ball, where it was estimated that each year some £1.5 million worth of jewels were worn by the guests.

The high point of the Season for most debutantes was being presented before the enthroned king and queen in one of several spectacular court ceremonies in late spring. The practice first arose in the days of George II, when the granting of the honor not only entitled a young woman to receive invitations to English and foreign court activities but was tantamount to a certificate of virtue. (Illegitimate children could not be presented, no matter what their father's rank might be.) In 1938 court presentation and coming out in London was still a stamp of approval of class and family background.

During all the festivities London debutantes were treated as celebrities. Two thousand gate-crashers had scrambled over the pews of Brompton Oratory in 1933 to catch a glimpse of the wedding of Miss Margaret Whigham, debutante of the year, to Charles Sweeny. Some young women hired their own designers; gossip columnists like Tom Driberg, who wrote the William Hickey column for the London *Daily Express,* or the notorious Viscount Castlerosse recorded their every appearance at the Kit Kat or the Savoy. "The Whigham," with her vampish, unsmiling pose, had made it fashionable to wear ruby-red lipstick in a cupid bow, small hats at a peckish angle, and pearl-colored nail polish that glowed in the dark. She was even immortalized in a stanza of Cole Porter's song "You're the Top," a hit from his musical *Anything Goes:*

> You're the nimble tread of the feet of Fred Astaire,
> You're Mussolini,
> You're Mrs. Sweeny,
> You're Camembert.

In June the Kennedys attended their first Royal Ascot. The ambassador felt as if he had walked onto a Hollywood set when he caught sight of the open carriages of the Royal Procession, drawn by Windsor gray horses and attended by footmen in scarlet and gold livery, making their way down the straight grass course. Spectators at Ascot were divided between those who sat in the public stands and those holding vouchers signed by the palace. Because of Kennedy's position he and his wife, to their delight, had been escorted to the impeccably maintained emerald mound of the Royal Enclosure. After the races they were to dine with the king and queen.

During the afternoon all the young women seemed less interested in the races themselves than in who was wearing what garden-party ensemble and appearing on the arm of which escort in the customary gray morning dress and top hat. With photographers for the social weeklies scouring the spectators, an outlandish outfit could virtually guarantee a write-up. Mrs. Kennedy wore a black organdy gown and a matching picture hat. Although ice blue and cyclamen were the colors of the Season, she had made her selection, as she noted in her diary, to stand out from the "lavenders and pinks and other pastel shades of the crowd."

With so much publicity devoted to the clothing of debutantes and diplomatic wives, fashion had become a major consideration for Kick and her mother. Mrs. Kennedy's keen interest in designer clothing dated from the ambassador's days in Hollywood. She had, in fact, gotten her first taste of *haute couture* through Gloria Swanson. In 1929, while still involved with Gloria Productions, Joe Kennedy had sailed to London with both Rose and Gloria for a European premiere of the star's latest movie. For most of the trip he had doted on the object of his affection and pressed his wife to escort her around and protect her from clamoring fans. The two women visited the salons of Paris together. At the urging of the glamorous actress the designers fawning over her also outfitted her prim little matron friend.

In her present position as the American ambassador's wife Mrs. Kennedy believed that her clothing was a statement of diplomacy every bit as important as her husband's official pronouncements. In her diary she even noted in detail the ensembles of the royalty and aristocracy with whom she now socialized.

Kathleen spent many weekends in Paris on shopping sprees with her mother, assembling a spectacular array of gowns and formal town ensembles necessary for three solid months of festivities. Matched accessories were also essential, and it was considered highly eccentric to go anywhere without a hat. She and Mrs. Kennedy visited the best salons—Schiaparelli, Paquin, Chanel, Lelong—in France and England, examining the Victor Stiebel suits that were the current rage or the elaborate lace-over-net-over-satin creations of Molyneux, the foremost British designer and Mrs. Kennedy's favorite.

A month after her arrival Kathleen began appearing at parties in the floodlit gardens of townhouses in Belgravia. Invitations arrived for weekends at country house parties given by the parents of her new friends, where a half dozen older couples and the same number of young people would follow a crowded schedule of dining, dancing, and sport. Each guest list would be a carefully wrought mix of old and young, artists and politicians. Kick soon was mingling with the actor and playwright William Douglas-Home and Somerset Maugham's daughter; it was at such a weekend party that she met Winston Churchill, the Duke and Duchess of Kent, and many of the best political and literary minds in Britain.

During these weekends a gong would sound announcing dinner, attended by footmen in "semilivery," full state livery being reserved for formal parties in London. Housemaids would scurry into the room beforehand to sweep the rug so that all the pile lay in the same direction. After the guests retired, maids worked until dawn cleaning the steel grates that had contained coal fires with a chain-on-leather burnisher, rubbing rhythmically to produce a scratchless shine. A housemaid assigned to Kick would unpack her clothes, run her bath, squeeze toothpaste onto her brush, and leave a clean, pressed dress, underclothes, and stockings—turned down so that she could easily slip into them—all laid out on the bed before dinner.

Steaming hot water was brought to her four times a day in polished brass cans and left with pressed linen towels on the china washstand by her bed. The larger houses employed a groom of chambers, whose main task was to ensure that the writing table in every bedroom and study was correctly outfitted with stationery, and that the silver pens and water bottles used for wetting stamps were polished and arranged at a particular angle.

Kathleen spent one of her first country weekends at Hatfield House, a vast Jacobean palace requiring some hundred servants that was the seat of the Marquess of Salisbury and the Cecil family. It had been the childhood home of Queen Elizabeth I. Among the dozen young people there for the weekend she came across as a terrific novelty. Kathleen Kennedy was so brash and outspoken, so obviously American, that Robert Cecil and his friends from Oxford couldn't resist a joke at her expense. Noticing how proud Kick was of her neat little feet—she would often rotate an ankle admiringly in front of the other girls—the boys stole all her left shoes and hid them in the maze hedge. For the entire weekend Kick hobbled around on two right shoes. Veronica Fraser, Lord Lovat's daughter, and the other girls had been tipped off about the theft. They took turns being solicitous. "Why are you limping, Kick?"

"Oh," she shot back offhandedly, "Robert broke my leg before dinner."

What a terrific sport, Veronica Fraser thought. This American girl made no attempt to hide her amazement at life among the English upper class. At least ten times that day she'd nudged Veronica and asked ingenuously, "Okay, so what do I do *now?*" She was not really pretty, according to English standards, a bit plump, really, with a short neck made to look even shorter by her broad shoulders. What was so attractive about her was her curly golden brown hair, which she wore in a long bob without a permanent. Veronica had never seen a girl with such vitality—or informality. She would bound in from playing tennis, kick off her shoes in front of strangers, and make herself comfortable on the floor. British young ladies were taught to express opinions cautiously. But there was Kick, cheerfully expounding away on topics about which she obviously knew absolutely nothing. She was so wicked about almost everything they held sacred; she'd referred to the Duke of Marlborough as "Dukie Wookie." Nobody would dare be stuffy in the same room with this girl.

Kathleen adored the pomp and splendor of these country weekends and the odd reticence of these people. Just because she was American almost everything she did seemed to produce a laugh. She began to play up every last difference between herself and her new friends, and before long the young aristocrats were picking up all her slang. "Oh, kid, what's the sto-o-ory?" they said, trying to mimic what sounded like a flat drawl. They loved the way Kathleen laughed uncontrollably at her own jokes before she even got to the punch line. Her favorite was the one she'd heard about an American who tells an Englishman that his favorite breakfast is "a roll in bed with Honey." The Englishman then tells his friends at White's, an exclusive men's club (and here Kick would assume what she thought was a tremendously stuffy English accent): "I've heard a frightfully funny story from an American. I asked him, 'What's your favorite breakfast?'" By this time tears would be coming down Kick's cheeks, she would be laughing so hard. "'And do you know what he said to me?'" The accent was now more pronounced, as in a drama diction class. "'A rrroll in bed with strawb'ry jaaahm.'"

The joke itself was awful and a little crude, and so was her accent, but the delicious part of it was hearing a British accent with that terrible Boston twang. Kick had no gift for language (they'd heard her address Parisians by speaking English with a French accent), but she was quite aware of this failing and enjoyed being the butt of her own jokes. "Oh, do go on," Veronica Fraser would say. "Do speak English again, Kick."

During her first month in England, Kathleen was also invited to Cliveden, the Astor estate in Buckinghamshire. Nancy Astor, the eccentric American who had married well and succeeded her husband in Parliament as first woman MP, made a point of entertaining the families of prominent Americans in London. Lady Astor asked another debutante to look after the newcomer. The young woman soon discovered that Kathleen hardly needed anyone to make social introductions for her. Two days after the weekend Kathleen herself made the first friendly overture. She invited the girl and her father, an earl, to lunch at the embassy and introduced the peer to her father.

At Cliveden, Kathleen had also met Janie Kenyon-Slaney, who quickly became her best friend. Janie was blond, stylish, and theatrical—a real live wire. Her own collection of expressions ("It's soooo extraordinary") matched Kick's hyperbolic American slang. That weekend Kathleen had even won over her notoriously vehement anti-Catholic hostess. Lady Astor took an immediate dislike to Mr. Kennedy but virtually adopted his spunky daughter.

For the first time in her life Kathleen was not surrounded by Roman Catholics. Some of her new companions, like Lady Astor, muttered anti-Catholic remarks all the time. Kick usually laughed off the slurs. She didn't mind these people knowing she was Catholic. There wasn't any point in her pretending that she was something she wasn't.

One day in her room at Prince's Gate with several girls she had recently met, Kathleen was putting on her hat and jacket, preparing to leave with them on a shopping trip. When Luella Hennessy, the Kennedys' nurse, came in, Kick blurted out, as though the presence of the Irish Catholic suddenly reminded her, "Oh, Miss Hennessy! I haven't said my rosary this morning!" She turned to her friends. "You girls will excuse me, won't you?" Reaching for a set of beads, she closed her eyes, knelt down in front of them all, and spent the next fifteen minutes in silent prayer.

Even though the older generation disapproved of the new American ambassador, most of Kathleen's new friends were secretly fascinated by her family. David Ormsby-Gore, a student at Oxford and the heir to the Harlech barony, found the Kennedys refreshingly flamboyant. He and his friends came from families with far more wealth, yet it was considered bad form to display one's riches, apart from property accumulated through the family line. Even his aunt, the Duchess of Devonshire, one of the wealthiest women in England, would never have considered buying a first-class train ticket. David loved American jazz, and the Kennedys reminded him of it, they were so flippant and spontaneous—flying to France or phoning America on impulse, unreservedly offering unsolicited opinions to important members of the government. To be near them was to be unaware of limitation; if one wanted to play golf and didn't have the equipment, one simply went out and bought new clubs. Then there were what Janie Kenyon-Slaney referred to as the family's "pajama dinners." Every one of the family members —including the ambassador—would be seated around the long stately embassy dining table in his pajamas and robe. What was even stranger was that Kathleen seemed unaware of the fact that eating dinner in her nightgown might be considered bizarre.

One afternoon Veronica Fraser accepted an invitation to lunch at Prince's Gate. During the meal the ambassador dominated the conversation, taking what seemed to be an obsessive interest in the minutiae of his children's lives. All but ignoring Veronica, he approached all his children, one by one, requiring that they report on the petty details of their day, including their current weights. He even found a discreet way, she noticed to her amazement, of inquiring whether they'd had a bowel movement.

The first time that William Douglas-Home came to the embassy, a butler opened the door and asked him to wait in the drawing room. A few minutes later what Douglas-Home assumed was another butler walked in, carrying a tray of drinks.

"May I have a whiskey and soda?" Douglas-Home asked.

"I guess you may if you point it out," came the curt reply.

From the tone of voice Douglas-Home concluded that the man standing before him was Father Kennedy himself, come to look over the fellow who was going to be out with his daughter.

On May 12, when Kathleen made her formal entrance into society, she found herself in the midst of a controversy set off by her father. In 1938 making a bow to the queen was considered the pinnacle of social ambition for American debutantes. Since only thirty could be chosen from among the hundreds applying for the honor, the selection process, incumbent upon the American ambassador, had deteriorated to one of string pulling and political payoffs. On April 10, after conferring with Washington and Buckingham Palace, Kennedy had announced that henceforth no American debutantes would be presented because the existing selection process was "undemocratic." He had chosen to make his decision public with a reply to a letter sent by Massachusetts Senator Henry Cabot Lodge on behalf of a Boston debutante. Lodge had agreed to allow both letters to be published, but when they appeared without warning, the blue-blooded Bostonian was inadvertently made to appear reprimanded by the redheaded Irishman.

This new policy decision, however, did not put any restrictions upon the ambassador's own daughters, since he had determined that immediate family members of American officials or Americans living in England for business or professional reasons should be the exceptions to the rule. In reporting the decision the *Daily News* commented, "Even though his own pretty daughters would constitute 'official presentees,' Ambassador Kennedy had best be prepared for cries of 'foul' if one or more of 'em duck their plumed heads to King George VI and his Queen this season!"

In normal circumstances only those matrons who themselves had made their obeisance at court would have applications made on behalf of their daughters accepted by the palace; otherwise, a mother would have to be sponsored at court, and once presented, then present her daughter. But members of the diplomatic corps had special status in all respects; gilt seats were assigned to them where they would remain during the ceremony of some three hundred presentations. The Kennedys were to be presented at the first of four courts along with the wives and daughters of military attachés and would be about twentieth in line, preceding ordinary presentations, including those among the peerage.

The event required meticulous preparation. According to the palace, which determined the style of dress required, trains on gowns were to be no longer than two yards from the shoulders and fifty-four inches wide. Gloves were to have exactly twenty-one buttons. A tulle veil no longer than forty-five inches was to be worn at the base of the required three Prince of Wales plumes. The women were to be presented in pairs before the seated king and queen, at which point they were to perform a slow, sweeping curtsy. It was important to precisely fix the spaces between the pairs in the procession, so that trains would not be stepped on. After approaching the monarchs, the two debutantes were to curtsy in unison and then withdraw. Many English girls were tutored by dance mistresses in the art of curtsying, but Kick, Rosemary, and their mother needed no instruction, after years of automatic curtsying at convent school.

On the evening of the presentation Mrs. Kennedy, flanked by her two daughters, was swarmed by newspaper photographers upon their arrival at the palace. Kathleen and Rosemary wore similar gowns of white tulle—the recognized "court uniform"— trimmed with silver threads, but it was Mrs. Kennedy's gown that would be written up the following day. Like members of the Royal Family and the peerage, who favored metal threads that year, she had selected a magnificent Molyneux of white lace, with tiny silver and gold beads embroidered over a white satin foundation. The silver in the gowns of her daughters on either side of her only seemed to focus attention on the gold threads of her own. Although the girls carried small lily-of-the-valley bouquets, Mrs. Kennedy clutched a large ostrich fan. As a matron she was obliged to wear a tiara, and the one she had borrowed from Lady Bessborough glistened with rubies surrounding a large marquise diamond. After the evening was over, she would pack away the gown, and take it out only one more time, twenty-two years later, to wear for her son Jack's presidential inauguration in 1961.

The Associated Press later estimated that the Kennedys at court received ten times more news coverage than the titled dignitaries. But the publicity did not have the kind of slant that Kennedy had expected. Rather than emphasizing the groundbreaking nature of the occasion for an Irish-Catholic family, the stories focused on the ambassador's refusal to wear knee breeches and the presence of the Kennedy women as conspicuous exceptions to his own hard-and-fast ruling on American debutantes. The London *Evening Standard* noted: "Mr. Kennedy's desire to shield himself from the charge of flunkeyism achieved the somewhat paradoxical result that the only trousers at last night's court were those worn by himself and some of the less important waiters."

Several weeks later Mrs. Kennedy held a coming-out party for Kick and Rosemary. After a dinner party for eighty the two girls helped to receive three hundred guests, who walked into the embassy between avenues of varicolored lupins and crowded up the stairway to the paneled French ballroom on the second floor. Luella Hennessy and Betty Dunn, the governess to the younger children, were grateful to Kick and Mrs. Kennedy for their insistence that they take the lift down to the ground floor and enter the ballroom from the stairwell, as though they were among the invited guests. Mrs. Kennedy had selected a pink and mauve floral motif for the ballroom. Ambrose's Band, the most popular English swing band next to Ray Noble, hired away for the evening from the Mayfair Hotel, played its "sweet" music. America's trans-Atlantic stage and nightclub star Harry Richmond gave a rendition of "Thanks for the Memory" that brought down the house.

Despite the newspaper announcement and the engraved invitations it was common knowledge among the guests that the party was mainly for the ambassador's second daughter. By now everybody knew that Rosemary was a bit backward (many times they had seen Kick, always so patient, offering to relieve Luella and walk Rosemary around Hyde Park). Knowing how clumsy Rosemary usually was made it all the more astonishing to see how well she danced. She had a dance partner for every number this particular evening, but it was always the same man—Jack Kennedy, often called Ding Dong Jack or London Jack to distinguish him from his boss's son. He worked for the ambassador at the embassy, but tonight his duty was to fill up Rosemary's dance card and make sure that she did not feel left out.

All evening long Kathleen changed partners among noblemen and royalty, including Prince Frederick of Prussia and the Duke of Kent. The society papers would acclaim it as one of the "best boy and girl parties of the Season," and reporters in the States would speculate about which of Kathleen's titled dance partners would end up as a suitor. It was a social triumph for Kick, with every man in the ballroom seemingly captivated by her. Despite the publicity attending Debo Mitford and Sally Norton she had become the most exciting debutante of 1938.

The ambassador looked on with pride and probably even awe. It was just as much a breakthrough for himself as it was for his daughter. After only two months, and entirely on her own, Kathleen had achieved the position that he had longed for all his life.

Three

In July and August, as concern mounted over Germany's campaign to swallow up Europe, the Season grew noticeably subdued. Functions were held on a much more modest scale than in past years. Normally enthusiastically competitive in planning lavish evening parties, hostesses limited their entertaining to small cocktail parties. Numerous events were canceled because enough tickets were not sold. Every night the Royal Opera House, Covent Garden, greeted crowds without the usual array of dazzling jewelry. At Ascot women broke precedent by arriving in tailored suits and narrow-brimmed hats.

After hearing word that England was embarking on a massive rearmament program, members of the aristocracy breathed a sigh of relief. England, of course, would beat back the German bully, and stability abroad would be assured. The seminars being held on air raids and the trenches being dug in Hyde Park were just another sign of Chamberlain's intelligent caution. Occasionally the wireless picked up broadcasts from Germany of thunderous Nazi demonstrations demanding "justice" for the Sudeten Germans. But if Goodwood was still on, everything must be all right.

In mid-June, Joseph Kennedy sailed for the States to attend young Joe's graduation from Harvard. British newspapers variously predicted that the popular ambassador would manage, during his few weeks at home, to reshape foreign policy, end the stalemate holding up the signing of an Anglo-American trade agreement, help to devaluate the dollar, arrange for a planes-for-ships trade between the two countries, and settle Britain's debt to the United States from the last war. Upon his arrival in the United States, Kennedy discovered that the publicity about his family's social success and his political savvy in dealing with British leaders like Chamberlain had paid off. He was pleased to ward off constant rumors that he was the 1940 presidential candidate, the "Crown Prince of the Roosevelt regime," as the *Daily News* put it, and that in fact he was already practically elected.

When the ambassador returned to London in early July, accompanied by young Joe and Jack, the boys were immediately made to feel welcome in British society, largely through introductions to their younger sister's friends. Jack was quite stunned by Kick's success, but after dating a few English girls he told her she had no competition. One date of his broke an evening-long silence only once—to describe the brook at the bottom of her father's garden.

The young British aristocrats easily took to Jack, even though it was commonly assumed that he was Kick's younger brother. His American crew cut was so novel and his attractive frame so similar to that of English men. Kick's male friends marveled at Jack's easy conquests. After he'd only been in London a few weeks, a hush fell over the Ritz one lunchtime when Jack Kennedy arrived. On his arm was a staggeringly beautiful woman, dressed in a gray two-piece dress, a hat perched jauntily to one side of her head. Jack introduced her around as Honeychild Wilder, the Cotton Queen of Louisiana, who had just arrived in England to promote the cotton industry.

Joe, on the other hand, was received less enthusiastically. His manner seemed abrasive and his humor often uncomfortably sharp-edged. He lacked the finesse that had enabled Jack and Kick to adapt so readily to British ways. At debutante balls Joe brusquely cut in on dance partners, as he had done at Harvard functions, until he was curtly reminded that he would have to follow the dance programs.

He and his father had decided that he would take a year off between undergraduate studies and law school. Exploiting Mr. Kennedy's ambassadorship as a training ground of sorts, Joe would work as an embassy aide, travel to many strife-torn areas in Europe, and periodically mail back to his father his observations. At the moment Joe was less concerned with his social life than with his itinerary and with the image his father was cultivating of him as an apprentice politician.

He spent much of his time at the Four Hundred, an after-hours spot frequented by a crowd older than Kathleen's. The rivalry over women between Jack and Joe had continued across the Atlantic, with the elder brother clearly the loser. Although Joe made a hit with a number of young women—among them, Virginia Gilliat, a debutante of a few years back, often described as "Popular Girl Number One"—some aristocratic young women were shocked by what occasionally surfaced as sexual aggressiveness and a violent temper.

In late July, Mrs. Kennedy and the younger children left for a two-month vacation at Eden Roc on the French Riviera. The ambassador planned to join them in August with the older children visiting periodically. Although Joe and Jack wandered in and out of the embassy and the summer's events, Kathleen maintained a life apart from them as a participant in virtually every important social occasion.

It was an exhausting, intoxicating routine for her, attending parties night after night, shuttling from London to the English countryside, often moving through a string of house parties in a single weekend. She became as proficient as her English friends at lying to her parents about her whereabouts. She would elude her chaperone and leave well-supervised balls to head off to the deep velvet environment of the Four Hundred or the Café de Paris, with its ballroom pit, both considered far too "gay" for an eighteen-year-old girl. In the early morning hours beside a fountain at Hever, she had promised William Douglas-Home, by now a constant companion, that she would marry him; by morning she'd evidently forgotten all about it because she asked him to drive her to the home of another beau. Kathleen liked William a great deal, but, puzzled by his sardonic sense of humor and what seemed his frivolous approach to life, she often complained exasperatedly to Janie, "I *just* don't understand him." Another ardent suitor was Anthony, the Earl of Rosslyn, who had just succeeded to the title, but he was a little too reticent and inhibited for her taste.

In England, Kathleen had attracted an even larger collection of admirers than in the States, but at that point she was more in love with the Season and her whirlwind social life than with anyone in particular. The other British debutantes were so fond of her that they were quite magnanimous about her spectacular success with the boys. At the weekend parties that included the quizzically eyebrowed Debo Mitford; Sally Norton, an attractive girl with raven hair and fabulous legs; and Lady Astor's nieces, Dinah and Virginia Brand, Kick became part of a regular crowd. That summer she became very close to David Ormsby-Gore's girl friend, Sissy Lloyd-Thomas. After Sissy's father, Hugh, secretary to the Duke of Windsor, was killed in a steeplechase accident, Sissy came to stay with Kick at the embassy. Although as lighthearted as her friends, Sissy was serious about one aspect of her life—her religion. She was one of the only Catholics among Kathleen's British friends, and the two often attended Mass together.

Kathleen and her mother had soon discovered that girls among the British upper classes were not encouraged to pursue higher education. For the time being Kick abandoned any thought of college, intending, like her newly made friends, to concentrate instead on what seemed *really* important—the dances and shoots of the autumn Little Season.

Peter Grace had arranged to visit Kick in England during his summer break. He had had to take an additional week of absence with his vacation, with all the travel time it took to sail back and forth across the Atlantic. Arriving in mid-July, he made his way to the embassy only to be told by a butler that Kathleen was attending the races in Sussex. After all their elaborate planning he couldn't believe she'd forgotten his arrival date. When she returned to the embassy near the end of Peter's week in London, she admitted that she was involved with someone else. Bitter about the circumstances that had forced their four-month separation, Peter left that day for Southampton and caught the same boat home.

Kathleen's presence at that particular race meeting had been prominently mentioned in the society pages. *Queen* published a photograph of her in a demure little print dress and hat beside William Cavendish, the Marquess of Hartington, known to everyone as Billy. Dressed in the required double-breasted suit and trilby, the six-foot-two marquess towered over her, but he had the fine features and soft countenance of an English schoolboy. The first news of Billy's interest in Kick was the source of much comment and speculation among his parents' friends. Billy was the heir to the Duke of Devonshire, one of the wealthiest, most powerful men in England. On the lists drawn up by the mothers of debutantes, his was undoubtedly the first and most attractive name.

Kick had met him a few months before at a garden party through David Ormsby-Gore. Before long she was seeing more of Billy than of her other beaux; often they paired up with Sissy and David, who was Billy's cousin as well as his closest friend. Billy had a lanky, coltish charm. A former cricket player, he moved very gracefully for someone so tall, his hands often thrust deep into the pockets of his rumpled wool trousers. Kathleen's English girl friends invariably described Billy as "sweet." He was considered a typical Cavendish—placid and gentle, unlike his mercurial dark-haired younger brother, Andrew, whose rapid, hatling speech favored the Cecils, the maternal side of the family. (English aristocrats used their titles as surnames, so that Billy, who had one title, was known as Hartington, and his father and mother, who had another title, were known as Devonshire, even though their actual family name was Cavendish.)

At twenty Billy was quiet and purposeful, but for all his seriousness he lacked confidence and direction, perhaps because of the awesome responsibilities his future title held for him.

When he met Kathleen, he was at Cambridge. Like most of his friends, Billy was an indifferent student, spending much of his time at the racetrack or at London parties. Rumor had it that he was doing well at Cambridge because of the dissertation he was preparing on the Whig oligarchy, of which his family and their ancestors had been a prominent part. Andrew thought that Billy had struck it damn lucky when he got that subject approved because he had learned about it at his father's knee.

Although good-looking and eligible, Billy had few girl friends and little interest in making conquests. Many of his previous girls had been even quieter and more acquiescent than he. Billy's approach to dating, as to every other aspect of his life, had a certain purity about it, as though he had set himself the task of finding his lifelong mate. Kathleen was unlike any girl he had ever known. When Billy first told his brother Andrew that he fancied Kathleen Kennedy, Andrew was quite put out because he fancied her himself. She was so exciting, so exuberant, and somehow she was able to make him more so.

Kathleen knew it was quite a feather in her cap to have someone like Billy chasing her. He was so unlike any of the jocks she had dated, like Torby Macdonald or Peter Grace. Although proud of Kick's various conquests among the English upper crust, the ambassador did not take any of them seriously. Most of Billy's chums, however, had taken note of the budding romance and were very surprised by it. It was out of character for Billy to have fallen for an American and one who was not a great beauty. The two seemed to have so little in common. The real problem—even if it was a bit crass to think it—was that Kathleen did not have the right background. England's ruling class was democratic about accepting outsiders (the grander the family, the more tolerant, it was often said), but not as marriage partners. All those carefully gleaned lists and elaborately planned weekends had a none-too-subtle point—that such relationships should be kept, so to speak, in the family. Although Billy's uncle, Charles Cavendish, had married the American dancer Adele Astaire, Billy's future position made it imperative that he stick to young ladies from the peerage. His parents undoubtedly preferred the aristocratic girls he had been seeing before he met Kathleen.

The main question was what the duke and duchess would say about Kathleen's religion. Of all people to be dating a Roman Catholic! Billy's father was considered a pillar of the Anglican faith, and his anti-Catholicism was legendary. It was said that he contemplated changing bedrooms in his London townhouse because his present one looked out on the spire of Westminster Cathedral. The duke had a mischievous edge to his voice when he talked about Catholics (he was a great tease), but his humor derived nonetheless from a deep-seated bigotry shared by many members of his class. Many of the duke's contemporaries believed wholeheartedly in the existence of a conspiracy to recatholicize England. The "promises" that had to be made in a marriage to a Roman Catholic before the Church would sanctify the union—particularly the agreement, in writing, of the non-Catholic party to the marriage to raise the children as Catholics—were regarded as proof of this popish plot. The great fear was that their firstborn sons would be captured by Catholic girls, thus endangering the future of the family line. Boys like Billy Hartington usually shied away from serious involvements with Catholics, and the leading English Catholic families were as mindful as their Anglican counterparts of the invisible boundary between them. After the birth of a daughter to the Duke and Duchess of Norfolk in June of 1938, there had been talk that the king would like to stand as sponsor to the child. His majesty had not forgotten the work performed by the duke for the coronation the year before and wished to show him some mark of royal favor. The problem was that Norfolk was the premier Catholic of the realm. A Catholic baptism precluded a Protestant godparent, even a royal one.

If the Duke and Duchess of Devonshire were alarmed by Billy's sudden interest in the American ambassador's Roman Catholic daughter, they did not initially discourage it. Kathleen had stayed at Compton Place, the lovely ivy-covered Devonshire mansion in Eastbourne, during Goodwood Week. Later in the season she was a guest at Churchdale Hall, the Devonshire home in Ashford-in-the-Water. The village was located in the low country surrounding the "Peak," or two-thousand-foot Kinder Scout, in Derbyshire. Derbyshire was the idyllic heart of the English countryside, a boundary of sorts between the midlands and the north country, containing features of the geography of both: wild moorlands, grottoes, lush pastoral grazing land, and chalybeate, or warm-water, springs. It was land mainly fit for quarrying and tenant farming, and its villages, with their cloistered populations and customs, had changed very little over the centuries. Corn was still ground by water mill in Miller's Dale. Curfew was still rung in Chapel-en-le-Frith, the ancient deer forest of the king. It was in Derbyshire that Charlotte Brontë had elected to place Jane Eyre and the infamous Moor House, patterning Morton after a moorland village called Hathersage. Superstition was woven into the fabric of county history, fantastic stories of lost villages and clandestine elopements, doomed lovers on the limestone cliffs of the Winnats, hidden treasures beneath the moat of a Plantagenet castle. The Derbyshire villagers believed that the Crooked Spire in Chesterfield—the result of warped timber—crowning an otherwise magnificent fourteenth-century church like some bizarre crone's cap, had been cursed by the devil and would right itself at the moment when a virgin was married inside.

With only ten bedrooms Churchdale Hall, where Billy had been born and raised, was modest compared to the estates Kathleen had visited lately. For Billy's parents it had served merely as a way station, to be abandoned at the moment of succession. Five miles away stood Chatsworth, the house where Billy's grandfather had lived until his death a few months before, which his father now intended to occupy by Christmas, and where Billy himself would one day reside, his portrait taking its place in the Sketch Gallery beside those of his ten predecessors, seven of whom bore his name.

Chatsworth was not immediately visible from the tiny winding drive out of the village of Bakewell. After a deep bend in the road a Palladian mansion suddenly appeared, incongruously set in the midst of grazing land, with a steep wooded hill and rambling garden as its backdrop and the River Derwent in the foreground like a serpentine moat. The dramatic splendor of the scene resulted from the subtle balance of all the elements in it: the geometrical grid formed by the buildings and garden and the unbridled, almost menacing country behind them—untouched forest and domesticized farmland, where sheep and deer grazed, ambling idly across the narrow main road. Although seemingly random this composition had been arrived at after hundreds of years of planning and consultation with the best architects, gardeners, and landscape artists of several centuries. The intense beauty of the eleven-hundred-acre park was largely due to the genius of eighteenth-century landscape artist Lancelot "Capability" Brown, who had labored to arrive at his characteristically romantic look of happy accident. In selecting and planting hardwoods, he'd had the foresight to plan an effect that would only be fully realized one hundred fifty years later. Every possible approach had been considered and arranged so as to display the house to perfection. The road had been laid so that at certain positions the house and a small nobly proportioned bridge crossing the river would align in perfect perspective. With the trees acting as a frame and the magnificent classical facade of the mansion reflected in the river's blue waters Chatsworth appeared to be a scene from a nineteenth-century pastoral oil.

From the South Front, straight across the giant rectangle of Canal Pond, the house seemed to emerge from the water. The hundred acre grounds around it were less a garden than a collection of mystifying botanical delights. Largely because of the sixth duke (called the Bachelor Duke) and his protégé, chief gardener Joseph Paxton, who later achieved fame for the Crystal Palace he built in Hyde Park, Chatsworth contained the most elaborate waterworks of any private estate in Britain. Relying entirely upon gravity, manmade lakes—some nearly a mile in circumference—supplied water for the many natural fountains, including the two-hundred-ninety-foot geyser of the Emperor Fountain, named and designed especially for the intended (but never realized) visit of Czar Nicholas II of Russia. High up on a hill behind the house, through a series of fountains and jets initiating from a domed, winged structure, water danced and plummeted down the twenty-four steps of a cascade. Ravines, grottoes, and a greenhouse supplied the camelias and rare orchids that were cut and placed in frosted vases before the plates of dinner guests. The main square block of the house itself was a famous example of the William-and-Mary style, built of the stones from the neighboring quarry with the idea of making an unobtrusive addition to this natural setting. The original architects had intended to provide the first duke with England's Elysian Fields, and, indeed, over the centuries Chatsworth had come to be considered the most beautiful house in the world.

It was a shuttered storehouse, however, when Kathleen first toured through it, the only noise throughout the one hundred and seventy-five rooms the simultaneous chiming of clocks which were faithfully wound and set once a week. As Kathleen walked from room to room she could imagine the kind of life Chatsworth had been built to accommodate. The entrance was through the Painted Hall, an immense, breathtaking area of gilt ironwork balustrades, a red-carpeted stairwell, and wall and ceiling murals painted by Laguerre with scenes from the life of Julius Caesar. Proceeding through the vast state rooms, she viewed their ornate hand-carved overmantels, gilded leather wall hangings, and tapestries especially patterned after the drawings of Raphael. Murals of mythological scenes graced most of the state room ceilings. Door cases had been imported from Italy or fashioned from alabaster dug from the local quarries, as was the altar of the chapel, where several dukes had been married. The tortoiseshell surfaces of Boulle furniture were elaborately patterned and inlaid with brass.

On previous Christmases, when more than a hundred relatives stayed at Chatsworth as guests of his grandfather, Billy's immediate family were put up in the state rooms, which were considered among the best rooms of the house. (Service was always arranged according to precedence in the family line.) Billy had slept in the same bed as George II and opened his eyes in the morning to dazzling ceiling frescos of Aurora chasing away the night. The Cavendishes owned the bed in which one English king had died, and the chair in which another had been crowned. Rare Chinese wallpaper had been imported for the late-regency bedrooms. The landing of the Oak Staircase (everything seemed to have a name in capital letters) was lit by a novel chandelier of gilt stag heads containing real horns that had been given to the family by another English king. The music room, where guests had been entertained by small concerts, was easily identifiable by a hallmark of Chatsworth: the trompe l'oeil painting of a violin on an inner doorway. Some fifty servants were required to run the house when it was inhabited, with about twenty additional hands for the garden.

With opulent furnishings of this kind many of the real treasures of Chatsworth hung unnoticed. It was said that Billy's ancestors had amassed the greatest private collection of paintings and sculpture in England. An entire wing of the house had been constructed by the Bachelor Duke to properly display his impressive collection of neoclassic sculptures. Priceless oils by Rembrandt, Velasquez, Gainsborough, and Rubens adorned walls throughout Chatsworth, with others packed away or placed in unobtrusive corners. Sargent and Reynolds were among the master painters who had done ancestral portraits of family members. The Cavendishes were especially known for their collection of Holbein, Da Vinci, and Rembrandt drawings and engravings, and for the thousands of rare books in the library, a number printed before 1500.

Everywhere Kathleen turned, she saw evidence of Billy's distinguished forebears, many of whom she had read about in history books. The origin of the estate could be traced back to Bess of Hardwick, who persuaded her second husband, William Cavendish, to settle in what was then inhospitable country. The title had derived from Bess's great-great-grandson, who received the dukedom for assisting William of Orange to the English throne during the Glorious Revolution of 1688. Several bedrooms in the house had been named after Mary, Queen of Scots, an involuntary guest when Bess's fourth husband, the Earl of Shrewsbury, was appointed her custodian by Queen Elizabeth I.

Thomas Hobbes, author of *Leviathan,* had tutored several Cavendish children; Charles Dickens had been the sixth duke's good friend.

It was overwhelming to think of the extent of the riches owned by Billy's family; Chatsworth may have been the most magnificent of the Cavendish residences, but it was only one among many. Bess herself had built the Elizabethan masterpiece, Hardwick Hall, also a treasure-house of rare objects, where Billy's newly widowed grandmother, the dowager duchess, now resided. There were Lismore Castle in Ireland, Bolton Abbey in Scotland, Chiswick Villa, just outside of London, Compton Place in Eastbourne, and several townhouses in London. In all, the family owned some one hundred eighty thousand acres of land: in Derbyshire alone, besides the park of Chatsworth, the estate controlled twelve thousand acres, mostly farmland leased out to tenant farmers in much the same arrangement that ancestral manor lords had maintained in feudal societies. A good deal of the employment and activities of the area, often called the "dukeries," was dominated by the Duke of Devonshire and the Duke of Rutland, who owned the neighboring Haddon Hall, and its population was intensely loyal to the men they still largely viewed as their benefactors.

Billy's grandfather, fastidious about tending to his estate, had determined his place of residence according to holidays and sport. The three months surrounding Christmas were spent at Chatsworth; February through March at Lismore; April through July, the traditional months of the Season, in London; July and part of August, again at Chatsworth for the Bakewell Show, an agricultural and horticultural fair; August and part of September at Bolton Abbey for the start of grouse shooting; and finally October at Hardwick Hall for the partridge shoot.

"Chiswick?" Billy's grandmother was once heard to remark. "Oh, we sometimes used it for breakfast."

As future head of the family Billy would hold, besides the dukedom and marquessate (the latter to be passed on to his son as a courtesy title, as Billy's father had passed it on to him), two earldoms, two baronies, three Irish titles, one title each in Portugal and Spain, and a princedom in the Netherlands.

After seeing Chatsworth it was obvious to Kathleen that the greatest difference between her and Billy was not their religious one. She had no family pedigree; her father had been inventing a Kennedy history as he went along. Billy's father was a little eccentric, prone to wearing tattered suits with paper collars. But the fact that he didn't possess an overcoat made no difference to his standing in the community or to his electoral popularity; he had held key positions in both the House of Commons and the cabinet. The Duke of Devonshire hardly had to worry about maintaining a proper image, supporting a particular prime minister, or cultivating important newspaper people to ensure that his son received the right kind of exposure. Billy's future position as one of the most important men in England had been assured from the day he was born. The other great difference was that Billy's father—and his grandfather and great-grandfather—had never needed to make money. Chatsworth and other estates like it hadn't been built by stock-market deals or fast killings in the liquor business but through centuries of people like Billy marrying their own kind.

In early August Kathleen flew with the ambassador to Cannes to meet up with the rest of her family, while Billy headed up north to Bolton Abbey with his family for the start of the grouse-shooting season. By the end of that month Jack had returned to the States for the start of his junior year at Harvard, Kick and her father had returned to London, the young Kennedys, along with Luella Hennessy and Betty Dunn, had begun a week's trip to Scotland, and Mrs. Kennedy had stayed behind with Teddy, intending to spend all of September in France. Joe Jr. left on his first job as envoy to his father, working for William Bullitt, the American ambassador in Paris. The French government was in the midst of a crisis, and Joe Kennedy had thought that his son would benefit from being on hand as an eyewitness.

The family was still dispersed when Hitler grew increasingly intractable about the fate of the Sudeten Germans and set October 1 as the date when he would disclose whether or not he would go to war with the Czechs over the issue. Mrs. Kennedy returned with Teddy to London, and the ambassador made plans to send his children to Ireland.

Then, on September 15, Chamberlain met with Hitler in Berchtesgaden and agreed to the Führer's demands for a partition of the Sudetenland, a condition the Czechs would have to accept if they did not want to fight Germany alone. When it appeared that war had been avoided, the young children were sent back to school, and Kathleen went ahead with her plans to go to Scotland with friends for the final fortnight of the Scottish season. Mrs. Kennedy herself traveled alone to Perth, the hub of the social events up north, booking a room in the Gleneagles Hotel and telephoning Kick from time to time to keep her abreast of the political situation.

In late September, when Chamberlain journeyed to Godesberg to firm up his agreement, Hitler, to his astonishment, abandoned all his former terms, laying down a new set of demands, now calling for the cession of a larger area of the Sudetenland by October 1. Overnight, war had become inevitable. Trenches were dug around the parks and gas masks hurriedly dispensed to a shocked population. Workmen at the palace labored overtime, reinforcing the walls of the royal air-raid shelter with concrete and sandbags and installing gas-proof windows. The British cabinet declared a state of emergency. When Hitler responded to Chamberlain's plea for a settlement through an international commission by moving up the date of reckoning to September 28, the ambassador telephoned Mrs. Kennedy and told her that she and Kathleen should be prepared to come home at any moment.

Four

In London on September 28, 1938, a House of Commons meeting packed with spectators was dramatically interrupted when Chamberlain read off a cable that had just arrived from Berlin. At the eleventh hour Hitler had agreed to one last meeting with the British prime minister. There was still the hope of striking a bargain and averting war.

Kathleen and her mother were in Scotland that day at the Perth races. Normally swarming with tourists, the town had remained peculiarly empty, although the traditional festivities went on uninterruptedly. On the afternoon of September 28 there had been a picturesque gathering of the Scottish clans, where Kick was photographed in tweeds and in what British papers had come to refer to as her "hatless fashion." It was only that evening, when she ran into her mother at a cocktail party, that she caught up on the momentous news from London. Rose Kennedy had received a call from the ambassador. In view of Chamberlain's trip to Munich he had encouraged her to stay in Perth with Kick for the weekend. In the meantime, however, he was going ahead with plans to get the children ready to leave for the United States.

The ambassador himself had joined in the relieved cheering

following Chamberlain's announcement. Just the week before, Kennedy had entertained Colonel Charles Lindbergh, who had visited Germany at Hitler's invitation to view the much heralded Luftwaffe. Lindbergh's assessment of German air power, which he estimated to be more powerful than that of all the European nations and the United States put together, had so alarmed the ambassador that he had asked the aviator to write up his findings in a report to be subsequently passed on to the secretary of state and the President. As the ambassador now saw it, the British had no choice but to accede to German demands.

Kick was still in Scotland when word came of the prime minister's triumphant return. British newspapers jubilantly reported his meeting with Hitler as an astounding diplomatic coup: Neville Chamberlain had not only managed to stave off war and address Germany's grievances in terms favorable to both countries but had convinced Hitler to sign a treaty promising that the two countries would never again resort to arms to settle differences. It was the dawning of a new age, Chamberlain proclaimed, waving the treaty to crowds gathered outside his window at 10 Downing Street. "With this paper," he told his audience, he had managed to secure "peace in our time." In every newspaper photographs appeared of Chamberlain's triumphal return, umbrella in hand, disembarking from his small aircraft as he waved to a wildly cheering crowd. "A Very Great Englishman" read the caption for a shot of the prime minister opening a taxi door for his wife with a flamboyant flourish and a tip of his bowler. The grateful French planned to rename the Place de Isle in Cannes the Place de Neville Chamberlain. *The Spectator* nominated the statesman for the Nobel prize.

After their initial relief some of the British had uneasy second thoughts. The day after his thirteen-hour meeting with Hitler, Chamberlain had read the brutal terms of the agreement the Czechs would be forced to follow. Along with the Sudetenland, Hitler had demanded the heavily fortressed Czech borders, thereby leaving the country defenseless to attack.

In Winston Churchill's view the British had "sustained a total and unmitigated defeat" in signing the Munich pact. A number

of Kathleen's friends heartily agreed with him. Young men with
political aspirations like David Ormsby-Gore and Billy Hartington jeered at references to Chamberlain's tough negotiating ability and the implication that Britain had maintained peace with
honor. At best Chamberlain had bought time for Britain in a
shamelessly self-serving manner. Like most other young people,
however, they were also enormously relieved. In the last few
weeks they had become very aware of Britain's ill-preparedness,
and they had tried to come to terms with the terrifying prospect
of being drafted and going to war. In the Great War in which
their fathers had fought, the lists of the dead and wounded after
a single battle had often occupied eight full pages of the London
Times. Boys like David and Billy, however, believed that it was
one's duty to fight, no matter what the odds. There had been soldiers in every generation of their families. They had grown up on
stories of the "war to end all wars"—of an entire generation facing almost certain massacre, who had nevertheless gone off to
fight. Now in their own time their country cowered before a
common blackmailer. It seemed impossible that Britain's adver-
sary in the last war would dare to fight again with the victor a
mere twenty years later. England was, after all, the strongest,
most powerful nation on earth.

There was the suspicion, though, especially among those
who had been to Germany and observed the Nazi youth movement, that Hitler would not stop at merely carving up Czechoslovakia.

The ambassador still stubbornly supported the approach
Chamberlain had taken. Several weeks after the meeting at
Munich he made a Trafalgar Day speech before the Navy
League, in which he pleaded that democracies and dictatorships
could coexist as good neighbors:

> It is true that the democratic and dictator countries have im-
> portant and fundamental divergencies of outlook, which in
> certain areas go deeper than politics. But there is simply no
> sense, common or otherwise, in letting these differences
> grow into unrelenting antagonism. After all, we have to live
> together in the same world, whether we like it or not.

It was the first time Kennedy had made a public statement implying unequivocal American support of appeasement. Editors of United States newspapers were outraged and accused Kennedy of being a member of the Cliveden Set, the name coined by a left-leaning British publication to refer to those members of the upper classes who favored sympathetic negotiations with Hitler. Many American Jews immediately abandoned their support of Kennedy as a potential presidential candidate. This latest indiscretion infuriated Roosevelt, who had been deliberately following a noncommittal path with regard to Britain's foreign policy. Annoyed already by Kennedy's "confidential" memos to newspaper cronies about the state of the European crisis, Roosevelt decided that Kennedy needed, as he put it, his "wrists slapped rather hard." He administered the slap with a radio speech that unequivocally denounced Hitler's methods of negotiation by "sheer force" or "threat of war."

Later that fall Kennedy and Chamberlain lost further political ground. On November 9 and 10, in retaliation for the revenge murder of a German official by a Jewish refugee, Nazis had pillaged Jewish neighborhoods, burning and looting shops, murdering and raping, and arresting some twenty thousand people. When the government confiscated the insurance money due the Jewish people for their property damage and levied on them a fine of several million marks, it was clear that the raids and the violence had not been the handiwork of a small group of extremists but had been sanctioned by Berlin.

Facing a storm of criticism, particularly charges that he was out of touch with his countrymen in the United States, the ambassador decided to return home over Christmas. It became the responsibility of young Joe, back from a whirlwind tour of Berlin, Warsaw, and other European cities, to marshal the family to St. Moritz for the holidays. According to his diplomatic passport Joe had been abroad on "official business." After shepherding his mother and younger brothers and sisters back to London, he secured an ordinary passport as a "journalist," returned to France, and crossed the border into Spain with his father's embassy assistant Harvey Klemmer to take a look at the Spanish Civil War. In

February, when the ambassador arrived in London, he found a cable waiting for him from his oldest boy: "ARRIVED SAFELY VALENCIA, GOING TO MADRID TONIGHT." Madrid was under a state of siege. Kennedy told staff members at the embassy that he hoped his son would stay out of the firing line but was obviously pleased by the reputation Joe was fostering in the press as a "crisis hunter." As Joe sent him detailed accounts of the fall of Madrid the ambassador proudly showed them to Chamberlain, Halifax, and several American reporters.

Jack had come over on the ship with his father to begin work at the embassy—"to *begin* his education," Joe had remarked disparagingly in a letter to a friend. Like Joe he was entrusted by the ambassador with tasks considered too sensitive for professional employees to handle, and after accompanying the family in March to Italy, where the Kennedys were special United States representatives to the coronation of Pope Pius XII, Jack initiated his own "fact-finding" travel program to German-occupied areas of Europe. Career service people and diplomats honored the letters of introduction he carried from Ambassador Kennedy but presumably had more important work to do than to fill the itinerary of a youth with no official status.

Despite her father's dour prediction that war would come to Britain by the springtime, Kathleen threw herself into preparations for the 1939 Season. Social calendars were more hectic and parties and balls more elaborate than they had been for many years. The Duke and Duchess of Marlborough had purchased a mansion in London so that their debutante daughter, Lady Sarah Spencer-Churchill, could more conveniently attend the events. Her own party at Blenheim Palace, the Marlborough estate, was the most dazzling of the Season, with all the gardens floodlit and champagne flowing in nearly every room. Sally Norton's mother, Lady Grantley, at first planned a small beer and chips party for her daughter but ended by arranging a large New Orleans ball where jazz pianist Fats Waller played "My Very Good Friend, the Milkman" over and over to the delight of Sally and her friends. Swing had just caught on in America after all the saccharine music of the early thirties and had recently traveled across the Atlantic. All Kick's English friends were ardent fans; Sally had most of their favorites on gramophone records, including almost everything by a new bandleader named Glenn Miller. Hours were spent discussing the merits of the top musicians, but Benny Goodman with his "killer-diller" brass arrangements was the undisputed King of Swing. The Big Apple had been introduced that year, and Kathleen and her friends loved forming the big circle and ending with a bumpsadaisy—to the dismay of Mrs. Kennedy, who found the dance a little shocking.

This year it was Eunice's turn to come out, since she would be seventeen in June. She also collected a number of English beaux, including Veronica's brother, Hugh Fraser. One young Englishman in particular considered Eunice the earthiest of the Kennedy girls. (There was something of the *chienne* about her, he thought.) But most of the time Eunice was considered a little socially ill at ease. She fitted into the events of the Season as awkwardly as into the required wardrobe; her white straw hats shaped like wide saucers always seemed slapped on slightly askew. Once she'd even shown up for Royal Ascot in a sensible navy blue coat.

Fashion reporters still focused their attention on "K.K." Almost weekly note was made of her wardrobe—dainty little dresses with puffed sleeves for daytime and pink and white taffeta gowns at night, one with a very tight-fitting boned bodice held up by no visible means of support. She had grown to like flamboyant hats; her favorite was an Edwardian picture hat tied with a lavish bow of white tulle. This year Kathleen was treated like any other young member of English society. She was even invited to work on various committees, notably that of the Derby Ball. On two occasions, while Mrs. Kennedy traveled abroad, Kathleen took over her official functions, once at a reception at Buckingham Palace, and again at a fete given by the American Women's Club (Mrs. Kennedy was its honorary president). Opening the event with the first speech of her life, Kick received tremendous applause using a tried and true standing joke of her father's. Explaining that she was simply her mother's stand-in, she added, "And I rather wish that my father were here to deputize for me. He always has things to talk about—at least nine familiar subjects!"

In mid-March, Hitler broke his Munich pact. For several days, as Nazi troops stormed through Czechoslovakia, Neville Chamberlain held out hope that he could salvage the situation. Poland was the next obvious target, with Hitler demanding a corridor to the port of Danzig. Although Ambassador Kennedy made it quite clear to Chamberlain that he did not consider it worthwhile to have a showdown with Germany over Poland, the prime minister had no choice. He knew that the British people would not stand for another show of weakness. At the end of the month he reversed the policy the country had followed for five years and guaranteed the Poles military support.

As the prospect of war began to appear even more likely it became apparent to Kathleen's friends that Ambassador Kennedy was an ardent isolationist, intent on doing whatever was necessary to keep the United States out of war. Indeed, he appeared far more determined to avoid having his sons drafted than to win support for America's old ally in her hour of need. Even if he privately held these views, it was indiscreet of him to state them publicly. Kennedy's young embassy aide Page Huidekoper told the ambassador the current joke circulating in London about the two yellow races who would eventually fight it out together: the Japanese and the Americans. It was far from being the only anti-American remark going around at the time, but she thought he'd better hear this one from her first. Kathleen's friends came to agree with what their parents had suspected all along—that Joseph Kennedy was not adequately equipped to hold his post. There was even speculation that the Irish Catholic took secret pleasure in the twisting of the British lion's tail.

In the States as well criticism of Kennedy became more heated. Liberals who demanded his recall accused him of being Chamberlain's pawn and of being anti-Semitic (the ambassador was said to have complained that the American Jews were trying to get the United States into the war). Kennedy's main support came from the substantial body of conservatives at home who saw Hitler as a European problem, not an American one. After frequent, often hysterical phone calls to Roosevelt warning that war was imminent, the ambassador tried to book passage home in early summer, preferring to resign rather than continue to take abuse, but the President wouldn't hear of it.

If the ambassador's isolationist position was an embarrassment to Kathleen, she loyally refrained from mentioning it, and her friends made a point of avoiding political discussions with her. One night, however, Billy, David Ormsby-Gore, and Sissy Lloyd-Thomas inadvertently stumbled upon another sensitive issue. Someone made a disparaging comment during dinner about a man who was having an extramarital affair, and Kick reacted rather strongly.

"That's what all men do," she replied, with a little too much authority in her voice. "You know that women can never trust them."

David broke the embarrassed silence. Eventually the ambassador's name was tactfully mentioned. Kick's friends took turns explaining that his behavior was hardly typical and certainly not anything that a woman was automatically expected to put up with.

In late winter Kick visited Charlotte McDonnell and her sister Anne, who were in Rome for the year. One day, while the three of them were on a sight-seeing tour, an air-raid drill sounded. Everyone in the bus ran for shelter. After the All Clear had sounded and the passengers had filed back into the vehicle, Kathleen got separated from the McDonnells. Charlotte suddenly heard a familiar voice shriek authoritatively, "Stoppa the bus! Stoppa the bus!" For a minute she thought the commotion had something to do with the drill. After the driver had stopped for them, Kick told her friends that she'd been pinched by one of the Italian men. If she hadn't gotten off that instant, she was sure that something terrible would have happened to her.

During the next few months Kathleen followed the lead of her English circle in participating in the gaiety of the spring events. At country house weekends the imminence of war was discussed with a certain detachment, as though it were merely a topic of intellectual interest. It was not British to voice one's private terrors. Experts had predicted that in a war with Britain, Germany would rely on gas warfare and air raids and flatten English cities in a day. Sally Norton often envisioned a devastating scene of a thousand airplanes all dropping bombs simultaneously on London—H. G. Wells's *War of the Worlds* brought to life. Yet other thoughts of what war might bring had a certain appeal for her crowd. Billy decided to do a stint in the Army whether or not war was declared, and received his commission into officer's training for the Coldstream Guards. The previous year's debutantes talked of working as WRENS or in the Red Cross, or as decoders or parachutists. A girl looked especially pretty in an army hat or a factory uniform. Young people were constantly warned by their parents how uncomfortable and boring it had been in the first war and how one had to get used to going without, but the slight discomforts they might have to endure seemed insignificant beside the undeniable anticipation that each day now held for them. They knew they stood poised on the brink of some momentous event. There would be opportunities to match their fathers' heroism. They imagined terribly romantic good-bye scenes at airports, frantic all-night train rides to catch up with a beau for a few minutes of leave. And all the normally agonizing decisions about one's future and career could now be postponed indefinitely.

As in the two past summers Kathleen and her friends split up after Goodwood Week, most of them taking to the country or going away on holiday. Veronica Fraser spent most of the next two months at a house party in Derbyshire with eighteen other young people, working on an amateur charity production of *The Merchant of Venice*. Sally Norton traveled with her mother to the south of France. Roosevelt had talked the ambassador out of resigning, and he and Mrs. Kennedy had taken another villa in Cannes. Young Joe had returned from Spain a month before. In late July, Kick and Hugh Fraser traveled with Joe back through Madrid in a circuitous route that was to end up in southern France. It was the first time her brother had acknowledged her as a companion and potential friend. Joe had always

seemed so much older than she was and never more so than
during this past year on his intermittent visits to the embassy,
when he regaled the family with stories of his meetings with important foreign government officials and complicated analyses of
European political situations. The entire family was very proud
of him. In Madrid, Kathleen met some of his Spanish friends,
who had been impressed by his bravery. During the bloodiest
days of the siege Joe had often been the only American walking
about the streets. He had sent his father some thirty-six letters
from Spain, all eyewitness accounts of the war. The ambassador
intended to have them published under the title *Dear Dad*, but
even his fatherly prejudice didn't blind him to the fact that they
were ungrammatical and needed editing. He had called in Harvey Klemmer, who had written many Kennedy speeches. "Make
a book out of these," the ambassador said, tossing the batch at
him, "and send your kids through college."

After making her way with Joe to the south of France, Kathleen went to stay with Sally Norton at her mother's rented villa
in St. Maxime. Janie Kenyon-Slaney was a guest there as well,
and after several days she and Kick headed off to the Kennedys'
villa in Cannes, where Jack Kennedy had already arrived with
his traveling companion, Torby Macdonald. Jack immediately
developed a terrific crush on Janie, but she considered him too
brash and put him off. During midnight confidences in the bedroom she and Janie shared, Kathleen often chided her friend, "I
can't think why you're not being nicer to Jack." Torby was still
pursuing Kick—more and more unsuccessfully.

On August 15 and 16, when the Duke and Duchess of Devonshire held Billy Hartington's coming-of-age party at Chatsworth,
Kathleen was still away from England. Billy had turned twenty-
one the December before, but out of deference to his newly de-
ceased grandfather the family had decided to postpone the celebration until the summer. Despite the deteriorating political situation the Duke and Duchess of Devonshire had proceeded with
the lavish festivities. Nearly five thousand guests, mostly tenants
and employees of Chatsworth, gathered on the grounds in the
brilliant sunshine as the Coldstream Guards band played and a

carousel set up for children revolved. By the second day, after too much handshaking, the duchess wore her right hand in a sling.

Even though Kick couldn't attend the ceremony, all her closest friends assumed that she and Billy were "semiengaged." On the day of the party reports of a secret engagement were published in the Boston papers. Both the Duke of Devonshire and Joseph Kennedy denied the rumor, the ambassador dismissing it as though it were another Peter Grace story invented by one more reporter hungry for a scoop.

The truth was that the young couple had reached no such agreement. Every time that Billy thought of asking Kick to marry him, he ran up against the same insurmountable obstacle. Marrying a Roman Catholic seemed absolutely out of the question. How could he agree to the conditions of her Church? Once he became duke, he would have to appoint a number of Anglican ministers; he could hardly turn over that task one day to a Catholic son. Just imagine a Catholic Duke of Devonshire. His father's ridiculous prejudices were a common joke among his crowd, but he had to admit that he didn't really savor the idea of raising Catholic children. Besides, with all the coming-of-age festivities this was not the time to bring up the subject with his father. It was frightening enough just thinking about his father's likely reaction. Already his parents were embarrassed about his seeing Kick. They hadn't confronted him yet, but he'd found out that they were talking over the problem with their friends. Now that he was twenty-one, he had his own position and future to consider. Kick would just have to understand. Perhaps they could work out something at some point, as long as she didn't insist on marrying in her Church.

After Billy told her his position, Kathleen was even less ready to enter into an engagement. She was well aware of the dangers of marrying a non-Catholic. She could never forget the catechism answers she'd had to recite over and over at Noroton listing the only acceptable conditions for a mixed marriage. How could Billy expect her to marry outside the Church? That was the worst sin she could possibly commit. For the rest of her life she would be in mortal sin; when she died, she'd go to hell. Then there was her family's position to consider. Just think how marrying a Protestant would publicly humiliate her parents, especially after they had been chosen by the President to represent America at the papal coronation. What would it do to her father's career? Aside from everything else she wasn't sure how she felt about Billy. She liked him well enough, but going steady and getting engaged were so confining. There was all the time in the world to think about settling down.

The issue was resolved for the two of them when Germany invaded Poland on September 1. The Kennedys had learned of the imminent invasion the week before, while they were in the south of France; the ambassador had insisted that the children depart immediately for London. Kathleen and Janie were still wearing their tennis shorts when they were put aboard the train for Paris, their luggage following them through diplomatic channels. The return trip seemed like just another of the summer's many larks. Then, at one point along the way they observed trainload after trainload of British troops heading in the opposite direction. Kick and Janie suddenly grew frightened. It was finally obvious why they had been sent home early.

On September 3, seated in the public gallery of the House of Commons, Kathleen, with her brothers Joe and Jack, and Mrs. Kennedy, heard Chamberlain's heartbroken declaration of war and his statement of personal failure: "Everything that I have worked for, everything that I have hoped for, everything that I have believed in during my public life has crashed in ruins."

Shortly afterward Jack got his first visceral taste of the effects of war when his father dispatched him to Scotland to aid the survivors of the British liner, the *Athenia,* which had been torpedoed by a German submarine.

With air raids expected at any time in London, the ambassador attempted to secure homeward transportation for his children. For the time being he sent them out of the city to the J. Pierpont Morgan country home in Windsor Great Park. Americans were desperately flooding aboard neutral ships en route to the States, and space was extremely limited.

For two weeks Kathleen argued vehemently with her father. She was determined to stay in England. All her friends were frantically deciding what to do next. Billy and the rest of the boys were being called into service. Sally Norton, who had only been allowed to take three swing records with her from France, had been sent to stay with her grandmother in Scotland. Chatsworth was being packed up and handed over to Penrhos College, a girls' school, since the duke preferred to have young women inhabiting it rather than soldiers. Some of Kick's debutante friends were talking of working in factories, helping to build bombers. Kathleen desperately wanted to do her share. Her father was adamant, however; she was going home on the first available ship. The Kennedys' nurse, Luella Hennessy, who had also acquired a titled English boyfriend, a banker whom she had met at the English Speaking Union, was just as reluctant to leave England as Kick was. She approached the ambassador one day with a scheme the two of them had cooked up: They would stay in England together.

The ambassador laughed but wouldn't hear of it. "If you want to wait for the boat to turn right around and come back, that's your business," he replied to Luella. "But I brought you over here single and I'm returning you single."

In mid-September the ambassador gave a farewell party for his children. He would be staying on in England alone, along with Rosemary, who would continue to attend her present school in the country. His wife and the rest of his children would be crossing the Atlantic a few at a time, aboard several liners. Mr. and Mrs. Kennedy had always made it a rule that in case of an accident the children should never travel all together. After many toasts and much good-natured kidding the ambassador predicted that England was going to be "badly thrashed."

A day or two earlier, when she learned that her father had booked her aboard the crowded *Washington* with Eunice and Bobby, Kathleen had wept. But now, with her father's insistence that the British were going to lose, it was even harder to abandon her closest friends.

Five

"Everything is just the same," Kathleen wrote resignedly to her father on September 26, a week after she'd been back in Bronxville. "That's the amazing thing when one's been away, one expects things to have changed and they haven't. . . ." Actually, some of her friends believed that it was Kick who had changed. She seemed somehow more sophisticated, or perhaps, as Nancy Tenney thought, a bit more aloof—full of tales of titled people, weekends at country estates, and English expressions like "keen" and "darling." Nancy was rather shocked when Kathleen, visiting one weekend, left her shoes outside her bedroom door, as though she expected to find them neatly polished and returned by morning.

Immediately after her return Kathleen had tried to resume her interrupted education and had applied to Sarah Lawrence, influenced perhaps by Frances Ann Cannon, Jack's current flame, who attended the prestigious experimental women's college. Rejected, she enrolled in Finch, a popular finishing school in New York for nonacademically minded young ladies of prominent families, and decided to study art and design. "It is a junior college and one can get a diploma, which is something," Kick wrote in the same letter to her father. Although she signed off with the news that Jack was taking out Frances Ann that very weekend, "so we can all hardly wait," no engagement was imminent. That weekend the daughter of the South Carolina Cannon Mills family told Kathleen's disappointed brother that she had just become the fiancée of the writer John Hersey.

Frequent visits with Joe and Jack at Harvard, particularly during game weekends, provided Kick with relief from an uninspired school term. On other weekends her brothers and a group of their friends made trips to Manhattan. She began to be seen regularly with Joe and Jack, listening to Eve Symington sing the blues at the Persian Room of the Plaza Hotel or at a little swing club on Fifty-second Street, where the music went "down and around, below, *below*, BELOW." At the Stork Club, Jack and Kick became known as the Kennedy family's personality kids.

During Kathleen's years overseas New York had come alive with the Big Bands she loved—the Dorsey brothers, Artie Shaw, and Woody Herman at Roseland. At seven in the morning fans were lining up outside the Paramount in order to listen that evening to Benny Goodman. Kathleen was astounded to learn that Glenn Miller had played at Nancy Tenney's 1939 coming-out ball for a few hundred dollars just before his spectacular rise to stardom.

When not out on the town, Kick's brothers were working hard. Joe was in his first year of law school, and Jack, who was attempting to make up the lost term of the previous spring and graduate in May of that year with honors, had begun tackling the required thesis. Law study did not come easily to Joe, even with the help of the nightly tutoring sessions with Superior Judge John J. Burns that were set up for him by his father. His fellow students soon discovered, however, that if they wished to be friends of Joe Kennedy's, they'd better be prepared to give him the spotlight. Joe relished telling stories of his days in war-torn Spain. A rumor circulated that he had been thrown into a Spanish jail and strip-searched, and he did little to dispel it. He had been known to leave the room brusquely in the middle of a conversation if he felt that his narrative was not being properly appreciated. He also clearly preferred the exclusive company of his own family. Occasionally when Jack or Kick invited a friend along on one of their outings, Joe would grow sarcastic or withdrawn. If his brother or sister was not to be present, Joe would think nothing of standing up a schoolmate for dinner.

Although women may have found Joe attractive, he had not had a single serious girl friend in all his twenty-five years. He shied away from eligible Catholic girls, preferring the company of older women, usually show girls and singers from the Cocoanut Grove.

Kathleen went out with Peter Grace a few times but soon discovered that they had little in common. When their reconciliation proved short-lived, she took up with college friends of her brothers. Her experiences in England had closed whatever gap had existed between herself and the Kennedy boys. The young men they knew flocked around Kathleen, attracted by her independence. Johnny Coleman, or Zeke, as everybody called him, a serious-minded midwesterner from a good family, fell in love with her. She also saw a little of George Mead, a junior at Yale, whose family summered in a town next to HyannisPort. Lem Billings, an old Choate buddy of Jack's, claimed to be mad for Kick. When Kick wouldn't go out with him, he asked Eunice, and when Eunice turned him down, fifteen-year-old Pat. Charlotte suspected that Kathleen had a sneaker for Tom Killefer, Joe Jr.'s law school roommate.

Rumors mounted about a possible engagement between Kick and Winthrop Rockefeller. A *Boston American* reporter claimed he had come upon young Rockefeller selecting an expensive ski jacket from one of New York's smartest stores as a Christmas present for Kathleen. ". . . Since it isn't quite etiquette to send a girl one isn't engaged to anything but books, flowers and candy," the reporter wrote, "—well, draw your own conclusions."

Other reporters revived the old rumors of a supposed romance between Kick and Torby Macdonald after they were spotted together at Harvard functions and in Palm Springs over the Christmas holiday. Torby, still crazy about Kick, had continued to pursue her even after his marked lack of success in Europe. He would later maintain that he and Kick were secretly engaged that year, a betrothal the ambassador broke up by offering to make him a "corporate son-in-law," which independent-minded Torby regarded as conclusive evidence that he and Kick would never be free of her father. In fact, Kick allowed him to accompany her only when they were going out as part of a group. Despite the fact that Torby kept her picture on his bureau at school, everyone knew that his feelings were not reciprocated and that Kathleen would never entertain the possibility of marrying a gym teacher's son. Charlotte McDonnell laughed at the stories of the supposed engagement. Just that fall she and Kick had gone to Harvard to attend a game weekend with Joe and Torb. The evening of the dance the two girls had gotten into a bubble bath in their room at the Ritz. They were still in the bath when the boys arrived to pick them up, and they decided that they were too tired to go out. They never did make the dance that evening, preferring to stick around the hotel and simply attend the game the following day.

Nearly all Kick's boyfriends were the rugged all-American quarterback types she had dated before England, and she maintained her maddening habit of giving none of them preferential treatment. She would often arrive in New York with one date and leave with another. Both her older brothers—and Jack, in particular—disapproved of their little sister's having so much freedom. Occasionally Jack felt obliged to act as her chaperone and counselor. He'd lecture Kathleen sternly about what he considered her "insincerity" with his friends. One time during a truth-telling session he worked himself into a fatherly fury, quoting from various sources, pointing his finger at her, flushed with the weight of his duty. Kick stared at him in mock horror, one finger characteristically twisting itself around a strand of her honey-colored hair.

"Gosh, kid," she said, humoring him at first by listening intently, "that's too close to a knuckle." She had her suspicions that he enjoyed these sessions.

As Jack became more emphatic, trying to drive home his point or perhaps seeing whether he could reduce her to tears, she finally burst out laughing. "Oh, gosh, kid," she said between giggles. "Oh, come *on*."

It was difficult for her to take Jack's counsel seriously when she knew that he himself often treated dates cavalierly. That fall he had begun taking out Charlotte McDonnell. ("My first taste of a Catholic," he told his father.) He thought of Shatzy, as he called her, as a great pal. Once he approached her with the prospect of marriage, but only, as he bluntly informed her, because Lem Billings and Torby Macdonald had convinced him that it might be a good idea.

Apart from setting Kick a bad example, Jack should have known better than to try to talk her into anything. Even when it came to choosing a movie, she was determined to have her own way. Once Jack, his older law school chum Cam Newberry, and several others wanted to go to the movies. They decided on a serious film. Kick was vehemently opposed, intent instead on seeing *42nd Street*, a musical. A count was taken, yielding four in favor of the drama, with Kick the sole dissenter. "I don't see why you want to see a *stupid*, depressing movie like that," she said. She began arguing and ended by throwing a mock tantrum. In the end the group had gone to see *42nd Street*.

At the end of September, after the Nazi army had crushed Poland in eighteen days, Joseph Kennedy made known his feelings that England hadn't a "Chinaman's chance." An eerie quiet settled over Europe, with Hitler's much anticipated Western offensive yet to be launched. Troops sat poised on the Maginot Line, the much vaunted multi-billion-dollar underground fortress of barracks, ammunition, hospitals, and railways built by the French along the German border to prevent the kind of mass annihilation they had suffered at the hands of their neighbors in the Great War. German soldiers informed the French of their strict instructions not to fire unless fired upon. As the months went by with no movement from Hitler the term "phony war" made its way into conversation. Britons joked uneasily about the sitzkrieg. It became *de rigueur* in France to give as a present a terra-cotta figurine of a dog lifting its leg over a copy of *Mein Kampf.*

Nevertheless, pessimists like Kennedy believed that a German invasion of Britain was inevitable. Looking at figures supplied by Chamberlain and once again applying his bottom-line reasoning, Kennedy calculated that the cost of war would bankrupt England within a matter of months. Even with airplane factories bustling around the clock the poorly outfitted Royal Air Force would not be able to withstand the anticipated onslaught of the Luftwaffe. If Britain were going to lose anyway, the destroyers and other supplies sent to her by Americans would only fall into German hands and would ultimately be used against the United States. "If we had to fight to protect our lives," he kept insisting, "we would do better fighting in our own backyard."

With the President's statements ever more vehemently antifascist Kennedy's intense determination to keep the United States out of Europe's war was becoming something of a personal crusade. As he made his position clear he became the target of the once friendly British press; even the departure of the Kennedy family for the United States was looked upon as cowardly. Increasingly the ambassador found himself dining with Americans or staff members at the embassy, with invitations from British government officials and aristocrats no longer forthcoming. Government officials began to consider Kennedy's outspoken pessimism a threat to British security; his opinions, if transmitted to Washington, might influence Roosevelt to forego attempts to send Britain the arms that were considered critical to victory. Parliamentary officials complained to the British ambassador in Washington, Lord Lothian:

> It has come to our notice from various unofficial sources that Mr. Kennedy has been adopting a most defeatist attitude in his talks with a number of private individuals. . . . We have thought it well to let you know about his indiscreet utterances in case it should later become necessary to ask you to drop a hint in the proper quarter.

As the debate over America's role in the war heated up Eunice and the older boys assured their father in letters and during the minute-and-a-half phone conversations he had with each of his nine children every week that his isolationist position was a popular one at home. Student organizations like the America First Committee, which was dedicated to keeping the United States out of the European war, sprang up on campuses across the country, although most Americans polled believed in providing "all aid short of war" to assure an Allied victory. Charles Lindbergh bought radio time to announce that since England was sure to lose the battle, America would only be beaten if she stepped in at this stage. It was widely believed that in 1917 the United States had been blindly led into an international economic dispute. The dominant mood of the country was "never again."

Young Joe began delivering carefully written speeches on the necessity of America's remaining neutral. Although Joe did not join America First, his views were identical to those espoused by that organization. He believed that even if Britain were beaten, Germany would not invade the United States. He vehemently opposed the employment of American convoys to protect British merchant ships traveling across the North Atlantic because he felt that a single attack on an American ship would automatically thrust the United States into combat. Joe viewed the situation as his father did, in terms of dollars and cents. America, to his mind, would be better off striking a trade bargain with Hitler than bankrupting its economy in a total war.

Although not as staunchly America First as Joe, Jack had chosen as his thesis topic at Harvard the causes behind Chamberlain's appeasement of Hitler at Munich. With the American embassy staff supplying information and Kennedy senior offering advice, the paper was becoming essentially an exculpation of leaders like Chamberlain. In February 1940 Jack wrote the ambassador reassuringly, "Everyone is getting much more confident about our staying out of the war—probably because there is such a lull over there. . . ."

By early 1940 Kathleen had become an ardent proponent of intervention. She could not believe Britain would be lost. What she longed for most was to be contributing to the cause herself. The uncertainty produced by the so-called phony war was very difficult to bear from a distance. Despite the hardships that had already hit London—the blackout; one of the worst winters in forty-six years; the rationing of butter, bacon, and sugar—the letters that arrived from her friends were full of vital accounts of dramatic activity.

All the boys were being called up and undergoing training in the country; Billy was a reserve officer in the Coldstream Guards, stationed at Alton in southern England. War work for women was not yet compulsory, but many of the girls Kathleen knew had already decided to do their part. Sally Norton and her best friend, Osla Benning, both of whom disliked the idea of wearing uniforms, decided that it would be especially heroic to work in an airplane factory manufacturing the bomber planes badly needed by the Royal Air Force. And how amusing, they had thought, to arrive at Claridge's or the Ritz in a boiler suit. They had secured employment at the Hawker Siddeley Factory outside London and were taking a six-month training course in riveting and drilling in order to qualify as semiskilled mechanics, eventually to work on the Hurricane, a small bomber.

They soon discovered there was nothing chic about the work itself. It was a twelve-hour grind beginning at eight A.M. and relieved only by teatime and a one-hour lunch break. Sally lived for Wednesdays, when a swing band entertained them over lunch. She had a wind-up gramophone at the apartment she shared with Osla, but all her old swing records were buried under the daffodil garden behind her mother's villa in France (where her mother had also buried her jewels). She now listened to "We're Gonna Hang Out the Washing on the Siegfried Line" and other recent releases.

She and Osla worked side by side with working-class women who arrived at the factory in garish sweaters and cheap costume jewelry and whose endless talk about their petty personal lives was hopelessly boring. Sally soon learned not to talk about her family background. At first she felt a giddy unity with the other workers, particularly after joining a trades union; it was reassuring to know that the monotony of her present existence was indeed making a vital contribution to the winning of the war. She spent her day off every eighth day either in bed or in London, arriving to stay the night at Claridge's in sensible shoes and factory uniform, her heels and evening clothes in a bag. With all her friends scattered and the boys permitted leave only forty-eight hours a fortnight, she and the others had concocted a make-shift form of communications at Claridge's: They all checked in with Gibbs, the hall porter, upon arriving in the city. "Ah, Miss Norton," Gibbs would say, "Lord Hartington is in London, Miss Kenyon-Slaney is staying here. Lord Grantley is over at the Ritz, and here is his room number." There was a set pattern to these London evenings; everyone knew to congregate at the Ritz Bar at eight, where they would have a few drinks before heading off to the Mirabelle for dinner. Rely on Us, the taxi service that continued to operate during the blackout, would shuttle the group on to the Café de Paris in Leicester Square, or the "Caff," as they called it, where they would dance to Snake-hips Johnson and his swing band. Only at two or three in the morning would it be appropriate to move on to the dark, cavernous Four Hundred, where they would stay until it was time to take a milk train back to work or training camp. Many of the boys out on two-day leave would have taxis standing by to get them back in time for morning drill.

Kick's London friends had begun pairing off seriously that winter; the letters Kick received were filled with news of hurriedly announced engagements: Sissy Lloyd-Thomas and David Ormsby-Gore; Debo Mitford and Billy Hartington's younger brother, Andrew; Janie Kenyon-Slaney and Colonel Peter Lindsay. Billy himself had no special girl friend. He had taken up again with Irene Haig, his old flame from his Eton and Oxford days, and had also begun taking out Sally Norton during his time off in London. Kathleen longed to be mad for someone in the service, as her friends were, to be involved in an exciting, patriotic job, for life to be as focused as theirs so obviously was.

The worst part of it was being left out. In letters and telephone conversations she began a campaign to get over to London that summer in between school terms. Fearing for her safety, the ambassador ignored her pleas. Billy, who had been sent to France with the British Expeditionary Forces in the event of possible invasion, wrote Sally: "I got a letter from Kick the other day. She seemed doubtful if she would be coming over this summer as apparently her father doesn't want her to because he thinks there is too much anti-American feeling in England."

Although preoccupied with rewriting his senior thesis, which Arthur Krock and the ambassador suggested he publish, Jack took up Kick's cause. He wrote his father that he himself would like to come over during the summer "if there is anything of interest going on—otherwise, I shall stay and sail at the Cape.

"Kick is very keen to go over—and I wouldn't think the anti-American feeling would hurt her like it might us—due to her being a girl—especially as it would show that we hadn't merely left England when it got unpleasant."

On May 9 Kathleen, Charlotte, Jack, and a number of his Harvard friends traveled to Baltimore. It was the weekend of the Maryland Hunt Cup, the last of seven hunt steeplechases that began in South Carolina and moved progressively north. For the third year in a row Zeke Coleman's cousin Bill had invited his Harvard friends to attend the event as weekend guests at his parents' home. Along with the Kennedys and Colemans this time were Cam Newberry and Jim Rousmaniere, one of Jack's roommates. Cam, a photography buff, was what everyone called the "eyes" of the group, recording highlights of the weekend with his ever-present movie camera: Jack climbing out of the front seat of the Colemans' 1938 green Packard convertible and onto the running board, the wind whipping at his hair; all seven of the house guests lumbering across the fields to the course, hurdling fences and jumping puddles—with a close-up of Charlotte's mud-caked shoe; Bill Coleman, the clown of the group, trailing a giant snakelike balloon behind him. Experimenting with portraits, special angles, and freeze frames, Cam managed to capture each of his friends in a characteristic pose: Charlotte in a cheesecake pose, cross-legged on the gleaming Packard; Kick, bouncing animatedly on her suitcase, then pumping Zeke's arm in farewell; Bill, glassy-eyed and tipsy, lying on the ground, a glass balanced on his forehead; Jack straddling a fence and then joking with Jim and Zeke, looking tanned and astonishingly handsome in sunglasses against the intense blue Ektachrome sky. Abruptly the film jumped to jerky shots of the boys in white tie and tails and the girls in gowns, waving at the camera, with the dazed, punchy look of those who had had too much to drink and now desperately longed for sleep. Cam had taken this last footage upon their return from the Hunt Cup Ball, which began at midnight and went on until dawn, after which Kick and Charlotte dutifully changed and headed out for seven o'clock Mass. Out of habit more than a sense of duty Jack accompanied them; he had continued to go to church on Sunday, although recently, for the first time, he'd ignored his father's demand that he attend a holy day of obligation.

The day of the Hunt Cup, Nazi Germany abruptly ended its silence and unleashed a masterful and devastating blitzkrieg throughout Belgium, Luxembourg, and Holland, taking over the governments of all three countries in less than a week. In building the Maginot Line the French had not thought to extend it to the Franco-Belgian border since their neighbor had staunchly maintained neutrality. Within five days armored German corps advanced straight through from the Belgian border to Abbeville on the north coast of France, thus cutting off the British and the badly outfitted French forces in the north from those in the south. Billy Hartington, a second lieutenant, was among those British officers whose troops were beaten back to the coast of France and thought to be within days of annihilation by the Nazis.

On May 21 Kick dashed off a worried letter to her father:

At the moment, it looks as if the Germans will be in England before you receive this letter. In fact from the reports here they are just about taking over Claridge's now. I still keep telling everyone "the British lose the battles but they win the wars."

I have received some rather gloomy letters from Jane and Billy. Billy's letter was written from the Maginot Line. Daddy, I must know exactly what has happened to them all. Is Billy all right?

By the time the ambassador received the letter and was able to reply, three hundred thirty thousand men of the British Expeditionary Forces and French First Army had been evacuated through the brilliantly improvised scheme at Dunkirk, where a "Mosquito Armada" of destroyers, ferries, dinghies, and pleasure craft shuttled the starved, exhausted army to safety across the Channel. Billy and his battalion had only narrowly escaped a few days before. At Dunkirk the troops had been forced to leave their tanks and all weapons except rifles on the French shoreline, but the bulk of the force itself had been miraculously saved. It had been a devastating defeat for the British, with France certain to fall into German hands at any moment. Nevertheless, Winston Churchill, who had succeeded the foundering Chamberlain as prime minister and minister of war after the May 10 German invasion, stiffened the resolve of his people by treating Dunkirk as a victory. Defiantly he declared his intention of fighting to the last man—with eventual American support:

> . . . We shall fight on the beaches, we shall fight on the landing-grounds, we shall fight in the fields and in the streets, we shall fight in the hills. We shall never surrender. And even if, which I do not for a moment believe, this Island or a large part of it were subjugated or starving, then our Empire beyond the seas would carry on the struggle until, in God's good time, the New World, with all its power and might, step forth to the liberation and rescue of the Old.

With the fall of Paris in June and most of continental Europe under German or Axis domination, Churchill and his constituency were well aware that it was simply a matter of time before England was to be invaded. Sally and her friends wept at Churchill's inspired battle cry, which filled them with terror, pride, and a fierce, irrational certainty of victory despite every evidence that the country was desperately short of basic supplies and arms with which to defend itself. (Churchill himself had wryly declared to radio commentator Edward R. Murrow, after delivering his speech, "And if they do come, we shall hit them on the head with beer bottles, for that is all we shall have to fight them with.") A hastily formed home guard practiced drills with broomsticks. Civilians armed themselves with whatever weapons were available, such as boarding pikes from Nelson's ship, *Victory.* In a drive for scrap metal to melt down and fashion into guns, railings were cut down in London parks and pots and pans contributed. As the weeks went on the government improvised ways in which to confound the Germans, removing signposts, painting ships in camouflage, and silencing church bells, which were to ring only in the event of invading parachutists. As the country steeled itself against attack individuals created their own makeshift defenses, determined that, by whatever means, the Germans would be gotten rid of. Lady Grantley mixed rat poison in a giant jar of Canadian maple syrup; in the event that a German storm trooper sought shelter in her home, she would offer him the syrup with his tea.

Publicly Churchill appeared buoyant and confident, with boundless energy for inspecting plane factories and bomb shelters; his bowler hat, which he often waved aloft to the crowds on the end of a stick, became a symbol of British imperturbability in the face of adversity. Privately, however, he was racked with doubt, particularly as the summer dragged along, with Nazi submarines and dive bombers reducing the British destroyer fleet by half and seriously disrupting the import traffic that kept the nation alive. Churchill sent an urgent plea to Roosevelt for the promised destroyers and flying boats: "Mr. President," he said, "with great respect I must tell you that in the long history of the world this is a thing to do *now.*"

After Dunkirk, Jack revised his thesis for publication. What had begun as a detached, intellectual analysis was turning into a call to arms for America. Jack began spending night after night at the editorial offices of the *Harvard Crimson*, the campus newspaper, aligning himself with the campus interventionists, who favored American preparedness in the form of rearmament and a peacetime draft.

Recognizing that Americans were abandoning the isolationist position, Kennedy senior had warned Jack that it would be imprudent to exonerate Britain's last leaders, even his old friend Chamberlain, to the degree that he previously had. Kennedy also didn't seem to mind Jack praising Winston Churchill, who was as popular in America as in England, although Churchill at that very moment was trying to drive him from office.

By this time Roosevelt routinely bypassed the ambassador. He conducted secret communications directly with Churchill and, to Kennedy's humiliation, sent his own special envoy to Britain to assess her chances of survival. Churchill made it plain that he wished Kennedy's recall. Careful not to offend the isolationist camps and thus hamper his chances of reelection to a third term, the President nonetheless inched forward in his plans to ally with Britain. He even arranged to send the destroyers Churchill requested in return for leases on key military bases in the Commonwealth.

As his requests for reassignment went ignored, Kennedy considered himself in exile. He suspected that Roosevelt was keeping him out of the way in London so that the President's reelection plans would not be frustrated. Kennedy felt betrayed. He had simply assumed that Roosevelt would retire after two terms and that he would be the President's handpicked successor in 1940.

After winning a seat as a Massachusetts delegate Joe Jr. went that July to the Democratic Convention in Chicago. Despite his father's position in the administration Joe had pledged himself to Postmaster General James Farley, the instigator of a party revolt against Roosevelt's anticipated bid for a third term. During the steamy summer convention Roosevelt henchmen put intense pressure on Joe, implying that he would destroy his father's relationship with Roosevelt and his own future political career if he didn't switch his vote. They even telephoned the ambassador in London, urging him to talk sense into his boy. In the end Joe held firm for Farley. Afterward the ambassador would point proudly to Joe's position as evidence of his independence. He even seemed a little gleeful that his son could cast the protest vote against Roosevelt that he couldn't yet make.

With bombs expected to descend on London at any moment, there was no further talk of Kathleen's return. Rosemary had been sent home with the Moores at the end of May. The entire family, with the exception of the ambassador, whom Roosevelt had urged to stay on in England through the autumn, spent a typical HyannisPort summer of swimming and sailing. With Arthur Krock supplying the title *Why England Slept*, as well as the agent, the publisher, much of the final draft, and the narrative flow, Jack's thesis was hurriedly published that summer and snapped up by a public eager for any information on the European crisis.

Joe Jr. had written to his father after reading the original thesis, "It seemed to represent a lot of work but did not prove anything." Reviewers, however, thought differently. After laudatory reviews appeared in such magazines as *Time,* Jack's book became a candidate for *The New York Times* Best Seller List. He was applauded as a young intellectual who possessed great foresight. Although surprised and rather flippant about his own celebrity, Jack diligently made radio appearances and mailed out autographed copies.

Jack's literary agent wrote Joe Jr. to see if he also had plans for a book, but Joe had nothing to offer. His observations on the Spanish Civil War, still in Harvey Klemmer's hands, had become obsolete. Furthermore, as the agent pointed out, the timing of Jack's book, which appeared in the month of the Democratic Convention, had "stolen quite innocently to be sure . . . the thunder" of Joe's courageous stand.

By August, Germany was waging a battle of the air against Britain, with the Luftwaffe attacking major airfields along the

HOME

1. Kathleen, the Kennedy's fourth child, 1926. (Royal Atelier)

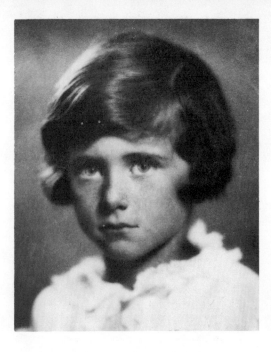

2. The Kennedy children and their governess, Alice Cahill, in Bronxville, 1932. *(left to right):* Eunice, Alice Cahill (holding infant Teddy) Bobby, Jean, Rosemary, and Kathleen. (Courtesy of Mrs. Arthur Bastien)

3. Twelve-year-old Kathleen with her infant brother, Teddy. (Courtesy of Mrs. Arthur Bastien)

4. Kathleen and her retarded elder sister, Rosemary, Palm Beach, 1935. (Courtesy of Mrs. Arthur Bastien)

5. The Kennedys in Palm Beach *(left to right):* Teddy, Jean, Bobby, Eunice, Pat, Kathleen, Rosemary, Jack, Mr. and Mrs. Kennedy (Joe Jr. missing). (Courtesy of Mrs. Arthur Bastien)

7. Rosemary on the beach in HyannisPort. (Courtesy of Mrs. Arthur Bastien)

6. Kick taking a dive in the pool behind the Kennedys' Palm Beach Spanish-style villa. (Courtesy of Mrs. Arthur Bastien)

8. The Kennedys and friends Sancy Falvey (far right) and Nancy Tenney (behind Teddy) engaged in their favorite sport—sailing. (Courtesy of Mrs. Arthur Bastien)

9. Eighteen-year-old Jack Kennedy and his steady girl, Olive Cawley. (Courtesy of Mrs. Arthur Bastien)

10. Rose Kennedy and her eldest son, Joe Jr., Palm Beach, 1935. (Courtesy of Mrs. Arthur Bastien)

11. Hockey goalie Peter Grace, heir to the Grace Shipping Lines, one of Kathleen's early beaux. (Courtesy of Peter Grace)

12. The Kennedys behind the American embassy residence in London soon after their arrival. *(left to right):* Kathleen, Ambassador Kennedy, Teddy, Mrs. Kennedy, Pat, Jean, and Bobby. (Courtesy of BBC Hulton Picture Library)

LONDON, 1938

13. Dinner at Prince's Gate. (Peter Hunter, Magnum)

14. Ambassador and Mrs. Kennedy at the embassy, 1939. (Peter Hunter, Magnum)

15. Kathleen, Rosemary, and Mrs. Kennedy being presented at the Court of St. James's, 1938. (Courtesy of the John F. Kennedy Library)

16. Kick Kennedy, the most popular London debutante of 1938. (Dorothy Wilding, courtesy of *Harper's and Queen*)

17. A Cecil Beaton study of Miss Sally Norton, another popular English deb, in her Victor Stiebel gown. (Courtesy of the Hon. Sarah Baring)

18. Jack Kennedy at the American embassy Independence Day garden party, 1939. (Courtesy of *Harper's and Queen*)

19. Kathleen at a race meeting at Goodwood, 1938, accompanied for the first time by William Cavendish, the Marquis of Hartington. (Courtesy of *Harper's and Queen*)

20. Billy's younger brother Andrew and his mother, the Duchess of Devonshire, at a grouse shoot at Bolton Abbey, 1938. (Courtesy of *Harper's and Queen*)

coast and in the south. For several days the fate of England and the rest of the free world seemed to rest on the abilities of a handful of eighteen-year-old bomber pilots, most of them sent up with only hours of flying experience. For days on end the three-to-one odds were kept from the public, with newspapers treating the outcome of each day's battle like a cricket game ("RAF v. GERMANS, 61 FOR 26—CLOSE OF PLAY TODAY," read one headline). Broadcasters like Charles Gardner of the BBC offered blow-by-blow accounts of dogfights between English Spitfires and German Messerschmitts with the noises of battle forming a macabre soundtrack. ("Oh, we just hit a Messerschmitt. Oh, that was beautiful. It's coming right down now. . . . Here he comes, he's going flat into the sea and there he goes . . . BAM! Oh, boy, I've never seen anything so good as this. The RAF fighters have really got these boys dead.")

It was a frustrating summer for Kick, who could do little but volunteer work at the Red Cross. She practiced bandage-making at the headquarters across from the tiny white-shingled St. Francis Xavier Church that she and her family attended every Sunday and began knitting a scarf for Billy, with twelve-year-old Jean following suit. Kathleen also occupied herself with planning a luncheon and fashion show for the Allied Relief Fund, which was to aid British seamen disabled in the war.

That fall Jack was marking time as well. To avoid further competition with Joe, he had decided not to enter Harvard Law School. With nothing in particular to occupy him until America made up her mind about the war, he decided to go to California and enroll in business school at Stanford University. The climate out there would be beneficial to his failing health. His chronic back trouble had kicked up again, and he was suffering from stomach disorders. He wanted to be in the California sun. Jack Kennedy made a fetish of sunbathing because he thought it made him look healthy. None of his Harvard friends ever saw him without a tan. In winter he even sat in front of a sun lamp.

The famous author of *Why England Slept* was the campus celebrity. He spent most of his time dating Flip Price, a beautiful brunette sorority girl with wide-set eyes, escorting her to Stanford football games in the brand-new 1941 green Buick convertible with leather seats he had purchased with the royalties from his book. But he kept his eye on the dire international situation and made Flip listen with him to every news broadcast on his car radio. Flip once switched the dial to a musical program and they had one of their worst fights. Jack declared angrily that his father expected him to keep abreast of current affairs. Early that fall a photograph appeared in newspapers of Jack registering for the draft, although he was to be allowed a deferment until the spring of 1941.

For a time the RAF successfully held off the Luftwaffe. Then, starting at dusk on September 7 and continuing for the next forty hours, Nazi bombers rained explosives upon the docks and shipyards along the Thames until the entire skyline of London appeared to be on fire. The flames were so intense that efforts to put them out were finally abandoned. For each of the following fifty-six nights there were raids on the city by more than two hundred planes. Entire sections of London were leveled and many famous landmarks destroyed or severely damaged. Americans viewing MovieTone newsreels finally woke up to England's desperate plight. They saw the fires that were allowed to burn themselves out once the city's water supply was exhausted; the old couples picking through rubble searching out the odd possession remaining intact; the neat piles in Hyde Park that grew higher each day of doors, salvaged wood, and bathroom porcelain from ruined houses. The world was awed by the cheery stoicism with which Londoners greeted this onslaught, queuing up matter-of-factly with blanket and pillow or simply a copy of the *Times* for shelter in a tube station at the sound of the air-raid siren at dusk, then calmly emerging at daybreak after the All Clear had sounded to go back about their business. Shops and services continued to operate, even with severe damage; boarded-up store windows were painted to resemble actual ones, and optimistic signs were put up, like those on

St. Thomas's Hospital: Down but Not Out. Please Help Us to Rebuild.

At first Kick's friends followed the directions of the ever present Air Raid Patrol, carrying gas masks, wearing luminous flowers and armbands at night, and staying behind their blacked-out and boarded-up windows after dusk. But before long they resumed their social lives; showing the Germans they weren't afraid of a few incendiaries seemed as important as firing antiaircraft guns at the bombers. For the first time there was no one to chaperon them, and it felt wonderfully wicked to defy the old rules of etiquette.

Sally Norton had begun seeing a great deal of Billy Hartington during their mutual days off, either in London or at Compton Place, the Devonshire estate at Eastbourne, where the family lived after their London home was bombed. After factory work proved too exhausting for her, Sally, who spoke fluent German, was reassigned by the Labor Exchange to MI-6, where she was to translate documents. Compelled to take a secrecy oath, she told no one of her new duties other than her roommate, Osla, who herself was employed by the same organization. Osla and Sally had made a pact: Whenever anyone inquired about their individual contributions toward winning the war, they would go on long and boringly about their new and "highly secret" tasks— locating and keeping records of those due to get war decorations. Their cover-up was so convincing, it had become a joke among their friends. "For God's sake," they would say, "whatever you do, *don't* ask Sally about her new job."

When Billy came up from Elstree, where he was stationed, to meet Sally in London for the evening, they followed their usual routine, from the Mirabelle, to the Café de Paris, to the Four Hundred. One particularly terrible night, as Sally noted in her diary, after three champagne cocktails at the Ritz:

> . . . the siren went off as we left. I wondered if it was going to be a bad night or not. I needn't have wondered; as soon as we got to the Mirabelle, the guns and bombs started. I've never heard them so loud or the bombs so near.

We had a delicious dinner and didn't have to interrupt our conversation once. . . .

We decided to go on to the Four Hundred, bombs or no bombs. The doorman managed to get us a taxi, and as we got to Piccadilly, we saw a big fire in the middle of the street. I was thrilled as I've always longed to do some firefighting. We leapt out of the taxi, only to find that they were not putting it out because of gas. By that time I was secretly relieved, because it looked much bigger near to. We got to the Four Hundred eventually by devious routes; bombs falling whilst one's in a taxi isn't very pleasant. We couldn't hear much once we got inside because of the band, but occasionally we got shot across the floor when the building rocked. About 1:30 I felt rather tired and wanted to go home, so Billy went outside to see if we couldn't make a dash for it, but he came in very fast. They were dropping high explosives in a circle all around us. From that moment it never ceased. The band stopped. Everytime I heard a whistle it seemed as though it couldn't miss us, but we thought we'd better play shelter games. But by that time I'd lost my sense of humor. One bomb behaved in a very odd manner. A tremendous whistle and I flung myself behind Billy, then the room began to shiver and shake silently, then after what seemed agonized minutes, a terrific crash like a high thump knocking you over, then much later on, bottles and glasses began to fall off the tables. . . .

By this time, I was almost paralytic with fear. I couldn't speak or move. This went on until 4 A.M. We then went out again to investigate and found the block next door was on fire. We'd had enough bombs without being a target, but to remain under an enormous fire was too much. The smell when we got outside was awful. My face felt scorched. We padded through the glass to the dear Rely on Us and then we scooted off to Claridge's, where we found the most fantastic party in the hall consisting of my mother, etc. We sat around a bit and had drinks, then it seemed fairly quiet. The All Clear went ten minutes after, so we went for a short walk. It was horribly beautiful, London at that moment. The sky was a brilliant red. As the All Clear faded out there was a complete and utter silence, except for the crackling of fires in the distance.

Their nocturnal circuit was only interrupted once, when the Café de Paris was bombed ten minutes before they arrived. As their taxi pulled up they were greeted by bodies being carried out on doors improvised as stretchers, the wounded wrapped in makeshift tourniquets and bandages made from swatches of cloth women diners had ripped from their gowns. Snakehips Johnson, all the members of his band, and most of the couples on the floor had been killed instantly when a bomb dropped on the dance floor right in the midst of the fast-tempoed "Oh, Johnny." Billy and another fellow went inside to investigate and returned with reports of the horror.

Sally tried to save the situation with the perky resourcefulness with which everyone lately had learned to greet the unspeakable: "Well, then, let's go on to the Four Hundred."

Joseph Kennedy, who expressed his astonished admiration for the ability of Londoners to withstand the prolonged assault, stayed on in England through the bombings for a month, as pledged, but retreated much of the time to his country house in Windsor Great Park. Rumors abounded that the American ambassador was shell-shocked and had lost his nerve. Embittered by attacks by the press and furious that his dire reports on the British situation were seemingly being ignored by Roosevelt, Kennedy leaked a story to the press that he was coming home to see the President, implying that he would not support FDR's candidacy. He sailed for New York in late October, the very week of Kick's Allied Relief Fund fashion show.

In early November, by a narrow margin, Roosevelt was elected for a third term partly because Kennedy purchased radio time at the last minute to dramatically announce his support. After his arrival the ambassador had been ushered to the White

House, where Roosevelt, with airy promises of future appointments and the boosting of young Joe's political career, managed
to pull Kennedy back into the fold, if not to convince him to stay
on as ambassador. As soon as the ambassador threw his support
behind Roosevelt, Joe Jr. followed suit, canvassing for the President and even accompanying him when he campaigned in
Boston.

Immediately after the election, however, the ambassador's customary off-the-record banter with reporters finally backfired.
Carelessly he remarked to Louis Lyons of *The Boston Globe*,
"Democracy is finished in England." Although Kennedy had been
referring to the wartime socialist measures the coalition government had been forced to enact and their ramifications in the
postwar world (". . . it comes to a question of feeding people.
It's all an economic question," he had said), Lyons quoted that
one blunt pronouncement verbatim and without its surrounding
context. It was reprinted in news releases around the world. Any
hope of the ambassador's making a graceful exit from his post or
of salvaging his strained relationship with Roosevelt had been
destroyed. Kennedy had resigned upon his return to the United
States and was only staying on until February, when Roosevelt
would appoint his successor. But the announcement of his resignation, coming straight on the heels of the Lyons article, made it
appear that he had been fired for his indiscretion. English newspapers were relentless in their indignant attacks; in a *Daily Mail*
article entitled "The Strange Case of Mr. Kennedy" George Mur-
ray wrote:

> We can forgive wrongheadedness, but not bad faith.
> How little you know us, after all. . . . Your three years as
> ambassador have given you no insight into the character
> and traditions of the British people. Plainly you know noth-
> ing of their fierce championship of freedom.

At home *The New York Times* chided Kennedy for his "un-
guarded talk," and after his resignation the *Herald Tribune*
claimed that many Americans "honestly concerned for their
country and her freedom will breathe more easily."

Although the ambassador repudiated the interview and, after Roosevelt's inauguration, bought radio time to clarify his views, it was too late. Throughout the winter months in Palm Beach he was listless and depressed. Now he would never become secretary of the Treasury—or anything in the political arena, for that matter. The autographed photograph of the President that Roosevelt had inscribed "To my new ambassador and old friend" on the day of Kennedy's swearing in was relegated to an obscure position on his office wall. He sold the Bronxville house and decided to make his permanent residence in Florida, where there was no income or inheritance tax.

When the family moved to Palm Beach that winter, Kathleen dropped out of Finch and enrolled in Florida Commercial College. Because of his ailments Jack returned there after only one semester at Stanford. Individually the Kennedy children tried to do what they could to boost their father's morale. Chuck Spalding, George Mead's Yale roommate, was a neighbor of Jack's in Palm Beach. One day he stood beside Jack watching the ambassador walking awkwardly with Mrs. Kennedy around the grounds of their Spanish-style mansion (even Chuck could see that their relationship was strained). Jack's eyes never left his father. "You know, they really beat him up and knock him for this and knock him for that," he finally said. "But you can't knock him for what he's done. Think of what he's *done*, Charlie."

That spring, as Roosevelt accelerated his program of aid to the beleaguered Allies, Joe Jr. returned to Harvard determined to wage an impassioned campaign to support his father's publicly stated intention to keep the United States out of the war. With a group of friends he organized the Harvard Committee Against Military Intervention in Europe, to which he devoted more attention than his studies. Announcing that he agreed with Charles Lindbergh's assessment that destruction of the British fleet would not be a serious blow to America, Joe declared during one of his emotionally charged speeches before a Boston town meeting, "All our trade would *not* be cut off if Britain lost."

On May 26 President Roosevelt declared a "state of national

emergency." Two days later Kick wrote Janie Lindsay a rather apologetic letter about her father's position and that of the rest of her country:

. . . After the President's speech last night everyone feels that we are in the war although there has been no official declaration. Of course we have gone so far it is silly to think of turning back. The only possible way we can get the tools to you is by convoys and once one of the convoys gets sunk we will be forced to declare war. Everyone is getting ready for the defense of the cities from air-raids. My imagination refuses to have anything to do with such impossible ideas. To me it is idiotic. I am sure people are much more excited here than they are over there. It is the American temperament to exaggerate things out of all recognition.

Daddy still feels the same way. All possible aid to you for the survival of the British Empire is the only way in which our economic, political and moral life will be safe for the future. [Originally Kathleen had written, "All possible aid to you for the reason that as long as you hold out we have time to get prepared." But perhaps realizing that these words implied that America would not get involved until England had been defeated, she carefully crossed them out.]

We do live in upsetting times. There is so little, if anything these days that is a sure thing. I suppose it seems funny for me to say this when we haven't begun to feel the horrors and uncertainties of real war. But sometimes I feel that almost anything is better than an existence that is neither one thing or another.

Kick's letter to Janie included the news that she had run into several English friends in Washington. Among them was Osla Benning, who was extremely annoyed that she had been sent to America by her parents and was missing out on all that was happening at home. She was thinking about returning to England via Portugal, the closest port of entry. "Her Portuguese visa seems very hard to secure," Kick wrote Janie, "and there is a very nice young man here who longs to marry her. I don't think she is mad about him or she wouldn't have such a hard time making up her mind. However she cannot go back to Canada and she has no American money so if she stays she will have to marry him and if she goes, God only knows where she will end up. I am sure she won't get back here in a hurry."

Kathleen also brought up the sudden rash of marriages among their other English friends. Janie herself had married Peter, Sissy had married David, and Debo had married Andrew in her parents' London townhouse, with rolls of wallpaper hanging over the windows that had been blown out by an air raid two days before. ("I received the funniest letter from her just before she got married. So absolutely typical.") Because marriage had become such a high priority among her old crowd, Kathleen felt she had to explain her own single status: "There are still no signs of marriage in the family. Sometimes I feel that I am never going to take that on. No one I have ever met ever made me completely forget myself and one cannot get married with that attitude."

At that point Kathleen didn't see the urgent need to pair off. On the contrary, she and Charlotte often talked of how they wished they could remain single forever and continue going out night after night on the town. Charlotte's sister Anne had married Henry Ford the year before in a ceremony society papers had labeled "the wedding of the century"; Ford, a member of the prominent Protestant family, had converted to Catholicism in order to marry Anne. Kathleen had been a bridesmaid at the spectacular Southampton affair. Unfortunately the priest presiding over the matrimonial Mass had seized upon the well publicized event as a perfect opportunity to deliver a tactless sermon about the evils of intermarriage before all the groom's Protestant guests. That spring Peter Grace—to Kick's amazement—suddenly married his pretty secretary, but no one else among her American crowd seemed in a rush to tie the knot.

With American involvement in the war simply a matter of time after Roosevelt's declaration of a state of emergency, Joe, who was facing a July call-up, enlisted in the Navy aviation cadet program to avoid a draft rank. After returning from an aimless tour of South America with Eunice and Mrs. Kennedy, Jack, who had failed an army physical on account of his weak back, managed (apparently with some intervention by his father) to secure a position in the Naval Reserves. Jack had been desperate to get taken by one of the services; he couldn't have stood being 4-F.

During this second frustrating summer of watching from the sidelines, Kathleen telephoned Page Huidekoper. Page had gotten a job on the *Washington Times-Herald* through Arthur Krock, who had been impressed by her political acumen and writing ability when he met her in London.

"Daddy says I've got to get a job and learn to earn my living," Kick said bluntly. Mr. Kennedy thought there might be something she could do on the *Times-Herald*.

She couldn't have called at a better time. Page had been working for the editor, Frank Waldrop, as a researcher/secretary but had recently been promoted. Once she moved on to the city desk, her old job would be vacant. "I think you'd be absolutely great at this," Page said encouragingly.

Six

When Frank Waldrop first interviewed Kathleen, he did not immediately realize that she was the former ambassador's daughter, even though he knew Joe Kennedy from his days in Washington. Her typing was terrible, and she knew nothing about reporting, but he sized her up immediately as a girl with a lot of natural curiosity and a gift for getting people to talk about themselves. These were the qualities he looked for in a fledgling reporter; after all, a good story that was badly written could always be handed over to a rewrite man. Waldrop hired Kick as his secretary at a starting salary of twenty dollars a week. If Kathleen worked out, Waldrop planned to move her, like Page, into the city room.

In September, shortly after Kathleen came to work for him, Waldrop received a call from Mr. Kennedy inviting him to lunch. It didn't take long for Waldrop to figure out that the lunch had been arranged so that Kennedy could give him the once-over now that he was in charge of his favorite daughter.

The *Times-Herald* was the least respected paper in Washington. Its editorial position was conservative and staunchly isolationist in a town that stood solidly behind Roosevelt. Waldrop himself was a southern conservative who agreed with Joe

Kennedy's politics concerning the war. Precisely because it was not the paper of choice in the capital, the *Times-Herald* had to make its mark with something more than news, and its character reflected the quirky, spasmodic interests of its publisher, Eleanor "Cissy" Patterson. Oftentimes these interests were sparked by whomever Mrs. Patterson had been seated next to at dinner the night before. She had launched an entire column called "Conquering Women" after she had been fascinated by a female aviator and been otherwise stumped as to how to include a story about her in the Sunday edition. In instructing one writer in what to say to the lovelorn in a column called "The Male Animal," she advised him, "Go to the very edge of propriety and *stay* there." One article under her byline disdainfully referred to her own son-in-law, investigative reporter Drew Pearson, as "flower-snuffing Drew."

Rumor had it that Mrs. Patterson had started the *Times-Herald* partly out of spite. When her own McCormick-Patterson relatives on the *Chicago Tribune* and New York *Daily News* had refused to give her a job because they did not think a woman fit to run a paper, Mrs. Patterson had gone to work for their competitor, William Randolph Hearst. Ultimately she purchased his two ailing papers, the morning *Herald* and the afternoon *Times*. Merging the two, Mrs. Patterson put out the first all-day newspaper in America.

The private eccentricities of Kathleen's employer were well known. At a party at Mrs. Patterson's Dupont Circle townhouse a noted beauty of Washington society attempted to pay her respects; obviously tipsy, she walked right past her hostess and tumbled down the spiral staircase. Leaning over the bannister, Mrs. Patterson surveyed the attractive figure knocked out in a sprawled heap across the landing. "Oh, my," she said in genuine admiration, "now isn't that Jane a *lovely* girl?"

That October, Frank Waldrop's new secretary was joined in Washington by her brother Jack, who had been assigned a desk job in the Office of Naval Intelligence, where he handled the writing of low-level security bulletins. He took a one-bedroom apartment in the Dorchester House on Twenty-first Street, over-looking a park, several blocks away from the small room Kathleen had rented. Through Arthur Krock they began meeting many powerful members of Washington society.

At the *Times-Herald* the editor delighted in his new charge, who quickly renamed him "Frank Ohhhhh-what-a-funny-name-you-have Waldrop." But once word got around that Kathleen was a working girl, the moneyed members of her old New York crowd were a little annoyed. A young lady from a wealthy family was not supposed to accept a paying job because she would be taking it away from someone who really needed it.

Many of Kick's coworkers were unaware, just as Waldrop had been at first, that she was Joseph Kennedy's daughter. Prefer-ring not to be considered wealthy or special, she would carry her mink coat to the newspaper office stuffed in a brown paper bag when her plans called for her to go out directly after work. The subterfuge was so convincing that it got her into trouble. One day several women reporters who discovered the mink concluded that innocent Kathleen, who could not possibly afford furs on her salary, had fallen prey to a rich boyfriend.

Kick soon became friendly with a twenty-eight-year-old col-umnist named Inga Arvad. Inga wrote "Did You Happen to See . . . ," a daily feature that ran on page two of the *Times-Herald*, introducing second- and third-echelon government offi-cials and newcomers in an open, uncritical fashion. Worldly and multilingual, she was seven years Kathleen's senior. There were hints that she had had a varied and exotic past, although she talked little of her life in Europe. It could be that she was even older than she let on. Supposedly she'd been Miss Denmark, and indeed she was stunning—a full-bodied blonde, who exuded a maturity about her own sexuality that Kathleen noticeably lacked. The two women were very much alike, however, in other ways, Inga being as outspoken, responsive, and effervescent as her younger friend. She had been recommended to Waldrop by Arthur Krock, who had discovered her at the Columbia School of Journalism, where she had been learning to write in English.

From the little Inga told people about herself she appeared to be an opportunist, who left men and situations when they got too complicated. She had first been married to an Egyptian foreign service officer but had divorced him after deciding that she couldn't bear her husband's native land. After returning to Copenhagen and making a movie she had married a Hungarian film director named Paul Fejos. She and Fejos traveled to the Dutch West Indies on an archeological dig, but she left him there after war had broken out. Inga's marriage was supposedly over, but she had not yet gotten divorced. Kathleen introduced Inga to Jack, who was immediately fascinated by her. With her gift for adapting to any situation Inga began accepting his casual invitations.

Kathleen's other new friend on the newspaper was John White, who first introduced himself by asking to borrow ten dollars. The son of a southern Episcopalian minister, who once called him a "feckless oaf," John at thirty admitted to no ambitions other than maintaining a string of girl friends and a reputation as an oddball. Light-haired and good-looking, he disliked fussing over his appearance, once showing up for work in a sweater so frayed that his coworkers, yanking at threads here and there as they walked by, unraveled the entire back, forcing him to work the rest of the day in his overcoat. Although impatient with social niceties, White had a wry, highly developed sense of humor. A garish tattoo of a serpent—Tattoo Bill's deluxe design—adorned his right biceps. White had gotten himself tattooed as a lark, charging the five dollars it cost to the newspaper, after the city editor, Mason Peters, had attempted a do-it-yourself job. Underneath the design were the letters *T.S.P.* White had dubbed himself "The Sublime Port," the name of a great Turkish ruler of old. But whenever anyone asked what the initials stood for, he replied ponderously, "Truth, Sincerity, and Purpose."

John White was the newspaper's star feature writer. At one point he authored five columns under five different names, including one on male fashion, which Mrs. Patterson had assigned him under a French pseudonym because it appealed to her sense of the absurd. As Aldous O'Brien, author of "The Male Animal," he had achieved notoriety from the first column. To a boorish letter writer complaining of the unreasonable demands of his wife and mistress and inquiring whether he should put an end to his own misery, White replied: "You sound like a cheap heel. Go ahead and kill yourself."

White's first encounter with Kathleen ended with her calling him a "big bag of wind." A day or so later in the office an argument between them about the Catholic Church grew so heated that she phoned him at home that evening to continue it, insisting, as she had earlier, that birth control was murder. Knowing that he would only infuriate her further, White countered that the Church espoused such a belief simply to keep up its membership. In his diary he referred to Kathleen disparagingly as the "Kennedy ♀" or the "Irish Catholic stupid fool," but he was undeniably intrigued by the willingness of this twenty-one-year-old to take him on.

He began inviting her out for lunch at a Hotshoppe in Arlington or for makeshift dinners of fish rolls and beans at the "cave," White's basement apartment in the Georgetown house owned by his older sister, Patsy, and her husband, Henry Field. Both movie buffs, White and Kathleen would sneak off from work for afternoon matinees. White dragged her to see his current favorite, Hitchcock's *Rebecca,* again and again. She would spend hours with him at Haines Point or Arlington Cemetery, where he would recount to her the method he had perfected for killing mosquitoes (entombing them with a bit of wet cloth) or his current campaign to work up to a thirteen-egg milkshake. He was always in the middle of a wide assortment of books and would read aloud to Kathleen from *Death in Venice* or *Seven Gothic Tales.* They would play whimsical word games, where Kathleen would hold her own, but White was the undisputed master. When thinking up various kinds of shrouds he produced "a flimsy shroud for those who have never lived."

White guessed that he appealed to the wild streak he occasionally glimpsed in Kathleen beneath what she liked to present as a surface of hard-boiled practicality. In a discussion they got into about the meaning of fairy tales, White pointed out to her that in most stories the princess is imprisoned in the tower and the prince in the dungeon. What did she think was the significance of that?

Kathleen was bored by that sort of question. "If you ask me," she said impatiently, "they'd both be better off on the ground."

Although curious about everything, Kathleen seemed particularly fascinated by a series on mental illness White was researching at the time. She snapped up any information he uncovered about causes and hopeful new treatments; when he visited an institution for the retarded, she begged to be allowed to come with him. He wondered from time to time about the source of her intense curiosity. One day as they were walking through a park discussing his progress on the series Kathleen suddenly fell silent. Then, in a small voice, as though revealing a shameful secret, she told him about her sister Rosemary.

Rosemary had grown increasingly intractable after her return from England. After all the progress she had made at her special school, she seemed to be regressing. Normally good-natured, she had begun throwing tantrums. The Kennedys were particularly worried now that she had reached sexual maturity. White understood that recently and only very reluctantly the family had decided to send Rosemary to St. Coletta's, a little convent in Jefferson, Wisconsin. Doctors there attributed her mood changes to a new neurological disturbance, and a number of "cures" were being contemplated, Kathleen said, including a prefrontal lobotomy, a new, controversial operation thought to disconnect the "bad" from the "good" side of the brain. From what Kathleen said, White gathered that Rosemary's worsening condition was seen by the Kennedys as a disgrace and a failure. The battle to overcome her handicap had finally been lost.

Kathleen and John White spent most of their time together arguing. They would start the moment they saw each other and end late at night with one phoning the other soon after they'd parted to continue where they had left off. White himself did not have to be at work until after lunch, but he fell into the habit of getting up early to drive Kathleen to work in the temperamental yellow Plymouth roadster he had purchased two years before for thirty-five dollars and aptly named the Broken and Contrite Heart. As soon as Kathleen closed the car door they began, seizing on any subject, both feigning great seriousness and purporting to take great offense at the other's position. One time they even fought back and forth over White's height. "Here I am, getting out of my sack to take you to work early in the morning, so shut up," White finally snapped in mock exasperation. "Who's doing what for *whom?* Just keep that in mind."

Kathleen called White "shrinking, bald-headed, and irritable." He called her an "ignorant, thickheaded Mick." She disapproved of his refusal to observe what she considered the most insignificant of social conventions, such as wearing a tie, and chided him relentlessly for his swearing, his poor manners in public, and the dismal state of his clothes. He hammered away at her for being too conventional and retaliated by putting together even more threadbare combinations, once mixing a garish green suit with a wildly clashing blue shirt in order to "please her," as he announced on arrival.

White was particularly impressed by Kathleen's ability to argue. It seemed to come from a peculiar mixture of ingenuity and ingenuousness, the latter masking what he considered her shrewd powers of observation. He liked to tease her that someone that dumb on the surface had to be that dumb underneath. On first meeting, Kathleen appeared to strangers so innocent and nonjudgmental that they were always astonished by how masterful she was at manipulation. Often during an argument with White, Kathleen would go at him from a very intellectual angle, then suddenly turn all female. "It's a shame, really, that you have to be so schoolmarmish on a night like this with a full moon," she said once, just as he was finally beginning to drive his point home. Another time, when it appeared that he was going to win, she shrugged and said, "Oh, now, it's not all *that* important, is it really?" as though soothing an overexcited child, and changed the subject. She was the first to point out that he was turning pompous and boring. White had always thought that he was good at this kind of verbal parrying, but he had to admit that she was just a damn sight better than he was.

What astonished him most was that such a bright, inquisitive mind should be weighed down by such rigid, conventional notions. Kathleen's knee-jerk responses to most philosophical arguments—whether about birth control, ambition, the Church, or the meaning of success—appeared to be the pat notions that had been provided by her schooling and her parents: It was important to marry well. Certain beliefs of the Church were inviolate. Success in life was fulfilling the expectation of others. Many social conventions should be adhered to merely because they had been adhered to for centuries. White guessed—indeed hoped—that Kathleen was only holding on to certain opinions in desperation, terrified that if she were to question them, the framework on which her entire belief system rested would collapse. He liked to think that she was waiting for someone like him to come along and pry the first brick loose for her.

It wasn't difficult to see why Kathleen's training had been so firmly implanted. One evening soon after they had begun seeing each other, she turned to White and made a coquettish reference to North Carolina. *How the hell does she know where I'm from?* he had wondered. Later she dropped bits and pieces of knowledge about his background that he was certain he had not given her. Finally he had to ask, "Where the Christ are you getting all this information about me?" Her reply left him speechless. "Every time one of us goes out with somebody new, we have to call our father." He was stunned to hear that Mr. Kennedy would proceed with a background check on each prospective suitor or girl friend.

At first White thought she must be joking. Apart from the controversy surrounding Kennedy's resignation from his ambassadorial post, he had only a very hazy knowledge of Mr. Kennedy and little notion of the extent of his wealth or power. Kathleen needled White for knowing so little about her father; she simply assumed that everybody was familiar with his *modus operandi.* After she'd clued him in, White had a fantasy of Mr. Kennedy lying in bed in some luxury hotel far from home, his nine children all obliged to know his exact whereabouts so that they could check in at the end of each evening. He could just picture the twenty-four-year-old Jack Kennedy, obviously an experienced skirt chaser, asking, "Daddy, can I go out with so-and-so?" and the ambassador replying thoughtfully, "Well, Jack, I'll have to check on that." But what he thought of as a bizarre flight of fancy was evidently not far from the truth. Kathleen told him that she was fully expected to steer clear of anyone who did not meet with her father's approval.

"Has he run a check on me?" White asked.

"You bet he has," she replied.

"Then how on earth can he let you go out with me?!"

Kathleen laughed. "Oh, he considers you frivolous but harmless."

Kathleen sounded resigned when she told White about the required procedure, as though she had realized long before that there was no point in rebelling against it. He didn't know much about her family but gathered that they were all very close, too close, in fact, for her liking. Kathleen was supposed to check in frequently with her father before bedtime, but she let it be known that Mr. Kennedy was not her "total boss" and that she did not intend to spend her life being run by him. She seemed to be making her first tentative moves to break from her father's grip (her involvement with him was evidence of that), but she obviously wished to proceed cautiously, without fanfare.

Referring to Kathleen in his diary as "clay to be molded," White took it upon himself to be a mentor, constantly attacking many of her fixed views and enumerating what he considered her various faults. His good intentions were often undermined by his volatile emotions and brusque manner, causing him, as he once noted, to "probe at her coldly and ineptly." Once they got into a fearful argument about friendship. Kathleen had claimed that she made and held friends by letting them talk about themselves. That was no sort of friendship, White replied exasperatedly, if she was merely a receptacle for someone and got nothing out of it herself. Just to make his point, as a matter of fact, he was going to "quit" her group of "yapping half-friends."

That year Kathleen's old friends Nancy Tenney and Dinah Brand were both living in Washington, and Lem Billings and

Torby Macdonald made periodic visits, as did George Mead, who had joined the Marines and was stationed nearby in Quantico, Virginia. The truth was White disliked most of these people and was hardly bowled over by Kathleen's brother Jack, with whom they had begun double-dating. Jack seemed to be a lightweight without much intellectual equipment, little more than a calculating playboy, the kind who maintained a black book and methodically ticked off the names. In his diary White referred disparagingly to "Fort George Mead" or "that Billings creature." Only Mead's Yale chum Chuck Spalding met with White's approval. Spalding had a self-mocking sense of humor and intellectual curiosity similar to White's but a more ingratiating social manner.

White noticed that no matter what was said, Kathleen and her friends had a quick, witty comeback. This system of communication amused him until he heard the same wisecracks repeated over and over again. Among her set indecision, inefficiency, and laziness were always derided. It was important to be constantly on the move. It was essential to win. Until he had met Kathleen's circle, White had been perplexed and irritated by the competitiveness she had once displayed during a game of croquet; obviously furious that White hadn't backed her up properly, she had complained bitterly that he'd left her, as the English had been left, "to fight to the last Greek." With her family members Kathleen would say, "I have a T.L. for you," which meant trade-last, the idea being to offer to repeat to someone a compliment someone else had paid him if he will first report to you a compliment someone has given you. White found this mocking, juvenile humor distasteful. He hated to see so accomplished a conversationalist as Kathleen waste her talents. He also disliked hearing her called "Kick" and insisted on calling her by her Christian name.

Some of Kathleen's friends were equally unimpressed by John White, who appeared aloof and sullen, even if he demonstrated a certain degree of poise. The bickering that went on between them was so childish. White was obviously unnerved by his intense feelings for Kathleen. Nancy Tenney was shocked that Kick would be involved with a fellow with such an obvious chip on his shoulder; perhaps she was challenged by the first involvement in which she clearly did not have the upper hand. But, after all, Kathleen liked everybody and treated them all exactly alike. It was so typical of her to get hooked on the most oddball characters without being able to see them for what they were.

John was pleased that Kathleen was growing close to his sister, Patsy. Patsy's husband, Henry Field, was a distinguished anthropologist related to the Marshall Field family. Although Henry's career provided them with limited means, the Fields were very social and well connected. They held daily five o'clock teas, and each Sunday they would mix together a grab bag of guests from among the most distinguished members of Washington society for an impromptu luncheon. For these get-togethers Patsy usually laid out beans and applesauce or a large bowl of spaghetti accompanied by several bottles of wine. Sometimes Kathleen would arrive and find important associates of her father's like Jimmy Roosevelt or Lord Halifax, the present English ambassador, seated on the floor. White thought it would be educational for Kathleen to observe Patsy, who had married well (if not to money), had many high class friends, and also managed to get by with unorthodox opinions and behavior. She subscribed to the advice their freewheeling mother had given her as a child: "Observe every small convention and break every big one."

By this time Jack Kennedy and Inga Arvad had become embroiled in a deeply passionate affair that was an open secret in Kathleen's circle. Kathleen told White that her father approved of the older, experienced Inga as a sexual instructor for her brother; she herself was amused by the relationship. Jack, who was crazy about Inga, called her Inga Binga. For her part Inga was by turns loving and motherly. White noted that Kathleen greatly admired Inga's beauty and sophistication and frequently sought her older friend's advice in romantic matters. Apparently it didn't concern her that her brother was sexually involved with a married woman. In her relationship with White, however, she fended off even the most innocent passes with the automatic responses she had been taught as a girl. Although she had had many boyfriends and enumerated them for him, it was soon evident that she was totally inexperienced sexually. Once she confided that one of her current flames, a friend of Jack's, was twenty-four and had never kissed her—or any other girl, for that matter. It had even become a joke between them. She told him that her priest forbade any sort of sexual contact. He told her to get special dispensation.

By September of 1941, after an American destroyer that had been escorting a convoy of British merchant vessels had been fired upon by a Nazi submarine, the United States Navy had begun operating under wartime conditions. Americans had expected such action by Germany ever since March of that year, when Congress signed the Lend-Lease bill, giving Roosevelt the power to authorize all aid to Britain and to provide naval protection for merchant ships delivering supplies. Now they held a daily death watch for the first United States ship to be sunk by the Nazis. The most immediate threat of war, however, was posed by Japan. In 1937, when Japan had waged war against China, the United States had responded to that and subsequent territorial aggression by imposing increasingly strict economic embargoes, which were crippling the Japanese economy. Then, in 1940, Japan had formed a military alliance with Italy and Germany. In the year that followed there were further futile negotiations between the United States and Japan as Japan continued to develop a commanding position on the Asian mainland and in the South Pacific, and America responded by tightening its economic stranglehold. In November of 1941 relations between the two countries were so strained that Japan finally cut off all communications. The United States government braced itself for war.

On Sunday, December 7, when Kathleen and White came back from lunch at their Hotshoppe, they learned that Japanese bombers in a surprise attack had crippled the United States Pacific Fleet at Pearl Harbor. Emperor Hirohito had then declared war. The news made the argument they had just had seem crazily ironic. Convinced that America would soon become involved in the European conflict, Kathleen had asked White which branch of the service he would enter. Teasing her as usual, he had maintained that he wouldn't dream of entering any branch at all. In fact, White, although outraged by the attack on Pearl Harbor, was glad that the Japanese had finally forced Roosevelt's hand. Long disgusted with the editorial slant of the *Times-Herald*, he wrote in his diary on the day of the attack that he and the rest of his household had "jumped for joy" at the news. "The future would be filled with great things, the last moment of the old world, maybe." He immediately decided to join the Navy, the branch of service most popular among Ivy League graduates, even though he had some doubts that he would pass the physical. He had suffered from a serious ulcer in 1938, an automatic ground for rejection.

The following day word got around the city room of the *Times-Herald* that several of the magnificent cherry trees given to the capital by the Japanese government and planted along the Tidal Basin had been chopped down. White and a photographer were assigned to the story. It was clear, once they'd arrived and inspected the freshly amputated stumps, that the perpetrator had meant his actions to be a retaliation against the Japanese for Pearl Harbor, but there was no evidence to support a story to that effect. Glancing around to make sure there were no witnesses, White took a pencil and scrawled across the stump of one of the felled trees, "TO HELL WITH THOSE JAPANESE." He went over it once again to make it dark enough to be photographed. Newsmen were always accused of doing such things, but he'd never resorted to anything like this before. He was fully aware that the kind of person capable of chopping down trees in a fit of bigoted rage would hardly leave behind such a tame epithet, but if he used stronger language, they would not be able to use the photograph in a family newspaper, and certainly not on the front page.

Two days later Frank Waldrop asked White and Page Huidekoper to investigate the house of a suspected Nazi sympathizer thought to have fled after Pearl Harbor. The milk bottles and newspapers piling up outside her door seemed evidence of a hasty departure. After White climbed into a second-story window, the two of them searched the house, producing several incriminating letters and a Nazi medal. They were heading back to the office in White's Plymouth roadster when they realized that they were being sandwiched between two sinister black limousines. The cars were inching ever closer, frustrating White's attempts to pass them, when they both suddenly disappeared. Page and White arrived at the *Times-Herald* with what they thought was a good story only to have Waldrop give them a sound scolding. He had been informed by the FBI, which had the house under surveillance, that two of his reporters had been spotted breaking in. Waldrop laughed over their reportorial doggedness, but claimed not to have given them instructions to go to such lengths to get the story. "If you want to get them out of there," he had told the bureau, "please feel free to do so."

Now that even the isolationist *Times-Herald* was under suspicion for possible espionage, Inga Arvad's past began to prompt disturbing questions. A month before Pearl Harbor, Page had been in the morgue of the newspaper when a fellow reporter had called out, "Hey, have you seen this picture of Inga with Hitler?" The photograph showed Inga in a box with Hitler at the 1936 Olympics, which had been held in Berlin. Page had felt compelled to report her coworker's discovery to Frank Waldrop, who had suggested that she talk to the FBI. Although devoted to Inga, Page had agreed that it was her duty to do so, but only after she first informed Inga of her intention. Inga had shrugged upon hearing the news. "I'm not a bit surprised," she replied. "I hear this all the time."

Inga's story was that her association with Hitler coincided with the start of her journalistic career. While she was visiting Germany in the mid-1930s she heard a rumor that Reichsmarschall Hermann Goering was getting married. Posing as a reporter, Inga had wangled an exclusive about his impending wedding and then managed to sell the story to a Danish newspaper. Inga's tenacity impressed the newspaper, which gave her press credentials as its Berlin correspondent. She met Adolf Hitler while covering Goering's wedding. Enchanted by Inga and referring to her in a much quoted (and troublesome) remark as a per-

21. Chatsworth, South Front. (Sydney W. Newbery)

22. Chatsworth, interior—the Painted Hall. (Sydney W. Newbery)

23. Kathleen at the races, wearing one of her more flamboyant hats. (Courtesy of Jane Compton)

24. Kick chatting with beau William Douglas-Home at Eunice's London coming-out ball, 1939. (Peter Hunter, Magnum)

25. A member of the Derby Ball Committee in 1939, Kathleen (far right), unlike the rest of her family, was welcomed into English society. (Courtesy of *Harper's and Queen*)

26. Kathleen and Billy Hartington en route to a dressy affair. All London waited for the pair to announce their engagement. (Courtesy of Richardson's)

27. Goodwood, July 1939: Picnicking at a race meeting, Kathleen's English crowd carried on with the Season as usual, even though war loomed. (*Courtesy of Harper's and Queen*)

28. Joe Jr., Kick, and Jack rushing to a special sitting of the House of Commons on September 3, 1939, to hear British Prime Minister Neville Chamberlain declare war on Germany. (Courtesy of *Harper's and Queen*)

29. Ambassador Kennedy, ostracized by the British after his candid pronouncements that England was going to lose the war, returned home October 1940 out of favor with Roosevelt. (Courtesy of John F. Kennedy Library)

WASHINGTON

30. Kick, Jack, and their American crowd, including three of Kathleen's all-American boyfriends (*left to right*): Tom Killefer, John "Zeke" Coleman, Charlotte McDonnell, Jack, Kick, Lem Billings. (Courtesy of Charlotte McDonnell Harris)

31. Jack and his favorite sister. (Courtesy of the John F. Kennedy Library)

32. Joe Jr., Palm Beach, 1941. (Courtesy of Cam Newberry)

33. Eunice, Palm Beach. (Courtesy of Cam Newberry)

4. Jack at the Hunt Cup, 1941. (Courtesy of Cam Newberry)

5. Kick with her ever-present Kodak camera at the Hunt Cup. (Courtesy of Cam Newberry)

6. Charlotte McDonnell atop a convertible the day of the Maryland Hunt Cup, 1941. (Courtesy of Cam Newberry)

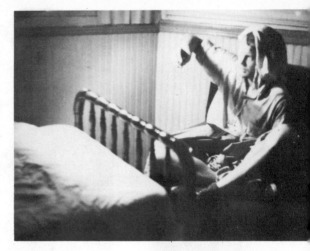

37. Beautiful *Times-Herald* columnist Inga Arvad, whom fledging reporter Kathleen introduced to her brother Jack. His affair with Inga, who was suspected of being a Nazi spy, almost got him cashiered from the Navy. (Courtesy of John B. White)

38. John White, holing up in the "cave," his basement Georgetown apartment, 1941. (Courtesy of John B. White)

39. As a U.S. Marine, White's military career was patchy. After a month overseas he landed in the brig on charges of espionage—charges later dismissed— for innocently photographing British destroyers. (Courtesy of John B. White)

40. As a navigator of transport airplanes White in a typical mug shot enlisted a crystal ball and wizard's cap to set his course. (Courtesy of John B. White)

fect example of Nordic beauty, the Führer had given her an interview and invited her to view the Olympic Games with him as a press member.

Adding to the intrigue about Inga were rumors that she had been asked by the Nazis to be a spy in Paris café society—an offer she said she had indignantly declined. She was also supposed to have been the mistress of Axel Wenner-Gren, a mysterious international industrialist said to have Nazi sympathies and suspected by Naval Intelligence of using his three-hundred-and-twenty-foot yacht to refuel Nazi submarines in the Gulf of Mexico. Inga maintained that her association with Wenner-Gren had been entirely through her estranged husband, since the industrialist had sponsored Fejos's archeological expedition to Chile.

With these kinds of rumors circulating, Inga and Jack thought it wise to be cautious about being seen together. The couple double-dated with Kathleen and White more frequently to maintain the appearance of propriety. Often they would begin their evening as a foursome and split up afterward, having made plans to reconvene before the end of the evening so as to create the impression that they had been together the entire time. Jack and Kick laughed frequently about the subterfuge. White understood that it was important for Jack and Inga not to be seen together by associates or employees of Mr. Kennedy's.

Seven

"No sooner in office than become embroiled in the great case of the Ambassador's Son and the Beautiful Blonde Spy," White noted in his diary on January 13. The source of the commotion was an item in Walter Winchell's column, published the previous day in the *New York Mirror:* "One of ex-Ambassador Kennedy's eligible sons is the target of a Washington gal columnist's affections. So much so she is divorcing her explorer-groom. Pa Kennedy no like." Upset by this smear on the family name, Jack had come into the office of the *Times-Herald* to consult with Frank Waldrop, who had turned livid when he learned that Winchell's source had been the FBI. After discussing the column with Mrs. Patterson, Waldrop considered writing a violent castigation of the bureau.

The next day, when White talked about the incident with Kathleen, he was surprised to find her shrugging off its seriousness and maintaining that her father, who had just passed through town, had found the great Inga scandal "very funny" and had told Jack to do just as he wished.

The Office of Naval Intelligence, however, had gotten wind of the affair. Their big concern was that Inga was a German spy who had been using Jack Kennedy to get information about the

Navy Department, even though the young ensign did not have access to anything of a highly sensitive nature. Jack's superior discussed the possibility of cashiering him from the Navy, then decided instead to move him to a harmless desk job in Charleston, South Carolina, and immediately informed him of his transfer. Several days after Winchell's column appeared, Jack had a sad farewell dinner with Kathleen, White, and Inga.

After Jack's departure Kathleen moved into his apartment, which she shared with Chuck Spalding's girl friend, Betty Coxe who was taking a course in foreign service. By this time Kathleen's relationship with White had intensified, and their differences were becoming steadily more apparent. White carped at her constantly for being cold and for allowing the occasional "indulgence," as he put it (a kiss, maybe), just to please him. He complained that she was "undersexed" and, by way of comparison, talked of his other women and their willingness to sleep with him. To Kathleen's astonishment he confessed to having recently kissed two other girls, but if he was unable to remain faithful, he hinted, it was due to her singular lack of warmth. He would begin an evening with her and Inga in high spirits, then suddenly grow sullen and withdrawn. When Kathleen was not responsive enough in greeting him, he would pick aimless fights with her for the rest of the evening. If they parted at an impasse, Kathleen, attempting a conciliation, would invariably telephone—against the advice of Inga, who labeled such behavior "crawling to the cross."

"L'Affair Kathleen rocks along its windy way, very verbose indeed," White complained in his diary. On February 3, under the heading "The Great Resolve," he wrote, "Too many words and no action. For two weeks as of this day, I shall not see her alone. . . . My God, that does sound terrible . . . but do it I shall to see if I can't get some sort of control of myself. I'm behaving terribly."

"She is not good enough for me," he wrote soon after. "I shall find another girl and slowly transfer affections in a serpentine fashion." At the same time he berated himself for being so "weak and hateful." Possibly as a result of his recent work on mental illness, he wondered whether some psychological disturbance was responsible for his being so "savage and sullen." Although he often blamed Kathleen's lack of physical responsiveness for his moodiness, at odd moments he admitted that his inability to maintain control largely stemmed from the fear he had of his own growing feelings for her and the likelihood that some commitment might be the net result. White had been engaged on several occasions. Each time, immediately after the announcement his behavior had markedly deteriorated as the full repercussions of his action began to sink in.

After Kathleen returned from a long weekend in Palm Springs in February to celebrate her twenty-second birthday, White came up with a compromise arrangement. He presented it to her coldly, as if he were closing a real estate deal. If she would make certain "overtures" (such as initiating the good-night kiss) within a reasonable period of time, he would stop pressing her to be more responsive. Although the plan met with Kathleen's assent, it soon dissatisfied him. "I want fire and freezing," he wrote, "not this placid, unexciting agreement."

Their most tender moments came at the end of an evening, after he had escorted her home. They would chat in her room, and once she had grown tired, she would run into the bathroom and return in her nightgown. Sometimes she would let White watch as she rolled up her hair in pincurls and put cream on her face. He would rub her back gently or read aloud to her until she drifted off to sleep, then quietly let himself out after leaving a note for her on her desk. The sight of Kathleen in a little flannel nightgown would completely disarm White; she reminded him of Claudette Colbert in *It Happened One Night*, and like Clark Gable he would feel honor-bound to keep the walls of Jericho standing. Kathleen always insisted on going to bed early and fell fast asleep immediately, even after the worst of their fights. Often White thought it was her way of escaping from him, and he would walk home dejectedly, pondering her unfair advantage.

Occasionally Kathleen would say her prayers in front of White. Her piety did not embarrass him. Although he had rejected his own church as too bland and clubbish, he considered himself religious and often prayed on his knees alone. Kathleen struck him as a pilgrim in search of a more honest relationship with her creator; she preferred to deal with God directly rather than through a church. She was like some of his other intelligent Catholic friends, who were also making private adjustments to the more illogical aspects of their religion. Once after he pressed her, Kathleen finally admitted that she could not believe that the actual physical body of the Blessed Virgin Mary had ascended into heaven on her death, as the Pope had recently affirmed. It was in the area of sex that Kathleen's religious training had obviously affected her most deeply. Sex was a sacred territory, reserved for marriage. White understood this and didn't push Kathleen to sleep with him. Once they had gone to bed, he would have to ask Kathleen to marry him, and only in his most farfetched imaginings could he allow himself to believe that such a marriage would work.

Jack Kennedy, meanwhile, continued to see Inga Arvad. They would meet in a Charleston hotel, their conversations and lovemaking all the while monitored by the FBI. Despite his earlier cavalier attitude about Jack's involvement with Inga, Joseph Kennedy became quite distraught that winter when Jack approached him about the prospect of marrying her. "Jack, she's *already* married!" he exploded. It was one thing to have a fling and quite another to contemplate matrimony with a non-Catholic divorcée currently under investigation as a Nazi spy. Jack's future would be irrevocably damaged, and the whole family would be under a cloud. He vehemently discouraged further contact with Inga.

In early March, Inga informed White and Kathleen that she and Jack had agreed to part. The following week when Jack called Kathleen, he sounded very lonely. Whatever assurances he had given his father, he was finding it difficult to give up Inga completely. Thereafter he saw her from time to time, an arrangement she found far from satisfactory. One day when she and White were covering a story together, she confided that although she still loved Jack Kennedy, she had always found him self-centered and a little cold. Rather bitterly she said Jack had an intense need to conquer women and was probably incapable of deep, long-lasting intimacy. Neither she nor White believed that was true of Kathleen.

Privately White found it rather ironic that Mr. Kennedy, who carried on his own affairs so flagrantly, was so adamant that his son maintain the appearance of propriety. But this was one opinion he never voiced to Kathleen. He had never been certain whether she knew about her father's philandering until one evening when they were at a party at the Hotel Mayflower and someone made a crack about Joe Kennedy's sexual swordsmanship. Kathleen overheard the remark and became visibly upset.

As the first six months of America's war against Japan dragged on the young men in Kathleen's circle became increasingly demoralized. Although most of them had immediately signed up for the armed forces, they were still waiting to be called into active service. Jack and his friends found it frustrating to watch as the Japanese successfully invaded Hong Kong, Malaya, Singapore, Burma, the East Indies, Guam, Wake Island, the Gilbert Islands, and the Philippines. The British forces were fighting fiercely on several fronts—in the Mediterranean, in the western desert of Egypt and Libya, and in the Atlantic—and the Russians were holding steady against the German invasion of the previous year. Since Roosevelt had declared war on Germany and Italy several days after Pearl Harbor, American troops were beginning to pour into Northern Ireland to train for the eventual Allied invasion of the Axis-dominated Continent.

Kathleen's older brothers longed to be doing something more vital than paper work and flight trials. White was dismayed when he was turned down by the Navy because of his ulcer. He considered signing up with the Marine Corps, which had formed a combat correspondence unit and was recruiting newspaper reporters and photographers. Since newsmen were notorious drinkers and were simply assumed to have poor health, the stringent physical requirements had been waived.

Even Joseph Kennedy's former isolationist sentiments had

been overridden by fervent patriotism. After Pearl Harbor he had cabled Roosevelt his emphatic support: "NAME THE BATTLE-FRONT. I'M YOURS TO COMMAND." There was no response from the President for four months. What the former ambassador had had in mind was a major commission post. What he was finally offered was the management of a pair of shipyards in Maine. To add to this humiliation, there was an immediate outcry in the press over the prospect of a "Nazi sympathizer" controlling American shipping. Kennedy turned down the job and ignominiously ended his public career. He could no longer ignore the fact that he was becoming a political liability to his eldest son. He turned once again to his private enterprises, speculating on war-inflated real estate.

The first among Kathleen's friends to be assigned active duty was George Mead. When George's orders came through that April, Kathleen and Betty Coxe left Washington for a farewell party at the Mead winter plantation in Aiken, South Carolina. George had been assigned to the Fifth Marine Regiment, which was preparing to embark for Guadalcanal in the South Pacific. Zeke Coleman, Chuck Spalding, and Jack Kennedy, who came up from Charleston, joined George and the girls. George's mother was especially anxious for her son to have one last good time. He was her eldest boy and her obvious favorite among the five Mead children. It was so typical of George to have enlisted in the Marines even before war had broken out. At Yale he had always taken the toughest courses, despite his failings as a scholar, and had gone out for the most rigorous athletics. He wouldn't have been satisfied with anything less than the most grueling military service.

For most of the weekend the group rode horses and played badminton. Lady Astor, who was visiting relatives in Virginia, joined them and participated in a spirited scavenger hunt at Chuck Spalding's invitation. One night George pulled out his tape recorder, and they amused themselves by mimicking a popular radio show, each pretending to be a commentator on the war. Jack took the part of a senator; Chuck became the famous staccato-voiced radio personality, H. V. Kaltenborn; Kathleen was an angry woman reporter; Betty represented the women's vote; and Zeke Coleman was an isolationist from the Midwest. "And now . . . another Roundtable Discussion," George, the host, began ponderously. "Mr. Kaltenborn, do you think this is the beginning of the beginning or the end of the beginning and the beginning of the end?" The game went on for hours, after which they played the tape back, delighted by their own cleverness.

George didn't seem his usual self that weekend, Chuck Spalding noticed. He seemed rather withdrawn and had welcomed his friends only lukewarmly. Finally George drew Chuck aside and made a shamefaced confession—he was frightened about going overseas, even though it was an honor to have been selected to participate in the first American offensive against the Japanese. He sounded as though he felt he had neglected some aspect of his training. Chuck groped for something comforting to say. They were all scared, as a matter of fact. Jack Kennedy believed that the trick was to avoid thinking you were going to get killed because those who worried about it were the ones who invariably got it in the end. Finally Chuck just fell back on all the weekend's heavy-handed jokes about how he and the others could all sleep a lot better knowing that a young man with George's consummate patriotism was going out to win the war for them.

That Monday Kathleen sent White a telegram from the Mead plantation: "SICKNESS PREVENTS MEETING." She had often criticized White's style of letter writing, which omitted salutations or closings—a space-saving device that he always defended. But her use of it on this occasion, when he was feeling rather jealous, wounded and infuriated him. He had been sleeping poorly and getting severe headaches, both reactions, he realized, to his anxiety about their relationship.

Throughout the week after Kathleen's return they fought. Finally, fed up with his own immaturity, White kissed her in front of the Dorchester House when he brought her home one night—and asked her what she thought about marrying him.

"Not the way you are now," she said quickly.

They had talked about the possibility of marriage before and had always concluded that they were impossibly mismatched. Once Kathleen had told White that if she ever did make up her mind about him, he would try to talk her out of it. Still he had always been sure Kathleen would make enormous compromises for him if only he would bend just a little. Now it was she who was backing off. To White's bewilderment Kathleen suddenly indicated that she was eager to return to England and hinted that some aristocratic young Englishman was still languishing for her. Billy Hartington, who had been writing her regularly, was evidently still smitten with her. Kathleen had finally learned to take the offensive with White; she dropped the reference to Billy deliberately to put him off guard. She may also have begun to tally up her alternative romantic prospects. White had managed to do all too good a job of convincing her that any long-range commitment to him was doomed.

For the next few days White continued to discuss marriage in a strained, intellectual way, enumerating his ideas as to how it should be approached and made to work. Then one evening as he was putting Kathleen to bed he was overwhelmed by his feelings. *What a sweet, sincere, good-hearted little thing she is,* he thought. "I love you, Kathleen," he whispered before she drifted off to sleep. The following day, nervous about his admission of the evening before, White took her home after dinner at his sister's house and said a curt good-night. He was on his way down the hall when she came after him. She was crying, which pleased him because he considered it evidence that she cared.

"Did you mean what you said last night?" she asked.

He nodded.

"I love you too, John," she said immediately. To White's deep shame she then apologized for any mistakes she had made in the past. "Think there are none," he noted later in his diary.

The following day, May 12, White finally enlisted in the Marines. He ordered a dozen roses to be delivered to Kathleen, and after taking her out for a final expensive luncheon—a sacrifice on his part since he hated fancy restaurants—said good-bye to her in front of the *Times-Herald* offices and headed off to Marine boot camp at Parris Island in South Carolina.

The same month White entered the service, Joe Kennedy, Jr., graduated from flight training school at Jacksonville, Florida, and received his commission as an ensign in the Naval Reserve. In June, Jack was informed he had been assigned sea duty while he was in a Boston hospital undergoing surgery on his back. In early summer he was sent to take an officer's training course at Northwestern University. He volunteered for PT boat duty after listening to a stirring speech about motor torpedo vessels in the South Pacific. Just before his back operation Jack had apparently been undergoing a crisis in his faith. On his way to Boston he had stopped off to see Kathleen. From what he'd told her he seemed on the verge of renouncing the Catholic Church. Kathleen had been rather shocked. She told White that although she could imagine leaving the Church herself without difficulty, she would never hurt her family unnecessarily.

After Jack had gone, Kathleen's friends began to leave Washington one by one. Inga Arvad moved to New York that July, and Kathleen took over her column, "Did You Happen to See . . ." Her reportorial duties provided her with a good excuse to get out and meet some of the people who were pouring into the city to fill the new jobs created by the war. One of her columns began:

> Ruth Welty is bursting with an idea. And such an idea! To say it is revolutionary is a clear case of understatement. A plan for the eventual abolition of war through the substitution of women for men in the governments of the world! . . . What about it, girls? Are you ready to take on the responsibilities of the world? Well, and what does the stronger sex think about this proposal to displace them?

In early August, John White returned to Washington on leave. He was to be sent to Northern Ireland, but no departure date had been set. In the interim he was to be posted at the Brooklyn Navy Yard.

Once White was stationed in New York, Kathleen flew up to spend weekends with him. One hot weekend in late August she invited him to accompany her to Jones Beach. White, who had never been there before, was made to understand that they were en route to a very exclusive beach community similar to Newport. After taking a circuitous route by train and bus they arrived at a public shoreline packed with bathers. They spent an idyllic day together, swimming, body-surfing, and sharing hamburgers and hot chocolate. White was in a playful mood that day, trying to kiss Kathleen underwater and laughing with her as their heads bobbed to the surface. After protectively fanning flies away from her as they sunned themselves on his heavy United States Marine blanket, White kissed her passionately in full view of the crowds walking near them on the boardwalk. Kathleen broke their embrace, a bit stunned. Even three months ago, she said, she would not have allowed herself to do that sort of thing in public.

That night, back in Manhattan, they stopped in to see Inga, who, after divorcing Fejos, had quickly remarried on the rebound from Jack Kennedy. She was living with her new husband, Nils Block, on Riverside Drive. Block seemed overwhelmed by Inga and very tense, as though threatened by the presence of anyone who might remind his wife of Jack Kennedy. During the evening Inga drew Kathleen aside and told her she still loved Jack. Kathleen agreed with White that the marriage would not last six months.

The rest of the weekend was nearly perfect. They shared brandy Alexanders and dinner at Rockefeller Center, with Kathleen paying for most of their entertainment since White was on a meager military salary. They saw *Porgy and Bess* on Broadway, then taxied up to Central Park. At the Bird Sanctuary, a little lagoon fringed with trees that reflected the buildings of the city, White fell to kissing Kathleen until she asked to be taken home at her usual bedtime. After he had escorted her back to the Chatham Hotel, where she always stayed in New York, they followed their typical routine. She changed into a nightgown which was several inches too long for her but then appeared nervous about his staying to put her to bed and insisted on leaving the door of her room ajar. Her father's assistant Eddie Moore stayed in the same hotel, and she was terrified that he would think—and tell her father—that she had spent the night with a man in her room.

On Labor Day, Kathleen invited White to come to Hyannis-Port and meet her family. After taking the wrong bus from Boston he arrived an hour and a half late at the bus station, where Kathleen met him in a huge, chauffeur-driven car. To his surprise the Kennedys' white clapboard house was indistinguishable from the neighboring ones, and certainly not as grand as he had imagined. Outside the bathroom White met Mr. Kennedy, who eyed him with disdain. "You missed your bus," he said coldly. Before lunch on the beach his wife extended a hand with the single pronouncement, "I am Mrs. Kennedy." It was obvious to White that Kathleen's parents knew who he was but had difficulty remaining civil toward him. John liked Kathleen's brothers and sisters well enough (particularly ten-year-old Teddy, who assured White with a patronizing air, "Maybe I'll drop down to Washington."). As the day wore on, however, with the Kennedys' relentless game playing and their insistence that he participate, he began to feel as though he were in an ants' nest and that he had to fight each family member off. When they played tennis, Kathleen was more competitive than usual. Although White saw her falling back into the habits of her family to some degree, he was pleased to observe that she was markedly less dependent on their approval than the others were. It was now apparent that Kathleen wanted to maintain her ties to her family, but by the same token didn't want them to overwhelm her. In that respect she was trying to pull off a delicate balancing act. His visit to HyannisPort was perhaps the first tangible evidence of Kathleen's quiet, determined rebellion.

That evening Kathleen and White said a hurried good-bye after a chauffeur drove them to Providence, where they boarded separate trains. He never saw any of the other family members again, apart from Eunice, who left several messages for him at the Navy Yard when she stayed in New York. Once she sent a note instructing him to call her hotel and signed it "From one Idiot to Another."

White asked a girl he knew to buy a nightgown for Kathleen, and he enlarged a snapshot he had taken of her the day they went to Jones Beach, but he never got the opportunity to give either to her in person. On September 23 he received notice that the following day he was to be transferred to Northern Ireland.

He called Kathleen that evening to say good-bye and good-naturedly complained that he hadn't heard from her.

She was in a despondent mood. "I'm sorry, I just haven't felt much like writing," she said. She told him she had recently learned from Mrs. Mead that George had been killed. When George's company had landed on Guadalcanal, he had led his platoon forward, ignoring Japanese fire. A bullet had hit him in the face and he had died instantly. He was to be posthumously awarded the Navy Cross.

White urged Kathleen to wait for him. Since he had returned from boot camp, he had tried harder to be more agreeable, even going so far as to introduce her to what he called "the Other White," but their fighting had resumed with its previous intensity, and Kathleen had become impatient with his inexplicable rages. On one peaceful last evening together in Washington, during which they had laughed about the impossibility of a future together, Kathleen had told White that she would marry him if she had not found herself another husband within five years. He had written in his diary that evening: "NOTE: KK WILL MARRY ME IN 1947."

Now he reminded her of that evening, insisting that he would be back for her in five years' time, and she laughingly agreed. He mailed her the nightgown, a little figurine, and a record of "Molly Malone Bluebird," Kathleen's favorite song besides "Joltin' Joe DiMaggio." He kept the enlargement of the photo for himself.

Before White left the States, he received a telegram from another girl named Shirley, to whom he had made the same offer as a backup: "THANKS HEAPS FOR CALLING ME. FIVE YEARS DOESN'T SEEM LIKE TOO LONG." He sent a dozen roses to a third girl. On board ship the following day White tacked up the photograph of Kathleen at Jones Beach in his berth and wrote her a long letter, describing in great detail what should have been their dream farewell.

George Mead's death had affected Kathleen deeply, as had the powerful, positive letter Mrs. Mead had mailed out to all George's friends. "The love in our hearts for George certainly is there stronger, if possible, than ever before and always will be," she wrote. "What is death, then, but a physical change which does not interfere in any way with our power to love? With that power and love and George in our hearts, how can we be unhappy! We can't."

Kathleen replied with a letter that would be quoted in a commemorative book that the Meads published privately. "If I don't write you of what is in my heart I think I shall burst," she said. ". . . Your words to us meant more than all the things I have ever read, learned or been taught about death, war, courage, strength. . . ." How proud they must be of George. She'd always admired people who respected their parents and tried to live up to their highest expectations:

I know that everyone who talks to you cannot help but know that what George did was just an act of obedience to you and Mr. Mead. You had always taught him love of duty and obedience to it. He was killed living up to that heritage.

Future days may bring bad news to us all, but remembering your words, and the way you have acted, one cannot help but feel—Please God, let me act in a similar fashion. . . .

That fall Jack was sent to Rhode Island for navigational training on PT boats, and Joe was stationed at Banana River, Florida, as a flying-boat instructor. He had volunteered for the work in order to clock in enough flying hours to qualify to pilot antisubmarine planes. The only new young men coming into Washington had either been rejected from the services or been among the war's first casualties. Kick's newest acquaintance was Richard Wood, the handsome youngest son of Lord Halifax, who had lost both his legs in Libya. Lord and Lady Halifax held regular dinner parties in Washington to help distract their son from his loss, and Kathleen had met him at one of them. He had captivated her and the other young American guests by his courageous handling of his disability. One wintry day Patsy Field had observed Richard outside a veterans' hospital slowly making his way on crutches across an icy stretch of sidewalk. All of a sudden he slipped and fell. He struggled back onto his crutches only with great difficulty.

"What are you doing?" one of his companions asked anxiously after Richard had repeatedly refused help.

He pointed toward the men staring at him from the hospital windows. "I'm just proving to them that it can be done," he replied.

John White's war career was less distinguished. After only a month overseas he returned to Washington in disgrace. While stationed in Londonderry he had innocently photographed British destroyers; when his superiors discovered the pictures, he had been arrested for possible espionage and put in the brig in the Washington Naval Yard awaiting general court martial on charges of treason. He managed to get a note to his sister, smuggled out in the shoe of a fellow prisoner. Finally he was released on Christmas Eve, after Frank Waldrop and Patsy and Henry Field had managed to convince the appropriate officials that no German agent in his right mind would trust John White with secret documents.

White stayed on in Washington waiting to be reassigned. Kathleen had visited him during his months of incarceration. They attempted now to revive their romance, but White's recent fiasco had settled any lingering doubts Kick may have had about the futility of trying to work out something permanent with him. Although finally admitting defeat, they were still devoted to each other as friends. In February, as White viewed it, Kathleen threw him a conciliatory bone, in the form of introducing him to Nancy Hoguet, the sister of Kick's old schoolmate Ellie from her

Parisian convent days. Kick announced to White that Nancy would be "good" for him and proved herself a competent matchmaker. Nancy liked White immediately; in the spirit of the moment they became engaged at the end of February. The Hoguets, a banking family who were numbered among the most respected Catholics in New York, were horrified. Their worst fears about White were confirmed when he sent Nancy a batch of photographs and her mother opened them by mistake. The photographs showed White in various dejected poses under a signpost that said: VD. No matter how many times Nancy explained, the Hoguets refused to believe the pictures had been a joke. They wondered what kind of fool White had to be, not simply to catch venereal disease but then to go ahead and boast about it.

In early March, White left with a group of Marines for the West Coast, where he was reassigned as a navigator of transport airplanes in the South Pacific. Jack had been sent off to pilot his own PT boat in Tulagi, and Joe Jr. was patrolling the waters off Puerto Rico, searching for German U-boats. As the last of the men Kathleen was close to were sent away on active duty she once again felt on the periphery. Her daily interviews with freshmen congressmen and long-established district architects began to seem more and more self-indulgent. All the women she knew were making important commitments, either to war work or to the men who were going off to fight. In rapid succession it seemed that all Kathleen's closest friends, including Nancy Tenney and Dinah Brand, suddenly had become war brides. Charlotte, to Kathleen's amazement, had lately become engaged to Richard Harris, a Southampton neighbor whom she had known all her life. Panicking at the thought of remaining unmarried with all the men leaving, Charlotte had consented to Richard's last-minute insistent proposal. Even career-minded Page Huidekoper decided to leave the *Times-Herald* to marry Fraser Dougherty, a serviceman from a good family without money. "But Page," Kathleen replied bluntly, "I thought you were *ambitious*."

Kathleen was certain that marrying well was a woman's

greatest achievement. Whatever else her parents had told her, they were right about that. Even if John had seriously proposed, in her heart she knew she would never have accepted. Perhaps it might have been different if his family had social standing. But she knew that if she didn't marry someone wealthy and powerful, she'd be calling her father every night for the rest of her life.

None of her American boyfriends had the stature of her English boyfriends, not even Winthrop Rockefeller. Whenever Tony Rosslyn and William Douglas-Home and all her other English beaux had written asking her to come back to England, she had had trouble deciding who among them was the most attractive. It had been very hard to explain that to her roommate, Betty Coxe, when she showed her their letters, without sounding conceited. But they'd all had their own special qualities. She could still recall watching the sunrise with William Douglas-Home beside the fountain at Hever, and driving with Billy Hartington in his Cadillac convertible through the Derbyshire hills. Billy had really been her favorite. It was almost exactly five years since she'd met him. She felt a little old thinking how long it had been since she'd been eighteen. At times she couldn't quite remember what Billy looked like. She could picture the hazy outline of someone tall and boyish, and that was all.

But ever since she and John White had broken up, she'd found herself talking of Billy more and more. Nancy and White had even begun to tease her about her "fathom lord," the fairy tale character she had conjured up and was going to turn from a toad into a prince.

She'd just wanted to return to England. Her English buddies were still the best friends she'd ever had. She'd sail the moment the war was over and all the boys were back from overseas. Nancy Astor would probably have them all to Cliveden the very first weekend. She'd always assumed she could make up her mind about Billy once she got there. But then Dinah Brand had read her the letter about Billy and Sally. Although she'd first heard about it months ago, she still couldn't believe they'd gotten engaged. Billy had known Sally all his life and had never expressed much interest in her. The gossip was that his parents, who disapproved of Sally's mother, were so unhappy about the engagement that they'd kept the announcement out of the newspapers. Probably they'd asked him to wait a year before setting a wedding day in the hope that time would break it up. All Kathleen's English friends had always thought Billy would wait for her.

How could he have thought that she wasn't going to come back? If only she had found a way to get back there early on in the war. If only Billy had just remained patient, they might have found a way around their religious difference. Even though they had reached an impasse five years ago, there had to be a hidden solution.

It wasn't that she bore Sally any ill will. She and Billy should never have been split up in the first place. This awful war that had killed George was wrecking her own life. Billy had been so crazy about her; he must still be—everybody told her so. It didn't make sense that he couldn't have waited a few years for the war to be over.

Now that John was leaving Washington, she'd been thinking more and more about leaving herself. There had to be something she could do more useful to the cause than writing a gossip column. All the girls she knew now were doing men's jobs. Sancy Falvey was welding on the Boston docks, but Kick wasn't sure she herself had the patience for that kind of work. It certainly wasn't like being out there on the front lines.

Early in 1943 Kathleen and Betty Coxe had read about Red Cross work being done overseas. With thousands of GI's in England and Northern Ireland and thousands more to follow, the Army had been in desperate need of organized lodging and recreation for American servicemen on leave, particularly in blitzed areas, like London, with severe housing shortages. The American Red Cross had been given the task of setting up clubs that offered cheap food and accommodation in London and Northern Ireland. The first clubs, installed in abandoned hotels and Queen Anne mansions, had been so popular that by early 1943 the ARC had embarked on an ambitious project to set up hostels through·

out England. And what could be a better morale-booster for a battle-weary GI than a pretty girl offering a doughnut and a smile? For servicemen in remote areas Harvey Gibson, the ARC commissioner for the European Theater of Operations, invented the "Donut Dugout," a Nissen hut equipped with a snack bar and a gramophone. He also had a vast number of Army-supplied General Motors trucks outfitted with doughnut machines and lounges so that "Clubmobiles" would travel right behind the front lines after D-Day.

The Red Cross began a publicity campaign to recruit American girls as staff members and had recently lowered the minimum age requirement to twenty-one. Photographs appeared in newspapers of pretty young women in smart blue-gray Red Cross uniforms distributing doughnuts and cigarettes to grateful GI's "somewhere in England" ("What a break, what chow, what a gal," read one caption). Although the boys and girls were usually shown having fun, the emphasis was on the contribution of this work toward achieving eventual victory. "This is strictly a non–glamour girl job," read the caption beneath a photo of two drenched workers making coffee. "With rain pouring down through the bomb-shattered roof at 2 A.M., it takes courage, inspiration and perspiration to lift heavy coffee urns containing more than 500 cups of java to the doughnut dollies. . . ."

Kathleen found in the Red Cross the excuse she had been looking for all along to return to England. By signing up, however, she would be taking something of a gamble. Since young women were not allowed to choose their assignments, she might very well land in the Mediterranean, or Iceland, or Northern Ireland. London was considered the choice location, and most of the positions there were quickly filled. With most clubs opening that spring in remote areas of the English countryside, the odds were that Kathleen would be assigned outside London, unless special provisions were made for her.

She decided to take the risk. In late March she informed her parents that she was signing up for Red Cross duty in the hope that she would be stationed in London. Since London was no longer being bombed and Kathleen's own roommate, Betty, was also signing up, Joe Kennedy could offer no objections.

By this time Kathleen had heard that the Devonshires' restrictions on Billy's engagement to Sally had had their desired effect. After only several months he had broken it off very clumsily—infuriating certain of her relatives, who thought Billy's family owed Sally more respect.

Without writing anyone in England of her plans Kathleen filled out an application at the Red Cross National Headquarters on April 6 and was accepted for duty. She had written "yes" under the question "Are you free to accept a position anywhere in the U.S.?" but then crossed it out and noted "yes" only for "abroad." Page Huidekoper signed the required form verifying that Kathleen wished to go overseas solely to perform Red Cross work, and not to be reunited with a loved one. The Red Cross required such a verification after many young women had rushed to sign up in order to be near their boyfriends in the services. Dinah Brand teased Kathleen mercilessly that after hearing the news about Billy Hartington she was getting on the first boat back to England.

Eight

After attending special Red Cross courses at American University, Kathleen was sent to Richmond, Virginia, for further training while she awaited her transfer abroad. John White had written her to keep an eye out for a fellow Red Cross recruit, Katharine "Tatty" Spaatz, the daughter of Lieutenant General Carl A. Spaatz, Allied air commander in North Africa and head of the United States Air Force in Britain. John had dated Tatty, a dark-haired, fine-featured girl, while she was at secretarial school in Washington. Perhaps because they were both his ex–girl friends, White thought Tatty and Kick would have a lot in common. He hardly suspected that they'd land in the same training group, much less the same boarding house. The two girls had a good laugh when they discovered that White, who was again covering all his bases, had sent them each adoring letters that were nearly identical word for word.

Tatty and Kick got to know each other in the next weeks as they were fitted for uniforms, given shots and dogtags, and shown how to drive a Clubmobile, change a tire, and service their truck in an emergency. They had been assigned officer status as second lieutenants in the United States Army so that they would receive maximum privileges if captured by the enemy.

Red Cross trainees were told to be prepared for any eventuality. Some neophyte staff assistants sent alone to remote areas of England had found themselves appointed directors of their clubs upon arrival. In normal circumstances, however, "personal service" was the most important aspect of the job. Most of the training period consisted in "getting to know the GI," which entailed being sent with other girls to local training camp bases for evening dances with homesick servicemen. Although the dances were held in dreary barracks, invariably a live band played, with local musicians patriotically donating their services.

For their last weeks in the States, Kick and Tatty were sent back to Washington, where they waited on tables at a canteen called Soldier and Sailor near Union Station. Tatty got a new permanent just before leaving so that she wouldn't have to bother with her hair in the field. On June 14 they received their orders. Before their departure from the Brooklyn Navy Yard they were given last-minute instructions on air-raid procedure and placed in gas chambers to simulate conditions in gas warfare. On June 25, a stiflingly humid day, Kathleen and Tatty boarded the *Queen Mary* wearing their winter uniforms under their raincoats, loaded down with gas masks, tin helmets, and thirty-five-pound musette bags, their canteens and first-aid kits strapped around their waists. As officers they received berths but were sandwiched together with seven other women, eight to a cabin. The eighteen thousand soldiers who were packed aboard the ship were forced to sleep in three shifts, lying down or standing on deck the rest of the time. "There are about 160 Army nurses and they certainly are a lot of tough babies," Kick wrote home. "There are also about 300 officers of every nationality. Most of the Red Cross girls don't pay attention to them as it certainly isn't any compliment to be sought after when the ratio is so uneven. . . . The girls are quite nice but you certainly get sick of a lot of giggling females and they still like to sit up until about 1:30 A.M. every night."

The *Queen Mary* traveled a circuitous route, swerving sharply to avoid German submarines. When not inching forward in line with her mess kit during meals, Kick spent much of her time on her bunk, the only place on board with breathing space. Tatty roomed with a bunch of lively USO girls, who entertained the soldiers but, in Tatty's view, appeared to be carrying their objective of "personalized service" a bit too far. As a wartime measure Mass was held in the synagogue every afternoon at three thirty. "I have been serving mass," Kathleen wrote home, "as the soldiers don't seem to show up."

After landing in Greenock, Scotland, Kathleen took an early morning train to London with the other Red Cross recruits. The first person she called was Sissy Ormsby-Gore. David, presently undergoing flying training as an air observation post pilot, was stationed in Hatfield, north of London. The two women plotted to surprise David with Kick's arrival. Sissy phoned him and asked mysteriously, "Can you get away for a few days? If you come up to London for lunch, there will be a lovely surprise for you." David rushed to their designated meeting spot several days later to find the two accomplices, giggling conspiratorially.

Word traveled rapidly that Kick Kennedy was back in London. Nancy Astor sent Kick a note of welcome from a family house in Plymouth, which had suffered more than fifty air raids by the Germans. No one was more delighted to learn of Kathleen's return than Billy Hartington, who was stationed with the Guards Armoured Division in Alton, an hour outside London. As soon as he could get leave, Billy came to London to take her out. The appearance of the two of them in their uniforms at the Four Hundred had all London society soon buzzing about the revival of the impossible romance between the Irish Catholic and the Protestant duke's heir.

Kathleen stayed with David and Sissy while awaiting her assignment. Tatty had been posted as a Clubmobile Ranger with the Eighth Air Force outside London, probably out of deference to her father. In early July, Kick learned that her own gamble had paid off. She was to be program assistant at the Hans Crescent Club, an officers-only club in a red-brick townhouse in Knightsbridge, one block away from Harrod's.

Special provisions had been made to accommodate Kathleen on the premises. In fact, another young woman named Irene

Stark was summarily dispatched to Londonderry in order to make room for her. A Red Cross report later noted that it was felt that Kathleen Kennedy's knowledge of the city and many influential people would enable her to make "ready contacts to the advantage of the Club and the programs initiated there for the Enlisted men."

"I received word last night that Kathleen has arrived safe and sound—and I presume it is England," Joseph Kennedy wrote Frank Waldrop on July 3. "I heard through the Army." It is doubtful that his daughter's assignment in London came as a surprise to Kennedy because he probably engineered it through his Army contacts. As ambassador Joe Kennedy had arranged for the Red Cross to set up operations in the 1940 blitz; undoubtedly he knew the organizational leaders, including Harvey Gibson, a banker and prominent member of New York society. When Kathleen arrived, Mrs. Gibson gave a tea in her honor to introduce her to some of the other girls—hardly a routine practice for new recruits.

In a letter to Jack in the South Pacific, Kathleen optimistically declared that London had not changed much physically and that the blitzed areas were not "obvious." Actually the London life she had known had changed profoundly. Most of the young men Kathleen had met five years before were scattered throughout remote areas of the country, along the coast and in the North, drilling in preparation for the invasion. Her women friends, even those with children, were now compelled to work. Sally was still buried away in MI-6 in Bletchley, outside London; Janie was in India, working for Force 136, a special wartime organization set up to aid resistance movements in Europe and Asia. Whatever novelty this arduous existence had offered in 1940 had worn thin as the country entered the fourth year of war. Kathleen's friends had settled into dreary, exhausting routines and experienced what was for many of them shocking deprivation. With shipping routes blockaded and factories almost exclusively manufacturing war materials, most food and commodities were in impossibly short supply. Almost all foodstuffs were rationed; meat was doled out at a few ounces a week per person, butter at a spare one ounce. Milk was under controlled distribution, and bananas and onions were given away as raffle prizes.

Four times a week women listened eagerly on the wireless to Ambrose Heath's *Food Facts from the Kitchen Front,* which provided recipes designed to help stretch meager rations to feed an entire family. In advertisements and radio campaigns the government represented frugal purchases and cooking as patriotic: "Better Pot-luck with Churchill Today than Humble Pie under Hitler Tomorrow"; "Waste the Food and Help the Hun." The *Kitchen Front* was considered every bit as vital to victory as the Front Line, and recipes were given heroic titles: Beet the Cold, All Clear Sandwiches, Victory Sponge. As meat and eggs grew scarcer, housewives were given recipes for unlikely alternatives—Sheep's Head Broth, Pigs Feet in Jelly, Eggs None for Breakfast (tinned apricots cooked in bacon fat and dressed out to look like eggs on toast)—or advice on how to cook an old duck. Soap was in such short supply (three ounces a week by 1943) that many of the women working in factories found it difficult to get clean. With most of England's arable land taken up with grazing and animal feed, the government launched a Dig for Victory campaign. Almost every household—even those in cities—planted seeds; in London even the moat surrounding the Tower of London and the flower tubs around Piccadilly Circus became vegetable gardens.

In 1940 the government had passed a Limitations of Supplies Order to ban the import and manufacture of "inessential goods," and by 1943 most shops were almost entirely bereft of basic household items. At pubs that had run out of drinking glasses people drank the regulation watered-down beer from jam jars. Midway through the war Parliament introduced Utility, a government-controlled standardized line of goods and clothing, which was rationed as well under a points system. Clothing designers like Norman Hartnell who had designed wedding gowns for the Whigham and other socialites among Kathleen's contemporaries were now being asked to design Utility clothing for the population at large. Silk stockings were unobtainable, and Ascot hats, which occasionally surfaced to brighten up society, were considered unpatriotic. Kathleen's friends, formerly so well turned out, were lucky by 1943 to purchase one dress a year. They had grown used to wool stockings, comfortable shoes, and scarves instead of hats; they traded clothing with each other or learned how to artfully redo a worn collar or sleeve in "make do and mend" classes. With cosmetics no longer manufactured or imported Sally Norton and her friends melted down old lipsticks and mixed them together or used black Meltonian shoe polish for mascara on special evenings on the town. Pipe cleaners doubled as hairpins; Victory rolls, a wartime hairdo, eliminated the need for a permanent.

Feeling a little guilty over their prewar lives, many of Kathleen's friends rationalized the austerity forced upon them. Sally, who published several stories in *The Baltimore Sun* about the conditions for young people in the war, cheerily wrote of present-day dress as a form of liberation: "I cannot imagine how we existed before the war, bound by the frequently hideous ties of fashion. Our hair was scrapped up, and held together by countless angry little pins, our waists were tied with steel, rapier-like pieces of bone pierced our ribs, enough to ruin any appetite, our feet were stilts, and we tottered about, every step like a bed of needles. . . . I must admit it is great fun to dress how you please, it breaks down that inherent tradition of wearing gloves in the train, and a hat on Sundays. Think! You can even wear blue with green."

Even though these hardships might go on indefinitely, Kathleen's friends maintained their good spirits. Being a soldier or standing on a factory line was the first work many of them had ever done in their lives. When Billy had been at school, no self-respecting Cambridge student would have allowed himself to be spotted in a library, swotting for exams. Now it felt good to have something really vital to do every day. As the ads on the wireless to recruit workers pointed out, women engaged in war work were every bit as heroic as the men on the battlefield. ("Bravo, the women flight mechanics! Ever thought of yourself as an electrician? Be a welder. Come into the factories!") The petty irritations of daily life only made a reunion of old friends that much more exciting. And since no one knew if today's party would be the last one for a long time, even the tiniest pleasures took on heightened significance. Guests at a party at Veronica Fraser Phipps's guiltily consuming a windfall tub of strawberries and a two-pound bag of sugar felt they were indulging in the most outlandish extravagance. Young women would drop everything at a moment's notice and travel any distance to spend a few hours' leave with their men. Veronica, who was married to a lieutenant in the Royal Navy, was so excited by the prospect of a reunion with her husband that she left her car at the top of a hill without the emergency brake on. She didn't give a damn when she returned and found the car smashed. What did that matter when she'd just seen her husband alive and well?

At first the war seemed to Kathleen just another kind of English social gathering. Preinvasion London was the center of leave-taking for British and American soldiers. Thousands of American GI's had invaded the city. The war-weary British were dazzled by these new arrivals in their sparkling, clean, pressed uniforms, full of enthusiastic resolve to "beat Jerry." British families invented mock hamburgers and renamed dishes "Beano MacRoosevelt" in an attempt to make GI houseguests feel welcome. It soon became apparent that these fast-talking allies from across the Atlantic had less wartime experience than many British children and more to eat each day than most English families were allowed for a week. Americans freely dispensed what appeared to be a limitless supply of cigarettes, candy, and chocolate to the astonished British, who had been forced long ago to drink their tea unsweetened. (English children quickly learned to ask, "Any gum, chum?") While some Yankee largesse was thought to be tactless and overbearing, young women without finery or male companionship looked upon the Americans who handed out nylons and cosmetics as glamorous stand-ins for their British boyfriends. By the fourth year of the war many young married women eagerly began to volunteer as dance partners for the hops and dances sponsored by British and American organizations to maintain troop morale. Factory workers often rolled up their hair in hair clips at lunchtime so that they could leave in buses for dances directly after work.

The most popular of all the dance halls were the American Red Cross Clubs, which operated like combination drugstores and service centers. Rainbow Corner, the largest, run for the GI's and their dates or guests, had been fashioned from a rambling five-story converted J. Lyons & Co. restaurant a block from Piccadilly Circus. Thousands of soldiers flooded through its doors each day to eat, take a bath, or get their uniforms cleaned and pressed. The front desk dispensed information about sight-seeing or furloughs in British homes, along with free theater tickets to West End shows. Taxi drivers shuttled GI's around on sight-seeing tours to famous points of interest. Along with a twenty-four-hour jukebox the smoky lounge downstairs contained a stage for plays and weekly gigs by local bands like the Flying Yankees or the occasional guest appearance of Glenn Miller and his new Army Air Force Band. In one corner "Ma" Whittaker sat ready to do darning or mending or to stitch on stripes or buttons, making sure to sew a lucky farthing under the stripe of every pilot getting ready to fly. "Dellie," or Adele Astaire Cavendish, who had married Billy Hartington's uncle, worked there eight hours a day writing home to the parents of soldiers. A first-aid room was devoted primarily to boys who needed sobering up before returning to their camps. Periodically the club taped its own radio show, *American Eagle Broadcasts,* which would feature music by traveling stars like Fred Astaire and Irving Berlin, speeches by such distinguished visitors as Eleanor Roosevelt, and messages from individual soldiers to their families in America.

The Hans Crescent Club, where Kathleen worked, resembled the smaller, more exclusive officers' clubs scattered around London, such as the Charles Street Club, where the director made a fetish of maintaining the best service, often buying strawberries and asparagus with her own money when she could not get such items through the ARC. At Hans Crescent, Kathleen was supposed to provide "general entertainment," which included greeting the boys, directing them to the club's various facilities, dancing, playing cards, and listening as they talked of individual problems and preinvasion jitters. Soldiers swamped Kathleen with constant requests to procure new leave passes, to write to their mothers, to find them someone to play the piano. One evening she had to scout out professional entertainers to put on a cabaret, then find beds for everybody in the audience after the show—in some cases on the club's lounge chairs. During her first weekend off, which she spent at Cliveden with the Astors, Kick wrote to Frank Waldrop:

> The job is a little more than I bargained for but life is full of surprizes [sic] so I guess one more won't hurt me. . . .
>
> I am stationed very near where I once lived and need I add that life is very different from those good old days. However my years with the old Times-Herald hardened me for come what may. You will be glad to hear that I am more pro-British than ever and spend my days telling the GIs about that great institution "the British Empire" (this is serious).
>
> As we get a day and a half off a week I am here recuperating from five days and a half of jitter-bugging, gin rummy, ping-pong, bridge and just being an American girl among 1500 doughboys a long way from home. (I'm not sure yet, but I don't think this is what I was born for). . . .

Kathleen signed off with "There'll Always Be an England"—a reference to a patriotic movie theme song that had lately become England's unofficial national anthem.

Some of the officers were a little awestruck when they learned they were jitterbugging with the former ambassador's daughter. At one point she wrote home, "The boys really crowd in here every night and most of them have gotten over the fear that I am some extraordinary being because I happened to have a father who really was (extraordinary, of course!)" Kathleen soon learned to keep her family connections a secret; one homesick sergeant whom Kick invited to attend Mass with her was later astounded to learn of her identity.

Meanwhile, in America, Joseph Kennedy made sure that Kathleen's participation in the war effort was well publicized. Her arrival in London had made the newspapers in England and America, and Kennedy had painstakingly monitored her press. Apparently to counteract what he felt was unfavorable publicity, he wrote to Frank Waldrop, with whom he had grown increasingly friendly:

> The Journal American had an article on her last Sunday but I didn't particularly like the material. Neither did her mother. But as you said that you would like to do an article on her sometime, I thought I'd send along a copy of the last picture that we had taken of her. It's not in uniform, but it's kind of cute. When you have decided whether or not you want to write a story, I'll send one . . . but I won't do anything about this until I hear from you.

One summer day a photographer on the *Daily Mail* in London photographed Kathleen in uniform on a bicycle pedaling to work. The photograph was promptly snapped up by *The Boston Globe* and reproduced in papers across the country as an apt symbol of the all-American girl coming to the aid of the boys abroad. "Larry Winship had a story in the Boston Globe last night . . . ," Kennedy wrote Frank Waldrop, "and said she had made a hit with the Red Cross, as I was sure she would. There are no two ways about it, she still thinks the British are the second best people on earth."

Actually Kathleen had not made a hit among her fellow workers, who sorely resented her preferential treatment. There was talk that Kathleen had used the Red Cross as a means of circumventing the travel ban so that she could return to England and marry the Marquess of Hartington. Joe Kennedy had probably pulled strings to get Irene Stark transferred so as to enable Kick to work in the most exclusive area of London. It wasn't fair that Kick had been stationed near her boyfriend when some of the married women weren't allowed to be near their spouses. Kathleen was given time off every weekend, while most of them were only off once a fortnight. Kathleen seemed to be spending more time entertaining her aristocratic friends, who had begun to drop by the club, than the officers themselves.

Even Lady Astor visited her periodically, searching out boys from Virginia, her home state, and once remarking to a sergeant, "You don't need to be entertained. I should give you a lecture on temperance." Eventually Kathleen's superiors were forced to speak with her about not paying sufficient attention to her work and allowing her social life to interfere with her responsibilities. Once upbraided, however, as the assistant director wrote in an evaluation sheet, ". . . Miss Kennedy was able to adjust herself to the situation quite admirably and did her utmost to perform her work satisfactorily."

As proud as Kathleen was of her Red Cross uniform, she lived for her time off. At every opportunity she rushed out of London, sometimes having to sit all night on her suitcase in an over-crowded train to travel up to the home of a friend in York-shire. Kathleen's romance with Billy was rekindling very rapidly. He was so attractive in his uniform, and he seemed even more so because they had so little time together—an occasional week-end at the country houses of mutual friends when Billy had a forty-eight-hour leave. He seemed so mature and confident as he regaled her with stories of the dramatic evacuation of France. After being promoted to the rank of captain in the Guards, Billy now commanded a group of soldiers. All his present work was top secret, but she knew he was undergoing months of training for the invasion. Occasionally Billy even talked of the discussions he had been having lately with his father, who thought it time for Billy to stand for Parliament. It was impressive to see him transformed over the three years from a languid Cambridge stu-dent into a prospective candidate for Churchill's government.

Billy now seemed willing to take on his parents over the pros-pect of marrying Kathleen. He began talking seriously of mar-riage from their first dates that summer but made it clear that he could never agree to the stipulations of the Catholic Church con-cerning mixed marriages. They would have to get married *his* way, in an Anglican ceremony and with the tacit understanding that future children would be brought up Protestant to carry on the Cavendish family line. Kathleen initially balked at Billy's de-mands. The convention in mixed marriages was for the Protestant to graciously capitulate to the demands of the Catholic Church; David Ormsby-Gore had done so when he'd married Sissy. Billy had to realize he was asking Kathleen to renounce everything she'd been taught to value.

During preliminary arguments with Billy, Kathleen wrote home about the burgeoning romance with deliberate flippancy in order to spare her family any undue concern. She treated her differences with Billy as a contest of wills in which she was determined not to be the loser:

> . . . It really is funny to see people put their heads together the minute we arrive any place. There's heavy betting on when we are going to announce it. Some people have gotten the idea that I'm going to give in. Little do they know. It just amuses me to see how worried they all are. . . .

In mid-July, after returning from a weekend with Billy at Compton Place, where his family continued to spend the summer months despite what had been heavy bombing, Kick wrote in a rather veiled manner to Jack. As though to elicit encouragement from him, she emphasized only her regret that because of religion she might be passing up a good catch:

> . . . Billy is just the same, a bit older, a bit more ducal, but we get on as well as ever. It is queer as he is so unlike anyone I have ever known at home or anyplace really. Of course I know he would never give in about the religion, and he knows I never would. It's all rather difficult as he is very, very fond of me and as long as I am about he'll never marry. However much he loved me I can easily understand his position. It's really too bad because I'm sure I would be a most efficient Duchess of Devonshire in the post-war world, and as I'd have a castle in Ireland, one in Scotland, one in Yorkshire, and one in Sussex, I could keep my old nautical brothers in their old age. But that's the way it goes. Everyone in London is buzzing with rumors, and no matter what happens we've given them something to talk about. I

can't really understand why I like Englishmen so much, as they treat one in quite an offhanded manner and aren't really as nice to their women as Americans, but I suppose it's just that sort of treatment that women really like. That's your technique isn't it?

In mid-August, Kathleen heard through the British newspapers that Jack's PT boat had been rammed and sunk by a Japanese destroyer in the South Pacific and that he and his men had been found after having been missing for a week. Eager for details, Kick rushed over to the London bureau of *The New York Times,* which had splashed the story across the front page under the headline:

KENNEDY'S SON IS HERO IN PACIFIC
AS DESTROYER SPLITS HIS PT BOAT

She wrote home immediately: "Of course the news about Jack is the most exciting I've ever heard. There wasn't a very big piece in the English newspapers but quite enough for me to gather that he did really big stuff."

Jack had been the skipper of the PT 109, which had been patrolling the waters around the Solomon Islands in the South Pacific. Its mission and that of its sister ships had been to impede the provisioning of Japanese-held bases by firing upon the "Tokyo Express," a flotilla of Japanese destroyers that delivered supplies at night. Kathleen read that on the night of August 2 a Japanese destroyer had sliced diagonally through the PT 109 in the Blackett Strait. After the crash Kennedy swam out to rescue several of his men who had been badly burned in a gasoline fire caused by the collision. With two dead the eleven survivors of the shipwreck had abandoned their sinking hull. For three hours the frail skipper swam for shore through the rough currents with an injured mate strapped to his back, the man's life-belt strap clenched between his teeth. Day after day without food or drink the eleven castaways waited for rescue on a tiny island. "On three nights, Lieutenant Kennedy, once a backstroke man on the Harvard swimming team, swam out into Ferguson Passage hoping to flag down PT boats going through on patrol," the story said.

On the fourth day two friendly natives had discovered the survivors and agreed to carry to a coastal base a message Kennedy had crudely carved on a green coconut husk:

> NAURO ISL
> NATIVE KNOWS POSIT
> HE CAN PILOT 11 ALIVE NEED
> SMALL BOAT
> KENNEDY

Finally, on the sixth day of the 109 crew's ordeal, a rescue boat, guided by a native pilot, made its way through the serpentine passages to meet Kennedy and pick up his crew.

Jack wrote to Kathleen while he was recuperating in a Navy base in the Solomons. "Goodness I was pleased to get your letter," she replied. "Ever since reading the news in all the newspapers over here I have been worried to death about you. All sorts of people have rung up about it and sent congratulations. I read the clippings from the New York Times but long to hear the whole story." Clare Booth Luce, who had become a Catholic convert, had given Jack a sacred medal, and Kick referred to it when she added, "Am sure Mrs. Luce is blaming your survival on 'her medal.' . . ."

Jack had written Kick from Guadalcanal, where he was waiting for a new boat to be refurbished so he could be sent out again on patrol. He had elected to return to sea rather than to take leave in New Zealand for a month in order to finish up his tour of duty and return home that much faster. While on Guadalcanal Jack sought out George Mead's grave. He found it in the very first row of a cemetery of crude year-old graves of those American soldiers who had died taking the island from the Japanese, and felt very moved when he read the epitaph on the simple aluminum plate:

> LT. GEORGE MEAD, AUGUST 20, 1942.
> A GREAT LEADER OF MEN—GOD BLESS HIM.

Jack wrote to the Meads about George's grave. He thought of that last weekend in Aiken—of George's tape recording, and their pathetic attempts to play polo, and Chuck's coup during the scavenger hunt in producing Lady Astor to satisfy the number ten requirement for an "odd object."

Jack had almost drowned one night out in the Ferguson Passage. After thrashing for hours against the fearsome current he had stopped caring whether or not he was going to make it back to shore. For six entire days he and his mates had been terrified of being discovered by the enemy or dying of thirst. One day, desperate for a drink of water, they had lain on their backs with their mouths open during a rainfall, hoping to catch a few drops. It had been a completely black time. Not only had he almost drowned but he had lost two of his crew members, one of whom had a wife and three children and had ridden with him his entire tour. Shaken by a bomb blast near the 109 a few days before the collision with the destroyer, the man had been convinced he was going to die. Jack had resolved to put the fellow off the boat as soon as he could and now couldn't shake the idea that he was somehow responsible for his loss.

He was a little embarrassed that his family name had put the story on page one. His actions were hardly extraordinary; all he had been trying to do was get help. If anything he might even have been a little rash and foolhardy to jump into perilous waters with his weak back. It would have demoralized the crew to lose their skipper.

Jack was impatient with the frequent battle cry of "unconditional surrender" made by commentators back home. "When I read that we will fight the Japs for years if necessary and will sacrifice hundreds and thousands if we must—I always like to check from where he is talking—it's seldom out here," he wrote his family. "People get so used to talking about billions of dollars and millions of soldiers that thousands of dead sounds like drops in a bucket. But if those thousands want to live as much as the ten I saw—they should measure their words with great, great care."

While waiting to take command of the PT 59 Jack sent off a letter to Inga:

Inga Binga. . . . I used to have a feeling that no matter what happened I'd live through. It's a funny thing that as long as you have that feeling you seem to get through. I've lost that feeling lately. As a matter of fact, I don't feel badly about it. If anything happens to me I have this knowledge that if I live to be 100 I could only improve the quantity of my life, not the quality. This sounds gloomy as hell but you are the only person I'd say it to anyway. As a matter of fact, knowing you has been the brightest part of an extremely bright 26 years. . . .

Far away in London, Kathleen knew little of Jack's state of mind. She had had difficulty at first associating the sickly, devil-may-care "Johnny," as she often teasingly called him, with the Harvard "backstroke champion" described in the story who had braved impossible waters and rescued his entire crew. She had expected that kind of performance from Joe. Jack had always been the family wit, who mimicked the Irish maid's brogue until he had her in tears. Suddenly the brother who had never taken anything seriously had amassed a list of weighty accomplishments. At twenty-six Jack was not only a best-selling author but a war hero.

Meanwhile Joe Jr., who had been transferred to Norfolk, Virginia, had grown increasingly frustrated over what he viewed as his own inconsequential contribution to the war. If his younger brother had already emerged as a hero in the South Pacific, Joe had yet to sink a submarine or even to see any real action. His letters home, however, full of braggadocio and inflated descriptions of various exploits, betrayed none of his real feeling. "Your brother is now sporting a moustache," he would write to his fifteen-year-old sister Jean. "There is some talk of looking like Gable. . . ."

In September, Joe got his wish. His squadron was selected as badly needed backup for the RAF Coastal Command to provide antisubmarine patrols in the Channel and Bay of Biscay in northern France. Joe flew up to HyannisPort to say good-bye to his family and participate in his father's fifty-fifth birthday celebration. Former Police Commissioner Timilty and a local judge were among the celebrants. During dinner the judge proposed a toast to "Ambassador Joe Kennedy, father of our hero, our *own* hero, Lieutenant John F. Kennedy of the United States Navy." Joe raised his glass cordially but had to struggle to maintain control. How could they have overlooked his own name in the toast when he himself was about to set off on dangerous patrols? At bedtime Timilty, who shared a room with Joe, found him on his bed, clenching and unclenching his fists in fury. "By God," he muttered, "I'll show them." After they'd retired, Timilty was kept awake by muffled sobbing from the other bed.

Before leaving, Joe had packed six dozen eggs from Hyannis-Port for Kathleen in his new airplane, a PB4Y Catalina. On the flight across the Atlantic via Greenland one of Joe's fellow pilots developed engine trouble. Joe radioed his friend that an emergency landing was out of the question. "I can't stick around and circle," he said. "I've got a crate of eggs for my sister."

In October, Joe's squadron settled temporarily in Cornwall on the southwest coast of England; from there Joe telephoned Kick several times a week. In the meanwhile Jack had finished duty and was being sent home, via New York. Jack had written his parents that he had word that Joe had been spotted in New York with the two most beautiful English girls in town before leaving for England. "I hope if Joe is planning to leave, he will leave a complete program with the names and numbers of the leading players."

Unable to extend genuine congratulations about Jack's heroism, Joe wrote that he was

> delighted to find you in such good health and such obvious anticipation of the pleasures which await you in the Big City. I know that you will be disappointed to hear that before leaving I succeeded in dispersing my first team in such various points that it will be impossible to cover all the territory. If you give me a rough idea of your itinerary I will try

to fit in a few enjoyable evenings for you en route. If you
ever get around Norfolk, you will get quite a welcome if you
mention the magic name of Kennedy, so I advise you to go
incognito.

Mentioning an old girl friend of Jack's, whom he had met after
Jack's sudden "burst onto the front pages," Joe wrote, "I was
tempted to take her out myself but knowing how you feel about
that sort of thing and knowing what a swell job you are doing in
winning the war I decided to lay off."

By late October, Joe had managed to arrange an assignment
to northern England to pick up some matériel and en route
landed in an airfield near London, where he delivered the crate
of eggs to Kick in person. They spent an evening together, ending up at the Four Hundred, after which Joe, unable to find lodging in crowded London, stayed with William Randolph Hearst,
Jr., who was there as a war correspondent. Joe had planned to
leave the following morning, but poor weather conditions forced
him to stay another entire day. That evening Hearst invited Joe
and Kick to dine with him at the Savoy, along with General
Robert Laycock, head of the British Commandos, and his wife
Angela and Virginia Gilliat, Joe's old girl friend, now married to
Sir Richard Sykes. Virginia had asked along Patricia Wilson, an
army wife.

Pat was a striking dark beauty with deep blue eyes. Her
chatty, open manner and infectious laugh were unusual compared to the reticence of most English women of her class. Joe
soon found out that she was in fact Australian, the daughter of a
sheep rancher from Cootamundra, New South Wales. When Pat
was seventeen, she had come with her mother to London ostensibly to attend school but primarily to participate in the English
Season—and, it was strongly implied, to find herself a husband.
Pat had come out the same year as Margaret Whigham, and by
odd coincidence a date with the Whigham's future husband led
Pat to hers. When Oxford student Charles Sweeny couldn't keep
a date with Pat one evening, he had asked his fellow student,
George Child-Villiers, the twenty-one-year-old Earl of Jersey, to

take her out instead. By autumn Pat had become engaged to the wealthy young peer, who had houses in Wales and throughout the south of England. Theirs had been the "dream match" of the year, with their spectacular wedding in St. Margaret's in Westminster held one week before Pat's eighteenth birthday. After a 'round-the-world honeymoon the young couple settled in Osterley Park, the eight-hundred-acre Child-Villiers estate outside London, noted for its Adam mansion and gardens. The couple's happiness, however, had been short-lived. It was said that theirs was a loveless marriage, with both partners before long pursuing separate lives. By 1936 George was being seen in the constant company of Virginia Sherrill, Cary Grant's ex-wife and Charlie Chaplin's leading lady in *City Lights*. A year later Pat divorced him. They had both since remarried, she to a banker in his late thirties named Robin Filmer Wilson.

By 1943 Wilson was a major in the British Army stationed in Libya and had been away for a couple of years. Pat had three small children from her two marriages and, after the onset of the war, had moved them to a little tile-roofed cottage called Crastock Farm in Woking, about one hour from London, where she worked part time in a factory. She had chosen that home not only to keep the children safe from bombing but also to be near her London friends. In the course of the evening Pat learned that Joe was to be stationed near Taunton in Somerset, which was on the same train line as Woking. The two of them got on very well immediately, and Pat casually asked him, as she did many of her other friends, to visit her on one of his leaves.

The next time Kathleen saw Joe was on his first week's leave in mid-November, when he and several of his fellow squadron members headed for London. Kick threw a party for them at the house of her mother's old friend and her old debutante chaperone, Marie Bruce. While Kathleen was getting dressed there Irving Berlin happened to telephone, and she asked him to come as well. All the Kennedys were dazzled by stars and notable people; Mrs. Kennedy often encouraged her children to approach the famous for autographs. "People don't pay much attention to celebrities over here and when he walked in he might have been

Joe Snooks for all the glances he got," Kick would write home in disgust about Berlin's presence at the party. At her urging Berlin agreed to play a few songs. Guests sang along as he played his new piece "My British Buddy," along with many of his old standards; he received a standing ovation for "Over There." The party was a terrific success for Kathleen, until a young Coldstream Guardsman, who had had too much to drink, set fire to the new evening dress of Billy's sister, Elizabeth Cavendish. "Before I was set on fire the boys didn't pay much attention to me," the young woman remarked, "but afterwards I was very popular."

During his leave Joe had taken out Chiquita Carcano, the daughter of the Argentinian ambassador, who was also dating Jakey Astor, Nancy Astor's youngest son. "He certainly is in right now, right after me," Joe wrote smugly to Jack. Jack had dated Chiquita's sister Bebe in 1939. "That ranch in the Argentine with all those cattle looks better all the time." In fact, Chiquita found Joe very disagreeable and arrogant, particularly one evening in a taxicab when he made a pass at her and was outraged when she refused. Joe's greatest social successes were among the young marrieds like Angela Laycock, who thought him a much more self-effacing and likable character than his brother Jack, whom she had met before the war. Angela knew of Joe's political ambitions, and she was genuinely touched when he confided to her that he was sure it was his brother Jack who would ultimately be President. She had the feeling Joe was in awe of Jack's intelligence and believed that his own was no match for it, particularly since his younger brother's recent triumphs.

"Joe seems to be having a good time, but no special girl friend," Kathleen wrote home. In the coming months, however, Joe began spending much of his leave time with Pat Wilson. None of Pat's friends were scandalized when they learned that she was seeing Joe Kennedy. By 1943 many young married women with absent husbands had taken up with American soldiers. Solitary British wives were thought to be fair game. Everyone was in love with someone. Because she wouldn't be seeking a permanent entanglement, Pat represented just another safe bet for Joe, but she was the first woman who had ever truly captured his attention.

Nine

In December 1943 Kathleen flew back to Palm Beach through travel arrangements made by her father to spend Christmas with her family. Over the holidays she saw her old friend Nancy Tenney, recently married to Demarest Lloyd, who was in Guam flying fighter planes for the Navy. Nancy was four months pregnant and depressed because it seemed unlikely Demarest would get home in time for the birth. Kathleen was thrilled when Nancy asked her to be the baby's godmother.

When she returned to England in early January, she found Billy in the thick of a political campaign. His uncle, Henry Hunloke, had resigned from Parliament, and the family had decided that it was time for Billy, who was now of age, to assume the seat that had been occupied by Cavendishes for all but five of the past two hundred and ten years. In 1938 the Duke of Devonshire had put up Hunloke as a candidate merely to keep the seat warm for his elder son. Since a regular serving officer could not become an MP, Billy resigned his commission as captain in the Coldstream Guards in order to campaign. He was placed in the Regular Army Reserve of Officers and would be called up immediately after the February election.

Billy went out to get votes on a gasoline-saving pony cart,

drawn by his sister Elizabeth's pony, Poppet, covered in ribbons the colors of the Union Jack. Churchill publicly came out in support of Billy as the National Government candidate. On her days off from the Hans Crescent Club, Kathleen rode around with him, handing out leaflets that read, "A vote for Hartington is a vote for Churchill." Billy seemed surprisingly comfortable on the podium. His sense of humor came alive. Kathleen looked on with pride as he hoisted his hands over his head and shouted, "Don't let the old side down!"

Billy's opponent, a paunchy fifty-three-year-old Derbyshire City Council alderman named Charles White, had declared his candidacy on an Independent Socialist ticket. The contest was a personal vendetta for White, whose father had been the only person to wrest the seat from a Cavendish in the last two centuries. White himself had stood unsuccessfully against Hunloke in 1938. Capitalizing on Billy's youth and the fact that the war was more than four years old, White turned the focus of the campaign away from war issues and toward those that would concern the population once the fighting was over. Ultimately the campaign was fought over class. White depicted it as a contest between a ducal heir and a cobbler's son. It was the common man up against the "Palace on the Peak." White accused Billy of choosing to stand only to avoid fighting in the war and claimed that he had received a special exemption to resign his army commission not open to common soldiers. The right of the Cavendish family to assume possession of a parliamentary seat was called into question, as was Churchill's right to dictate who Hunloke's successor would be. Even Billy's ability to milk a cow became a campaign issue. The Independent Socialist candidate claimed that Billy was incapable of doing so—all the more evidence of his distance from the common working man. Off the podium White attempted to link Billy's politics with those of Oswald Mosley, a fascist who had married Billy's brother's sister-in-law, Diana Mitford. White's smear campaign was successful. Day after day Billy was forced to correct newspaper statements implying that his resignation from the Coldstream Guards had resulted from a deal arranged by his father and to spend much of his time explaining to voters why he was campaigning rather than fighting on the front.

White had managed to gain the support of a recently formed political group calling themselves the Common Wealth. Organized by Sir Richard Acland, MP, the group claimed to concern itself with postwar issues and "anyone against the Tories." Common Wealth paid for most of White's expenses and flooded West Derbyshire with some hundred trained campaign workers, including a press agent who had successfully won a seat in Parliament for the party the month before. Caught totally off guard, the Cavendishes were overwhelmed by the tactics of the opposition. They had always relied upon family members and household help for vote-getting, and they were ill prepared for an organized professional campaign that would divide the district into sections and methodically canvass voters. They were also stunned that their constituency, which almost unfailingly voted Conservative, would consider the war as good as won and turn instead to postwar issues such as equality and socialism.

In the final days of the campaign Billy took the offensive, implying that his opponent's promises were empty by referring to him and the group supporting him as "Snow White and the Seven Common Wealth Dwarfs." Attending market day in Bakewell, where four young bulls were being weighed and sold, Billy jumped onto the auctioneer's rostrum to address the cowmen and farmers. "I think you are all too sensible to listen to chaps from Acland's West Country circus who come here talking revolution."

As the accusations that flew back and forth became more heated Billy suggested that he and his opponent stage an actual muck-raking contest. "I publicly challenge Mr. White to name any farm he likes in West Derbyshire and see which of us can rake the most muck in one hour, the loser to give five pounds to the Red Cross." To Billy's dismay, White didn't take him up on his dare.

On the eve-of-poll UPI reporters and MovieTone cameramen arrived to cover the last moments of what was termed "the most momentous campaign of the war."

The following day the residents of West Derbyshire went to the polls in hay carts and governess wagons. Hartington and White both expected the vote to be very close, but the results reported the following morning were astonishing. White had won by a landslide majority of sixteen thousand, receiving over five thousand more votes than Hartington—almost the identical numbers with which Billy's uncle had captured the seat from White in the previous election. News commentators had a field day speculating on the ramifications. Did the victory signify a decrease in Churchill's popularity? How much social reform would the war-weary British population press for after the war was won?

Billy made a final speech from his headquarters in Bakewell, announcing that he was returning to the front, to "fight, perhaps to die for you," and that he would stand again after the war, for either a local or a national seat.

In the United States, Frank Waldrop, who had been following the West Derbyshire election in the American press, wrote Kathleen a teasing note about how her "old pal the Marquess of Hartington got plastered the other day," and informed her he had seen photographs of her in Poppet's cart "spreading sweetness and light." Waldrop told Joe Kennedy that he thought Kathleen was going to England to get married, and in his letter he hinted again at an Anglo-American union: "I am sure that if you will continue along this line for a few years you will become the Lady Astor of 1956."

Waldrop had been writing frequently to Kick and his other former protégés, acting as a central depository of information about the activities of each. He arranged for Kick to receive copies of the *Times Heraldings,* a weekly house organ containing gossip and newsy bits about the activities of former employees involved in the war. Page, who was working in a factory, "expects to produce a genius in March," he wrote. "J. White is just about opposite your position at this time, if you were to project one of your hat pins through an orange." On February 29 he wrote Kick that her brother Jack had stopped in, fresh from a reunion with Inga Arvad, who had apparently left her third husband and moved to the West Coast. "He tells me he saw a former employee of ours in Los Angeles. He did not say how long he saw the same and he seemed very blasé about it all. I have not seen the said former employee or heard from same since the last time I had trouble on that front. . . ."

After taking command of the PT 59 and sinking three Japanese barges, Jack had been sent home after Christmas because of medical problems. He had contracted malaria, and his chronic problem with a disk in his lower back had worsened with the constant pounding of the patrol boats. His Los Angeles reunion with Inga was strained. The two had little in common now. Exhausted and painfully thin, traumatized by his war experiences, Jack had arrived to find Inga, who had temporarily taken over Sheilah Graham's syndicated gossip column, completely swept up in the Hollywood life. He regaled her with a lighthearted version of his PT boat adventures, joking that the Navy would either give him a medal or throw him out, but otherwise he seemed to have lost his sense of humor. Inga decided to write a column about his ordeal, but Jack insisted repeatedly throughout the interview, "None of that hero stuff about me. The real heroes are not the men who return, but those who stay out there, like plenty of them do, two of my men included."

From Los Angeles, Jack headed on to Palm Beach, where he was welcomed at the airport by Chuck Spalding, who was still waiting to be sent overseas. That first evening home Jack insisted that they head off to his favorite old haunt, the Patio, a nightclub with an open-air dance floor. Once they were inside, however, Jack was shocked by the gaiety of the dancers, the light conversation going on at the bar. Rage welled up in him as he sat with Chuck. Nobody in the room seemed to have the slightest understanding that a war was going on. In his short term home Jack had heard more than his fair share of inflated war stories told by civilians. Strangers learning of his patrol experiences invariably asked how many destroyers he had sunk, as though they could be picked off like decoys at a penny arcade. Jack had wept when he'd been ordered to leave the

South Pacific; right now he felt closer to his men than to anybody else in his life. He told Chuck he was going to call and write the sweethearts and families of his buddies left in the Solomons just to let them know their men were all right.

After his stay in Palm Beach, Jack ran into John Hersey, who'd married his old flame Frances Ann Cannon. Hersey, a budding writer intrigued by Kennedy's ordeal in the South Pacific, decided to write an article about it, which eventually was accepted by the *New Yorker*. Joseph Kennedy, Sr., also had in mind a story about Jack's heroics, but on a grander scale. Through some deft manipulating he managed to get the *New Yorker* article condensed into the *Reader's Digest*, the magazine with the largest circulation in the country.

When Billy Hartington returned to the Army in March, he was stationed at Alton in Hampshire, less than an hour from London and a short train ride from Woking. As Joe Kennedy had been seeing more of Pat Wilson and her house in Woking was easily accessible by train, Kick, Billy, Joe, and several other friends found Crastock Farm a convenient meeting place on weekends. They rechristened the house "Crash-bang." Each would arrive with an egg, a piece of meat, or a can of grapefruit juice, whatever they could manage to steal from Army, Navy, or Red Cross kitchens. They'd turn on the gramophone, play a little tennis, or enjoy hours of bridge and gin rummy out in the little wooded glen behind the cottage. Joe often berated Kathleen for what he considered her terrible card sense, but he had little success in his attempts to assert his authority over her. "You talk to me as though I were a member of your crew!" she complained once after being ordered around. The two of them argued a great deal over petty issues, particularly the ownership of Joe's Underwood portable typewriter, which Kick claimed was hers, but they were growing closer. Suddenly they found themselves fellow conspirators. Kathleen and her big brother were equals in their romantic predicaments—both were certain to incur their mother's wrath. It was gratifying for Kick to observe her eldest brother, always the family standard bearer, falling a little short of the family's high expectations. Lately she had seen him humbled by Jack's achievements, and now he was seeing a married woman with three small children. If Joe was interested in a woman whose husband was off fighting in Italy, then marrying Billy couldn't be the worst thing she could do, at least not as bad as it might have been before the war.

Many of Joe's squadron mates knew that he had become preoccupied with a woman and expected that an engagement would soon be announced. Only Mark Soden, Joe's boyish Wisconsin roommate, thought otherwise. Mark had known Joe from their days together in Norfolk, where they had spent many hours discussing Joe's political goals. During that time Joe had been involved with another married woman, whose husband Mark understood was an acquaintance of his brother Jack's. By now Mark assumed that Joe deliberately sought out women who were not candidates for marriage. Much as the present arrangement with Pat might serve a purpose, Mark believed that Joe would never allow a woman to interfere with his postwar ambitions. He was far too interested in high political stakes to take on the liability of a twice-divorced Protestant wife.

All Pat Wilson's friends knew about the romance, but they doubted that she would ever divorce her husband for Joe. Living as she did among a group of people who held Australians in slight contempt, Pat had probably grown up a little too conscious of class herself to ever marry an Irish Catholic. Many daughters of families interested in acquiring social status had been raised not to consider love and marriage synonymous. Pat's circle tended to regard her relationship with Joe as a heady fling brightening up an otherwise tedious time that would be cut off abruptly as soon as peace had been declared.

Kathleen, on the other hand, was in the throes of complicated discussions with Billy about matrimony. The invasion of Europe had been postponed, but Billy expected that it would be launched that summer. When he and Kathleen realized that he might be leaving in a few months, it became crucial for them to make their decision quickly. The danger Billy faced made him

WARTIME

41. Billy in his Coldstream Guards uniform, 1940. (Courtesy of Baron Harlech)

After war was declared, Kathleen's British friends quickly paired off:

42. Billy Hartington and Sally Norton at the "Caff," the Cafe de Paris, their nightime haunt during the London blitz. (Courtesy of *The Tatler*)

3. David and Sissy Ormsby-ore, one of the first couples marry, at the races. (Courtesy *Harper's and Queen*)

4. A uniformed Andrew Cavendish at his edding to Debo Mitford. Rolls of wallaper covered the windows that had been lown out by a bomb blast. (Courtesy of *arper's and Queen*)

45. "The Girl on the Bicycle"—the famous Daily Mail photograph of Kathleen pedaling to work at the American Red Cross Club. Reprinted in American newspapers, the photo became a symbol of the all-American girl coming to the aid of the boys abroad. (Courtesy of Keystone Press Agency Ltd.)

46. The American Red Cross Hans Crescent Club in Knightsbridge. (Wideworld Photos)

7. British army wife Pat Wilson with two of her three children—the woman who captivated Joe Jr. while he was in England flying for the Navy. (Courtesy of Patricia Laycock)

8. Pat Wilson and her children at "Crash-ing," her wartime cot-age in Woking where Joe, Kathleen, and Billy met on weekends. (Courtesy of Patricia Laycock)

9. Billy addressing farm-ers from an auctioneer's rostrum at the Bakewell Cattle Market during his 1944 by-election campaign. (Courtesy of Keystone Press Agency Ltd.)

50. Kathleen and Billy, flanked by the Duchess of Devonshire and Joe Jr., moments after their registry office wedding, May 1944. (Courtesy of the John F. Kennedy Library)

51. Joe Jr. in his Navy uniform chatting with Lady Virginia Sykes at the Eaton Square wedding reception held for Kathleen and Billy. Despite wartime restrictions chocolate cake without icing was served along with champagne. (A. V. Swaebe)

52. Labor Day, 1944: Jack invited his Navy buddies for a typical HyannisPort weekend despite the recent death of Joe Jr. (*left to right*): Paul "Red" Fay, Jack, Lennie Thom, Jim Reed, George "Barney" Ross, Bernie Lyons (kneeling), Teddy, and cousin Joe Gargan. (Courtesy John F. Kennedy Library)

AFTER THE WAR

53. Widowed Kathleen Hartington in Palm Beach, 1946. (Courtesy of Cam Newberry)

54. Disabled veteran Richard Wood at his 1947 wedding after he and Kathleen decided not to get engaged. (Courtesy of *Harper's and Queen*)

55. At Sledmere, the Sykeses' Yorkshire estate, Kick among her new postwar crowd, which included the glamorous Duchess of Kent (second from the left), wife to the king's brother. (Courtesy of Sir Tatton Sykes)

56. Debo, the new Marchioness of Hartington. (Courtesy of Sir Tatton Sykes)

57. Freshman MP Hugh Fraser mugging with a tennis racket at Sledmere. (Courtesy of Sir Tatton Sykes)

58. Peter, the eighth Earl Fitzwilliam.
(Courtesy of The Press Association Ltd.)

59. Peter with his estranged wife Olive
"Obby" Fitzwilliam, on the steps of
Wentworth Woodhouse (Courtesy of
Keystone Press Agency Ltd.)

60. A dashing Peter in his hunting pink coat, the host of a hunt ball at Coollatin,
his estate in Ireland. (Courtesy of *The Tatler*)

61. Peter and Obby racing at Newmarket, one month before his death. Even
while involved with Kathleen, Peter attended all public functions with his wife.
(Courtesy of *The Tatler*)

62. Kathleen, Marchioness of Hartington. (Courtesy of Popperfoto)

wildly attractive to Kathleen and the months they could have together more and more precious.

At first Kathleen had again taken a strong stand on the religious question. It would be impossible for her to marry Billy unless he agreed in writing to "promises" regarding the raising of
their children as Roman Catholics—a condition still utterly unacceptable to Billy's father.

Despite the present urgency surrounding the decision to marry
Kathleen, Billy remained the dutiful son. Aware of his parents'
alarm over the prospect of his marriage to a Roman Catholic,
Billy felt he could not go against their wishes. All the burden of
compromise was placed upon Kathleen. Although she understood that the demands of the Catholic Church seemed unreasonable to an Anglican family of the stature of Billy's, the di-
lemma she had been forced into was a very painful one.

She sought the advice of Father Martin D'Arcy, a Jesuit she
had befriended at the Church of the Immaculate Conception,
her Mayfair parish on Farm Street. D'Arcy had been responsible
for a number of conversions among the English intelligentsia,
notably that of novelist Evelyn Waugh. His responses to Kathleen's queries about the spiritual repercussions of marrying on
Billy's terms were as dogmatic as any she had heard from the
mothers at Noroton. If she went ahead and married outside the
Church, she had to be prepared to be viewed as living in sin. As
long as she and Billy were together, she would be unable to
make a true act of confession or to receive Holy Communion.
Were Billy to outlive her, she would never be able to repent and
would thus be eternally damned in the afterlife. In the view of
the Catholic Church, which taught that non-Catholics did not go
to heaven, she would be damning her own children by raising
them as Protestants. Her one hope of salvation—other than a re-
vision of Church law that had existed for centuries—would be for
Billy to die before her. Only then could she be absolved of the
sinful marriage. Father D'Arcy reminded her that the catechism
she had memorized used especially strong language in warning
of the consequences of a mixed marriage outside the Church: "It
is a sacrilege to contract marriage in mortal sin, or in disobedi-

ence to the laws of the Church, and, instead of a blessing, the guilty parties draw down upon themselves the anger of God."

Nothing Kathleen could do would hurt her mother as much as the act she was now contemplating. Her mother valued obedience to religious law above anything else; it was unthinkable that a child of hers would live in sin. The worst of it was that as the first of her brothers and sisters to marry, she would be setting a terrible example for the others.

She still had to think of the possible effect that marrying Billy might have on her family's political aspirations. The reputation of the united, happy, talented family that her father had painstakingly built up would be destroyed. As it was, Joe was going to have to struggle very hard to overcome religious prejudice if he was to become the first Catholic in the White House. And a Protestant brother-in-law might alienate the Catholic vote by casting doubt on the family's piety.

Because of the family's ambitions and its Irish American constituency, Billy was probably the worst possible marriage partner for her. Billy's ancestors had played a leading role in the spread of Protestantism throughout England and Ireland. On Billy's mother's side Robert Cecil, chief minister to James I, had refused to permit the Prince of Wales to marry the Spanish Infanta because she was a Roman Catholic. Generation after generation of Billy's ancestors, as occupants of high office in the English government of Ireland, had contributed to the domination of the Irish Catholics and had suppressed the Republican movement. As secretary of state for Ireland in 1870 the eighth duke broke with his Liberal Party and, in direct defiance of the prime minister, formed his own party to oppose Irish home rule. Directed toward the Cavendish side of the family was the longstanding hatred of the Irish Republicans. When the eighth duke resigned his post in 1882, his brother took over for him. After a single day in office he was shot and killed by an Irish Republican Army gunman in Dublin's Phoenix Park.

When she had been in Palm Beach over the Christmas holiday, Kathleen had avoided any mention of her intentions. She waited until early spring to write her parents that she and Billy were planning to get married. The Kennedys were aghast. They sought the advice of many of their friends highly placed in the Church, including Cardinal Archibald Spellman. At first Kennedy, who had once gone as far as to request a special dispensation to set up a separate household with Gloria Swanson in a vain attempt to get the Church to sanction their adulterous affair, was optimistic that something could be worked out. But he was soon briskly informed that no exception could be made, even for so eminent a Catholic family. The marriage could be sanctified only if Kathleen were married according to the laws of the Church. After this ruling Mr. and Mrs. Kennedy launched a campaign of strongly disapproving telegrams to their daughter. Kathleen was made to understand that the other family members, particularly Eunice, were shocked by her plans—all except Jack, who was too ill to put up much of a fight in her behalf.

Although Kathleen had expected this reaction from her mother, she was bewildered by the vehemence of her father's objections. Weren't Billy and the life he offered what her father had wanted for her all along? Mr. Kennedy was the one who had encouraged her to date young aristocrats like Billy in her debutante days in 1939. Hadn't he realized that she might end up marrying one? Hadn't he himself attempted—mostly unsuccessfully—to socialize with the likes of Billy's parents? It seemed absurd that her parents would disapprove of a marital partner like Billy. Billy was the greatest catch in England. He would have been considered an appropriate suitor for Princess Elizabeth. When he succeeded to the family title, his wife would have a position second only to the queen's. If anything, Billy was the one who was marrying beneath himself in taking an untitled foreigner as his bride. If the Duke and Duchess of Devonshire disapproved of someone like Sally, who was Lord Mountbatten's goddaughter, what must they think of an Irish Catholic? If only Billy had been Roman Catholic, her parents would be on top of the world.

One weekend Kathleen arrived at Crash-bang noticeably distressed by the latest telegram from her mother. With all her other close women friends so scattered, she sought out Pat Wilson as a confidante. For religious advice she usually turned to the devoutly Catholic Sissy Ormsby-Gore. After her own husband—Billy's cousin—had been so reasonable in the identical situation, Billy's attitude surprised Sissy. How selfish of him to allow the interests of his family to take precedence over Kathleen's spiritual needs. David had not found it difficult to raise their children as Catholics, even though their son was heir to the Harlech barony and many members of David's family had been nearly as bigoted as Billy's. Sissy wondered if Billy really understood what he was asking Kick to do. He was going to give up nothing, while she was going to be made to give up so much.

To Kathleen's surprise she also found a staunch ally in her brother Joe, although Joe was still so devout that he knelt by his bed every night in front of his squadron mates to say his prayers aloud. Nevertheless, Joe urged his sister to take whatever course of action she thought best. He would stand by her if she married Billy, even though he might very well be held accountable by the family for her decision.

Kathleen hated the idea of a civil ceremony. All wartime weddings were necessarily austere, but the thought of a five-minute registry office wedding seemed so shameful. She had always dreamed of a ceremony at Westminster Cathedral. In England civil weddings also had an unsavory connotation—as the last resort of divorcées and others who could not receive God's blessing. For a time Kathleen thought it might be better to be totally accepted by Billy's church than to live in lifelong estrangement from her own. At least she would be taking a course that would please one set of parents rather than settling on a compromise that would finally please no one. Desperately hoping to win over the Duke and Duchess of Devonshire, she consulted Lord and Lady Halifax, who were back in England from the States. They arranged for her to discuss the possibility of conversion with their old friend Father Torbert, an Anglican monk in the Community of the Resurrection Monastery in Yorkshire. After a few meetings with Torbert, Kathleen abandoned the idea. She feared a conversion would hurt her mother more than a registry office wedding would. A Catholic marrying outside the Church could still hope for eventual redemption. But conversion could only be viewed as a blatant abandonment of the faith.

With Torbert, Kathleen also explored some halfway measures. A typical custom among the peerage for preserving the family line in a mixed marriage was to raise the daughters as Catholics and the sons as Protestants. But such a course would still not be acceptable to the Catholic Church. There was also the possibility of marrying in an Anglican church but remaining Catholic. But the demands of the Anglican church proved unacceptable to Kathleen.

Billy, meanwhile, stubbornly refused to yield on any point. Kathleen agonized for a few weeks, then finally capitulated. She consented to marry him in a civil ceremony and to bring up their children as Anglican, even though she knew this arrangement would cause great pain to her mother, embarrass her parents publicly, hamper Joe's political future, and condemn her in the eyes of the Church. With the rumors of imminent landings of Allied forces on the French coast, every consideration seemed to pale beside the prospect of Billy's departure. She would simply have to deal with the ramifications of her decision later on. Surely her father would be able to work something out. Joseph Kennedy had always managed to put the fix in for her in every other area of her life. Even if it turned out that her father could do nothing, the Catholic Church might someday come to take a different view of mixed marriages and receive her back in a state of grace. With Joe on her side surely her mother would forgive her in time.

On May 4 Billy and Kick released an announcement of their engagement. They did not specify the date or place in the hope of avoiding what was expected to be a flood of adverse publicity. Joe Jr. had remained circumspect about his sister's plans until just before the announcement, when he solicited clothing coupons from his squadron mates for her trousseau. British and American newspapers pounced upon the unobtrusive announcement and pointed up the implications of the union. The London *Evening News* commented that "Parnell's ghost must be smiling sardonically. . . . It was the Lord Hartington of the

'eighties who headed the Liberal-Unionist revolt that wrecked
Gladstone's Home Rule Bill. Hartington it was who moved the
second rejection of the Bill, and the hopes of Parnell and Irish-
America vanished in the division lobbies. Now a Hartington is to
marry a Catholic Irish-American who comes from one of the
great Home Rule Families of Boston."

Reporters hounded the duke's private secretary, pressing him
to disclose whether or not there was to be a religious ceremony.
British newspapers speculated as to whether the Kennedy family
would attempt to arrange for a lifting of the travel ban to England in order to attend Kick's wedding. Ultimately the only
Cavendish family member allowing herself to be quoted in
newspapers prior to the ceremony was Adele Astaire Cavendish,
who professed to be thrilled at the prospect of another American
in the family.

Although avoiding any public statements, Joseph Kennedy
finally softened several days before the wedding and cabled
Kathleen his blessing: "WITH YOUR FAITH IN GOD YOU CAN'T MAKE
A MISTAKE. REMEMBER YOU ARE STILL AND ALWAYS WILL BE TOPS
WITH ME." Kathleen heard nothing directly from her mother.

Kick's grandfather Honey Fitz was the only family member
reached for comment after the announcement of the engagement. He was quoted as saying that it had come in a "rush" and
claimed not to know anything of the wedding plans. He offered
the opinion that quite apart from her family and training, his
granddaughter was "by choice and firm conviction a Catholic."

On Saturday, May 6, only two days after notice of her engagement, Kathleen, escorted by her brother Joe, rushed inside the
small red brick building of the Chelsea Register Office to avoid
reporters and the throng outside who had received word of the
wedding date. She wore a very pale pink matte crepe street-
length dress with a diamond brooch at her throat. Lace was very
scarce, so like many other war brides Kathleen wore a little half
hat; it was made of blue and pink ostrich feathers and had a
pink veil. Mrs. Kennedy's friend Marie Bruce, who had supervised the making of the outfit and offered great support, had
contributed a gold mesh bag with sapphires and diamonds,

which the bride carried as "something old and something new." The Duke of Devonshire had delivered from Chatsworth the pink camelias that had been fashioned into her bouquet. Although many war brides had to borrow wedding dresses (one gown was worn on seven occasions), Kathleen's had been made the day before by the best fitter in London. Marie Bruce had obtained the material, her milkman contributing clothing coupons when she found herself short. Since the fitter did not have time to make an original design, she had copied one of Kick's American dresses and had stayed up the entire night before the wedding to finish it.

Ushered into a drab little room, brightened only by vases of pink carnations, the bride met the groom, who was wearing his Coldstream Guards uniform. Representing Billy's side were the Duke and Duchess of Devonshire, an aunt, and his younger sisters, Elizabeth and Anne. Anne was mortified to be wearing badly torn stockings, but she had had no coupons with which to purchase new ones. Besides Joe, Kathleen was represented only by Mrs. Bruce and Lady Astor, who had come because she thought the Kennedy women, in their stark disapproval, were being unkind to Kathleen. The presence of the Christian Scientist Lady Astor was considered highly unusual because of her morbid fear of the machinations of the Catholic Church—which she referred to darkly as "the candlestick plot." It had been four years since David Ormsby-Gore had married Sissy Lloyd-Thomas in a Catholic church and still Lady Astor would demand of him on every meeting, "How *could* you, David?" In the present circumstances, however, a Catholic was acceding to the terms of a Protestant, and in that respect Kathleen's wedding represented a victory for Lady Astor's cause.

In the ten-minute ceremony before the registrar, during which no marriage vows were taken, Joe gave away the bride, and Billy slipped a family heirloom on Kathleen's finger. Joe and the Duke of Devonshire signed as witnesses. Billy's old chum Charles Granby, the son of the Duke of Rutland, acted as Billy's best man. He had never before attended a registry-office wedding and was shocked by the austerity of the room and the truncated nature of the ceremony.

Since rice was nearly as scarce as lace, the wedding guests threw flower petals on the couple as they emerged from the building. For a few moments before heading off to the reception, they stood awkwardly at the door to be photographed. Billy, who was furious about all the publicity, forced a smile.

As their bombed London home had not been repaired, the Duke and Duchess of Devonshire received some two hundred guests that afternoon at a relative's townhouse in Eaton Square. It was almost impossible to get a decent cake, with eggs and butter so severely rationed, but the resourceful Marie Bruce had slipped five pounds to the headwaiter at Claridge's, who produced a chocolate cake without icing, which was served along with the champagne. As wedding presents Mrs. Bruce contributed all her own new Porthault lingerie, and the Duke of Devonshire gave Kick a diamond bracelet. Dressed in a cherry-colored coat with a pink and white print dress and a white hat trimmed with matching gardenias, Kick bade farewell to her guests as she and Billy boarded a train for Eastbourne. Upon arriving, they walked the half mile to Compton Place, where they received a private, unpublicized Anglican blessing and spent a week's honeymoon.

The day after the wedding American newspapers turned away from the religious controversy of the union and concentrated instead on Kathleen's achievement. She was the envy of millions of girls and the ascendant to "dizzying heights of glory and power." They referred to her as the future "first lady of the realm after royalty," predicting that she, like the Duchess of Devonshire, would be automatically appointed Mistress of the Robes to the Queen, the official head of all Her Majesty's ladies-in-waiting.

For two weeks prior to Kathleen's moment of triumph the mother of the bride had been sequestered away in a hospital bed. She had checked into the New England Baptist Hospital at the suggestion of Kennedy's newspaper crony, New York *Daily News* publisher Joseph Patterson, who had thought it the best way for Mrs. Kennedy to avoid being plagued by reporters. On the day that Kathleen had become the Marchioness of Hartington, Mrs. Kennedy had released herself and headed for the Boston airport for a midday flight to New York, where she was met by her husband. She was then to go on to Hot Springs, Virginia, for a "much needed rest."

Mrs. Kennedy allowed herself to be photographed entering the airplane for New York but refused to answer any questions from reporters. Through an airline official she instead issued a short statement: The family had been unable to communicate with their daughter, "much as we should like to," because of wartime cable restrictions. She herself was "physically unfit to discuss the wedding with anyone."

Ten

Roman Catholics on both sides of the Atlantic were appalled by Kathleen Kennedy's "apostasy." While still on her honeymoon, Kathleen received several anonymous letters from Catholics, denouncing her for placing her secular interests above spiritual ones. Even Evelyn Waugh took time out from his work on *Brideshead Revisited* to expostulate on the marriage to his wife: "Her heathen friends have persuaded her that it is a purely English law that her children must be brought up Catholic, and that she can get married in U.S.A. after the war. It is second front nerves that has driven her to this grave sin and I am sorry for the girl."

Back in the States the Kennedys steadfastly refrained from public comment about their own reactions, although the widely published newspaper photograph that showed the wedding couple flanked by Billy's parents with only Joe Jr. representing the bride's family conspicuously advertised their attitude toward the union. Mrs. Kennedy wrote Joe a letter complaining about the manner in which she had been harassed by reporters and praising him for standing by Kathleen in her moment of trial. But her religious convictions apparently did not allow her to send her daughter some sign of her support.

After a week of luxuriating at Compton Place the newlyweds moved into a cramped little room full of mismatched furniture in the Swan Hotel in Alton, a small country inn outside Billy's camp. The Army had shown unexpected generosity in giving Billy wedding leave and in allowing him to live with his wife outside his company's quarters, but the newlyweds were all too aware of the cause of such largesse. Top Secret envelopes describing Operation Overlord had arrived in Billy's battalion; the invasion of Europe was to commence in a matter of weeks.

After all the frantic activity at the Hans Crescent Club, Kathleen's first few weeks as an army wife were tedious in comparison—days spent swapping stories with local women and nights spent waiting for Billy to return from his duties. In a thank you note to Mark Soden for the clothing coupons that "Brother Joe" had yet to produce, Kick wrote, "At the moment I am a camp follower. . . . I spend my days listening to all the old ladies talking about what a hard war they are having. It's rather a change from G.I. conversation to say the least." There was a flood of letters in those weeks from American friends who had heard of Kathleen's wedding from the newspapers. Even Charlotte McDonnell Harris had not been informed of the marriage by the Kennedy family. John White had received a newspaper announcement of Kick's engagement from Nancy Hoguet on which she had scrawled: "K. K.'s fathom lord! How about that!" "So there our little Irish girl goes," White wrote in his diary. "He looks to be something of a fool, but I feel good about it and I wrote her a sincere, enthusiastic letter. Dear good little girl." After receiving White's congratulations Kathleen replied, "At the moment I am living in a 'pub' but don't worry, things will get better and I've been in worse places (mainly with you!)"

Along with individual notes from Inga Arvad and Frank Waldrop, Kathleen received congratulations from the entire staff of the *Times-Herald*. "I often think of you all and would give anything to have a look at the fifth floor of the *Times-Herald* building," she wrote. "When the revolution comes I shall come begging for another go at 'Did You Happen to See . . .'"

D-Day finally arrived on June 6. In a carefully orchestrated maneuver British and American forces landed on five beaches along the northern coast of France, with wave after wave of Allied troops to follow. Thousands of men gathered in the Epping Forest waited for the loudspeaker droning day and night to call out their serial numbers, the signal that they were to be sent across the Channel into Normandy.

Billy's company was finally called on June 20. After one month and one week together he and Kathleen said good-bye. She would have to wait indefinitely for a husband she'd barely gotten to know, while her own life hung in the balance. With Billy leaving so quickly she would be left to deal with the aftereffects of her marriage alone. At least she could take comfort in the widespread predictions that Germany couldn't last more than a few months against the Allied offensive. With any luck British soldiers would be home by autumn.

Kathleen had resigned from her job several days before her wedding. Although she had taken a flat in Mayfair and had arranged to continue to work at the Club on a volunteer basis, she did not return immediately to London but spent the summer at Compton Place with the duke and duchess, where she began to assume some of the duties of the wife of the Devonshire heir. Without the support of Billy's presence Kathleen found herself in the awkward position of having to be on intimate terms with a formidable set of in-laws who hadn't wanted her to marry their son. She dealt with the situation with her usual playful candor, as well as a certain initial degree of bravado. Kick found immediate allies in Billy's younger sisters, Anne and Elizabeth. Even the duke, who had so vehemently opposed the marriage, couldn't help but warm to his new daughter-in-law, who typically greeted him, "Hi, Duke."

At Compton Place, Kathleen was made immediately aware of her change in status and the power her new title gave her. She greatly enjoyed the prestige of being ennobled, but the preferential treatment that went along with being Lady Hartington embarrassed her. During a forty-eight-hour leave in early July, Joe and several of his squadron mates spent a weekend with Kathleen at the Imperial Hotel, an exclusive resort at Torquay on the

Devon coast. The young Americans couldn't help noticing that Kathleen was treated with particular solicitude by the employees of the hotel, who addressed her as "My Lady." Mark Soden, who had never before been in the company of a member of the peerage, was fascinated by the strict observance of class maintained by the British. Pretending to be oblivious, Kathleen handled the extra attention so matter-of-factly that Mark was impressed by how gracefully she had assumed her new position.

That summer she continued to spend weekends at Crastock Farm with Joe and Pat Wilson. She also frequently visited Sissy Ormsby-Gore. David was back from his training. On Sundays he drove his wife and Kathleen to church. Kathleen stubbornly refused to acknowledge that her relationship with the Church had altered. Week after week she determinedly attended Mass, although now only as a spectator. During Communion she watched numbly as Sissy rose and approached the altar while she remained in her pew. She often remarked to David and Sissy how difficult it was for her to attend Mass week after week and not to take Communion herself. Every week her exclusion from Communion served as a fresh reminder of her sacrilege, and no amount of prayer, charitable works, or good intentions would alter her state of sin in the eyes of the Church. It infuriated Kathleen to be so humiliated. Why should she be condemned for her marriage when Billy in every way was such a model choice for a husband?

At midnight exactly one week after D-Day the Germans had launched their retaliation in the form of the *Vergeltungswaffen*, or "revenge weapon," a pilotless flying bomb. The V-1's were to have been sent off from the northern coast of France on D-Day itself, but Goering had miscalculated by a week. This new weapon, a gyro-controlled jet craft loaded with dynamite and fired from a steam-propelled carriage, could fly short distances at three hundred and fifty miles an hour, then drop wherever directed. Within three days the Germans had mounted their full offensive, sending seventy-three of these buzz bombs raining down on London. People were terrified by this new pilotless weapon that could strike at any point, day or night. It would pop along like a wheezing truck, then the engine would suddenly quit; fifteen seconds of terrifying silence would follow, signaling that the bomb was about to drop. Weeks before Operation Overlord had begun, the first V-1 sites had been photographed and identified on the northern coast of France. Bombers had been sent across to destroy them—with negligible results. When the troops who crossed the Channel on D-Day were attacked by this strange new weaponry, the sites, which resembled ski lifts or crossbows on a reconnaissance map, were thought to be an elaborately prepared hoax, and forgotten. Then the V-1 attacks began in earnest and continued through that summer, and the bombing of these sites was again assigned top priority.

Since the bombers had had so little success, extraordinary measures were soon being planned for the destruction of the ski lifts. General Spaatz suggested that the robot-bomb sites be attacked by the very weapon they launched, and discussions commenced between the Army and Navy as to how best to produce an American version of the V-1.

Eventually "Aphrodite" was born—a campaign that would employ a makeshift flying bomb. Obsolete fighter airplanes were to be gutted and packed with explosives. A pilot and copilot would be responsible for getting the plane off the ground and stabilizing the flight pattern. When this had been accomplished, pilots aboard two "mother" aircraft would take over and pilot the "baby," or "drone," by remote control, using a radar screen. The pilots of the "baby" would then parachute out, leaving the plane to be guided by the mother craft into the target with some dozen tons of TNT—a load twelve times that of a V-1. Aphrodite was a pet experimental project of both the Army and the Navy because it was thought to be the only possible retaliation to Germany's secret and deadly bombing capability. Allied intelligence was convinced that Hitler was preparing superweapons that would reverse the advances made after D-Day and threaten American cities as well as London. Germany was thought to be perfecting the atom bomb. Although the Navy had been test-piloting Aphrodite in Norfolk, Virginia, with B-24

Liberators, it was decided that the pilots for the actual missions would be chosen from among the most experienced in the Dunkeswell Squadron.

By D-Day, Joe Kennedy had completed his required thirty-five patrols and was due to return home, even though he had hit no targets. His only direct encounter with the enemy had come in the Bay of Biscay, when he was attacked by several ME-210's. Joe had heard that Jack, who was in the hospital recuperating from an operation on his lower back, was to be awarded a Navy and Marine Corps medal for heroism. Still desperate to prove himself a hero, Joe had volunteered for a special assignment off the Cornwall coast after finishing his tour of duty; when that came to nothing, he had volunteered for a second. He had been assigned to CORK, a special operation aimed at disarming German U-boats during the Allies' crossing of the Channel on D-Day. Although he had performed his duties competently, he had won no special recognition. Mark Soden realized that Joe, unlike all his squadron mates, who were finishing up duty and looking forward to going home, intended to stay in active service until he was given the mission that he was looking for. Once, when telling Mark about his experiences in the Spanish Civil War, Joe had asked, almost challengingly, if Mark had ever been in a bombing; he had talked about his own close calls as if he believed he was somehow immune in situations that would imperil ordinary men.

In late June, after hearing of Aphrodite, Joe went on a campaign to be named a pilot; when it appeared doubtful that he would be selected, he hinted that he would use his father's influence. In July the assignment came through and Joe was transferred to a special army-navy attack unit in Winfarthing-Fersfield, north of London, where he was sworn to secrecy and put in training until the target date of mid-August. No one, including Kick, knew the nature of Joe's mission—only that he had finally found what he was looking for, and that it appeared to be cloak-and-dagger material. Joe spent his last free weekend at Crastock Farm before his transfer. A V-1 had hit near the farm, and Joe talked Pat Wilson into using her precious gas coupons to drive out and see the smoking shell. Pat was to spend August at Sledmere, Virginia Sykes's estate in Yorkshire, and Joe planned to meet her there the day after his task was completed.

In early August the Army and the Navy worked in tandem, training men for Aphrodite. Of the six army missions sent off before Joe's, none had reached its target. One pilot had been killed and two severely injured in their attempts to evacuate the bomb-laden crafts. Furthermore, in the naval project, code-named "Anvil," Earl Olsen, the electronics officer, had discovered serious flaws in the circuitry of the arming panel, which was to ignite the explosives. He believed there was a fair chance that the plane would blow up prematurely. Olsen wanted to rewire the circuit, but his superiors—one of whom had designed the mechanism himself—overruled him. With the Army thus far unsuccessful, the Navy was eager to be the first to score. Joe's was to be the first navy mission, and the senior officers on Anvil, determined that it go forward, set the target date for August 11.

On August 10 Joe shared a last meal with his bunk mate, Jim Simpson, a shy Texas Baptist. Joe kept a little satin-lined pirate chest—a gift from Kick—filled with eggs. He offered to make scrambled eggs if Simpson would steal into the company mess and return with a pound of butter, a slab of bacon, and enough coal to heat Kennedy's frying pan. The two feasted on scrambled egg and bacon sandwiches dripping with butter—an outrageous indulgence with butter so scarce—after which Joe produced expensive Cuban cigars and bourbon from the supply of liquor he had gotten through his American embassy connections. Simpson, who had grown up in an impoverished Port Arthur family, had never met anyone like his millionaire bunk mate. He was impressed by the authority that Joe exerted over others. Several nights before, at two A.M., a poker game on the other side of the hut had kept them awake. Suddenly Joe had sat up in bed and called out sternly to the players, "You people put that light out and get to bed!" Despite the fact that many of the players were senior officers—one an army major—within five minutes after Joe's command the game was over.

That afternoon Simpson had had a talk with Olsen about the

anticipated problems with the circuitry. Simpson had sorely wanted to be chosen as Joe's copilot; even after he knew of the personal risk involved, he was still determined to fly with Joe. He had been treated as a raw ensign at the base and would do anything—even take on a dangerous mission—to gain the respect of his peers. Nothing would accomplish that faster than a Distinguished Flying Medal. That evening, however, he thought Joe had better know about his conversation with Olsen.

When he tried to bring it up, however, Joe cut him off. "Jimmy," he said, "I've been all around Robin Hood's barn about the mission. People have been asking me all kinds of things, suggesting all kinds of things, and I've developed a policy about the whole matter. And you know what that policy is."

"To keep quiet and obey orders?" Simpson replied timidly.

"That's the way it is."

The following morning Kennedy was irritated when he learned that the mission was to be postponed a day due to bad weather. Pat would be worried if he didn't show up at Sledmere that weekend, but he was not permitted off the airbase to tell her about the change in plans. Whether or not Joe was in love with Pat, not a night passed without his buddies, biking into the nearest town, noticing him in a red phone booth there, pumping in coins and talking to someone in intimate tones. Joe often hinted that he had romantic plans after the mission was over and did nothing to dispel a rumor that he was going to meet with his titled English girl friend after his parachute drop from the drone and drive off for a secret marriage. The night before the mission he finally received permission from his senior officers to pedal to the nearest pay phone outside the base. He left word at Kathleen's flat that Pat should be informed he would be a day late.

That afternoon Joe ran into the electronics officer, Earl Olsen, who had been trying without success to either postpone the mission or have the arming mechanism of the explosives altered. Olsen had finally decided to make his pitch to Kennedy. "Joe, there's something I have to tell you," he said. "I think you're risking your neck unnecessarily. The system isn't working right. I want to make some changes to make it safe, but I can't get any cooperation."

Kennedy was genuinely surprised. "Gosh, I don't know what to tell you, Oley," he said. "I appreciate what you're trying to do, but I don't have any say about things like that. I just volunteered to fly."

"Sure, you volunteered, and you can unvolunteer too, don't you see?" Olsen said agitatedly. "You're risking your neck for nothing."

When Kennedy asked about the dangers, Olsen decided he'd better couch his warning in oblique language so that he wouldn't frighten the pilot into aborting the mission altogether, after he'd taken off. "Well, maybe you're not exactly risking your neck," he said, "but I don't think the mission can be successful. I'm sure the plane will malfunction before it gets to the target."

"I can't do anything about that, Oley."

"You can go to the skipper," Olsen said, "and tell him to fix up your plane."

"No," Kennedy replied after a moment. "I don't think I will. I think I'm gonna fly it." He walked off and then turned and waved affably. "Thanks anyway, Oley, I know you mean well. I appreciate it."

The following morning Joe learned that the mission was on for that day and that, to Simpson's dismay, Bud Wiley, a senior officer involved in Anvil, had been chosen as his copilot. Finally Kennedy was told his target: Mimoyecques, a tiny village in Pas-de-Calais in northern France, the V-1 site closest to England. As he was boarding the plane Kennedy turned to Simpson and some of the other men who had crowded around to wish him luck. "If I don't come back," he said, leaning out the window, "you fellows can have the rest of my eggs." Simpson in particular chuckled, for he knew that they had eaten all but three the night before.

Packed with eleven tons of explosives, *Zootsuit Black,* the code name of Kennedy's airplane, left on schedule. When the drone reached its checkpoint, Kennedy called out "Spade Flush" on his radio, the signal for *Zootsuit Red,* one of the mother airplanes, to take control. Once on remote, Kennedy's plane veered off its flight path slightly, an easily remedied situation, but nothing else was apparently amiss. Twenty-eight minutes into the flight, as one of the mother pilots gently guided *Zootsuit Black* to the left, the crew from the mother planes heard two ear-splitting blasts. A blinding flash suddenly lit the entire sky. Where Kennedy's plane had been, there was a white hourglass of fire. The force of the explosion over Newdelight Wood near Blythburgh, a little town near the east coast of England, was so severe that it damaged fifty-nine buildings, knocking out plate glass and ceilings and scattering debris from the plane within a one-mile radius in the largest nonatomic explosion ever engineered by man.

The Kennedy family had finished an outdoor lunch in HyannisPort on August 13 when two priests arrived with an urgent message for Mr. and Mrs. Kennedy. Since the former ambassador was upstairs napping, they delivered it to Rose alone: Joe Jr. was missing in action and presumed dead.

Mrs. Kennedy rushed upstairs and, after waking her husband, blurted out the news. He jumped out of bed and hurried downstairs to confer with the priests. The information about Joe's mission was highly classified, but from what little information the priests had Mr. and Mrs. Kennedy gathered that Joe had volunteered for an exceedingly dangerous kind of flight. With the plane lost there was virtually no hope that he was alive.

Mr. Kennedy had taken the news stoically, and after the priests left, he was too devastated to cry. For some time he and Rose held on to each other wordlessly. Neither of them was accustomed to outward displays of emotion; Mrs. Kennedy looked to religion as an outlet for grief, Mr. Kennedy, to constant motion. He was the one to break the news to the children, urging them to be brave, as their older brother would have wanted. At his insistence the Kennedy children carried on with their sailing races that day—all but Jack, who was home for the weekend from the Chelsea Naval Hospital, where he was still recuperating from his operation. He spent the afternoon pacing back and forth along the stretch of beach in front of his parents' house.

Earlier that day in England, Pat Wilson, who knew nothing about the nature of Joe's mission, had been anxiously awaiting his arrival at Sledmere. She had not seen him since mid-July, when he'd taken on his new assignment and moved to his secret location. Just the day before, settling up a bridge debt, she'd written Joe's roommate Mark Soden, who had visited her at Crastock: "When Kennedy has organized himself back to normal you must come up to Crash-bang with him—We did have fun, didn't we? Say chum, have you got any more juice? There must be a lot of tins going abegging now!"

That afternoon British officials in the RAF, attempting to locate Lady Kathleen Hartington, called Virginia Sykes and told her about Joe. She, in turn, had to break the news to Pat. Two days later, before Pat had scarcely had time to mourn Joe's death, she learned that her husband had been killed when he and his men were ambushed by German soldiers in Italy.

A few weeks afterward Pat and her friends heard about a disquieting remark Joe had made to one of her guests during his last weekend at Crash-bang. He had been walking home from Mass with Frankie More O'Farrell, a horse-racing enthusiast. Always the gambler, Joe had made a pound bet with More O'Farrell about the distance back to the farm. Then, with typical self-assurance, he had remarked offhandedly that he'd found the mission he'd been looking for but that there was a fifty-fifty chance he wouldn't make it back alive. When Pat and the others also learned that Joe had left very detailed instructions about the distribution of his gear, it was evident that he had known the exact risk he faced all along.

Kathleen was in London when the RAF reached her. Mark Soden called her up a day later to extend his condolences and to tell her of her brother's last wish. If he did not return, Joe had told Mark, certain items of his that were difficult to get in wartime England—a Victrola, a Zeiss camera, a Zenith radio, and the disputed Underwood typewriter—were to go to his sister. Kathleen sobbed at the other end of the phone.

That evening, in a letter telling Mark where to send the items, she wrote:

> I'm so sorry I broke down tonight. It never makes things easier.
>
> . . . I don't know whether I'll even want to use the much discussed typewriter but it will make me always think of that hard-talker Joe.
>
> I still can't believe it. It's hard to write. I don't feel sorry for Joe—just for you . . . and everyone that knew him 'cause no matter how he yelled, argued etc. he was the best guy in the world.

The worst part of losing Joe was that she'd only really gotten to know him during the last year. She'd probably felt closer to him in the last few months than to any other family member—including Jack, whom she hadn't seen in two years. As soon as she heard about Joe's death, the only thing that seemed important was to get home. She made arrangements immediately through her father to fly to the States on an army transport plane.

When her plane landed in Boston, Jack was waiting for her in the airport. "Hi, Kick," he said, greeting her in a weary voice she'd never heard before. She was appalled by his appearance. He couldn't have weighed more than a hundred and twenty-five pounds. His cheek and jaw bones jutted out prominently, and his skin had a terrible yellow cast to it, after his bout with malaria. The operation on his back had been a failure, and the corrective steel plate that had been implanted was visible through a festering open wound. That evening in HyannisPort, before returning to the hospital, Jack asked Kick to come with him to see the pastor of St. Francis Xavier, their parish. Whatever their individual spiritual doubts, they returned to the familiar little church for solace as automatically as they did to the white clapboard house on the bluff.

Now that Kathleen was home, everyone seemed determined

to act as though it was just another summer at the Cape, her brothers and sisters as energetically involved as ever in swimming and sailing competitions. As Mr. Kennedy put it, the family was determined to "take care of the living." But although he made a pretense of going about his business, he was obviously shattered by the death of the son in whom he had placed all his hopes. There were times when he ignored the advice he had given his children and locked himself away in his room.

Joe's final mission was going to earn him a special award, possibly even the Congressional Medal of Honor, the country's most distinguished military award. His performance finally and for all time had surpassed Jack's. Joe was now rarely spoken of except in terms of the example he had set in dying for an important cause. He had come to symbolize an unattainable ideal, particularly for Jack, who felt himself completely powerless to comfort his inconsolable father.

Like the rest of her family Kathleen attempted to bury her grief. Frank Waldrop had written Kennedy a letter of condolence, but she made no reference to it or to her brother's death in the cheery letter she wrote a few days after she'd returned home.

It's a great treat to be back in the land of "the free!!! & the brave"—No place like it.

Should like to hear how Washington's greatest newspaper is progressing—Shall be around for about a month. Any chance of your being in N.Y. the middle of Sept.?

. . . Your devoted ex-secretary, office girl, teamaker & star columnist

Miss Ken

In a postscript Kathleen asked Waldrop to mail her some clippings on her wedding that had appeared in the *Times-Herald*. She was still flushed with happiness over her marriage and it alleviated some of the pain of Joe's death. She had carried home with her a little pillowcase embroidered with the Devonshire family crest, and she showed it to her brothers and sisters with the pride of someone who has pulled off something of a coup.

The crested pillowcase may also have been a kind of reassuring talisman for her. If she had arrived in HyannisPort uncertain about her reception among the Kennedys, she'd carried with her the evidence that she belonged to another family now.

Although newspapers had made much of the fact that this was her first trip home, as if to suggest that her controversial marriage had caused a rift between her and her parents, at first Kathleen did not notice anything very different in her family's attitude toward her. Her grief-stricken father treated her as lovingly as always, and her brothers and sisters typically followed suit. After a time, however, she realized that her mother was a little aloof, an attitude communicated through reproachful looks and a slight extra emphasis in her voice when inviting her daughter to accompany her to Mass. After Joe's death Mrs. Kennedy had sought solace in the Church by attending Mass early every morning, a practice she would continue in the future. As usual Mrs. Kennedy wouldn't state her thoughts out loud but made her point through her behavior. Kathleen had expected that she and her mother would forget the strain caused by her marriage in their mutual grief. Mrs. Kennedy made it plain that she could not.

Despite the Kennedys' determination that life would go on as usual, the summer was grim and quiet. Almost every Hyannis-Port neighbor had recently lost someone to the war. Nancy Lloyd's husband, Demarest, had been killed in June, his plane shot down by Japanese antiaircraft fire. Nancy had been feeding her infant daughter, Tangley, when she'd received the unmarked telegram announcing that Demarest was missing in action. She had ripped it open unconcernedly because she'd thought that telegrams containing bad news would arrive in envelopes bearing stars. Nancy had received three letters from Demarest that day, and his letters had continued arriving after he'd been killed. She'd found his last letter in among his effects; it was half-finished because he'd been writing it when he was sent up to fly for the last time. In Guam fighter pilots were needed in the air almost constantly. Demarest had flown on four sorties that day when his superior officer announced that he needed men to fly another mission. Aware that all the pilots were exhausted, he had asked only for volunteers. When one of Demarest's buddies had jokingly held up Demarest's arm and the officer had called out "Lloyd, okay," Demarest had felt obligated to make the flight.

Like Joe Kennedy he had died a hero and was due to receive several important medals. Although he had been buried in Guam, his family had asked Nancy to select an epitaph for a memorial stone on the family's Massachusetts estate. Nancy had chosen the words Demarest had sent her on a card with his engagement present a few months before he'd enlisted in the Navy. They were the famous lines from "To Lucasta: Going to the Wars" by the seventeenth-century poet Richard Lovelace:

> I could not love thee, dear, so much,
> Lov'd I not honour more.

Because her husband had died so heroically, Nancy considered it unpatriotic to cry. To be dignified and strong, she had to avoid talking about his death even to good friends like Sancy Falvey and Kick; at the merest mention of Demarest her eyes would well up with tears. For the last several months Nancy had borne her loss in silent rage. She knew families like the Kennedys who had lost sons and brothers recently to the war, but no one who had lost her husband. It infuriated her to be a widow at twenty-four—two months after their first anniversary, with their daughter, Tangley, only eight weeks old. This anger seemed to surface at inappropriate times; she would find herself exploding in fury while watching a movie that didn't to her mind adequately portray grief. A HyannisPort neighbor who had been visiting Nancy shortly after the telegram arrived had looked on in amazement as Nancy opened the mailbox and dozens of letters spilled out on the ground. "Oh," the woman said ingenuously, for she didn't know about Demarest, "do you always get that much mail?" Nancy had stared at her furiously. She'd wanted to scream out what had happened to her husband but caught herself just in time. Through the summer she found herself embroiled in little dramas walking along the beach and approaching neighbors, wondering always if the person knew or didn't know. When people went on as if nothing had happened, she always wondered if they knew but didn't want to say or simply didn't know how to say they knew. When somebody gave her some indication that they'd heard about Demarest, Nancy was very relieved because it meant that she didn't have to tell them or didn't have to worry about crying. How she wished to be spared these little humiliations and the need to suppress her terrifying, uncontrollable outrage.

For Labor Day weekend Jack invited a houseful of guests from among his PT buddies. The group included Red Fay, Barney Ross, Bernie Lyons Jewel and Jim Reed, and Kate and Lennie Thom. They spent a typical Kennedy Saturday of frenetic activity, everyone dividing up into little clusters for afternoon sports. Red Fay, who went golfing with Kick, ribbed her mercilessly about her title. To Kathleen's utter chagrin he announced officiously to two matrons who were holding up their game, "Excuse me, the Marchioness of Hartington is trying to get through." After the matrons graciously yielded the green, Kathleen was even more embarrassed when she hit her ball out into the woods and held the women up while looking for it.

After dinner and the evening movie the older children and their guests headed out on the bluff. Barney Ross, who had been the clown of the group in the South Pacific, had developed a standing joke with the men about a funny episode in which he had greeted an old friend after passing through a revolving door by falling flat on his face. His buddies persuaded him to go through his routine again, after which everyone was roaring with laughter. Suddenly the window flew open in one of the upstairs bedrooms of the Kennedy house and an authoritative voice bellowed out, "Jack, don't you and your friends have any respect for your dead brother? You get in here! You're making a nuisance of yourselves with the neighbors."

Jack tried to continue the conversation, but the guests had fallen into an embarrassed silence and the party clearly was over. Nineteen-year-old Bobby Kennedy burst out the front door onto the porch and said in a hushed voice, "Dad's awfully mad."

Kick, who had been walking in beside Jewel, whirled on him. "You're frightening our houseguests out of their wits!" She was fuming over her father's outburst. She thought that her father owed his guests more respect and had no business treating married people like children or dragging in a private family matter. She had also been irritated with her parents for maintaining their practice of serving a single cocktail before dinner to what were a group of hard-drinking navy men. Earlier that evening, after the cooks had left, she and Jack had helped the others sneak into the kitchen to get the scotch. Bobby had caught them there and threatened to call their father, but Kick shooed him out, telling him to get lost.

By mid-August, Billy Hartington had spent three grueling weeks in Normandy. There had been almost ceaseless fighting, and the number of casualties among officers was so high that survivors received promotions and new orders constantly. By Labor Day, Billy had been promoted to major and put in command of No. 3 Company. For several days he had been in charge of the entire Fifth Battalion until a replacement could be found for the commanding officer, who had been killed.

Billy exhibited great calm in battle, but he hated the physical discomfort of war—the slit trenches where they had to sleep, the ever-present whine of shells overhead, the stretchers carting off the dead and wounded. His predecessor in No. 3 Company, Baron Adeane, had insisted on spreading a white tablecloth on his mess table, no matter where he set up camp. Billy also believed that it would help morale to observe certain social niceties on the battlefield. After capturing a town in Normandy his company took up residence in an abandoned, ransacked building. When the officers of another company came to Billy's quarters, he had his orderly, Ingles, hand out glasses of rum and then insisted, with obvious pride, as though escorting his guests around the grounds of one of his family's estates, that they accompany him on a tour of his company's position. Billy was equally meticulous about maintaining his personal appearance in makeshift circumstances. As soon as his company had taken up

residence in the French house, he arranged to have a bath, or-
dering Ingles to lay hairbrushes and socks out neatly amid the
shambles of the room. Even in the field he liked to keep himself
as smartly turned out as possible. In his left breast pocket he
carried a little steel mirror, which he would pull out every morning and prop up on his company Jeep in order to shave.

Many of the Guardsmen of Billy's new company immediately
warmed to their new commander, who maintained a sense of humor about the more absurd aspects of military life. Billy and his
new sergeant-major, James Cowley, quickly developed a standing joke. Billy would see Cowley behind him but would turn his
back, pretending that he hadn't.

"Company Sergeant-Major!" Billy would bark in his most
officious manner.

"I'm right behind you, sir," Cowley would answer.

"I knew you would be," Billy would reply affably.

The company carried with them a table and chair for Billy.
Whenever they set up camp, he would survey the open field and
remark thoughtfully, as though weighing a multitude of possi-
bilities, "Now . . . where is the company office going to be?"
After a great mock deliberation he would point to a section of
land and announce grandly, "Ah, we'll have it *here*."

Billy's men often mimicked his constant commands to his faithful orderly. They would assume their best version of an Etonian
accent and shout in a shrill voice, "In*gles!* Some watah for my
feet!" It was a private joke they kept among themselves, made in
the spirit of good fun. Although the men expected that Billy
would laugh good-naturedly if he heard them, it would never do
for them to ridicule a peer of the realm. Protocol demanded
that Billy be the one to initiate the humor. Cowley would never
even presume to ask his company commander if he had had
word from his wife or family.

After taking over No. 3 Company, Billy became friendly with
John Knatchbull, one of his platoon commanders. At night in the
trenches the two would often share a drink together. Although
Billy said little about his recent marriage, he once complained
bitterly to Knatchbull about the adverse publicity he and Kath-

leen had received over the registry office wedding and his wife's supposed abandonment of her faith.

By the end of August, Billy and his fellow officers had become giddy with optimism. Suddenly and inexplicably the Germans had begun to retreat. The Fifth Battalion began advancing through eastern France. The men even crossed the Somme River, the site of mass slaughter in the Great War, with only an occasional skirmish. Then, on September 3, traveling ninety-three miles from Douai to Brussels, the battalion made the longest advance of the war. It was a euphoric drive of liberation. In the mining villages and industrial towns along their route, young women, dressed in black, yellow, and red, the colors of the Belgian flag, waved from windows, shouting, "Vive les Alliés! Vive la libération!" Townspeople tossed the British soldiers ripe apples and plums, draped garlands of flowers around them, and wrote in chalk on the passing vehicles, "Good luck, Tommy" and "Fifi loves the RAF." By midnight, as the battalion reached Brussels, crowds, twenty deep along the road, delirious from celebrating, clambered onto the army vehicles, embracing their liberators and singing "It's a Long Way to Tipperary."

After their virtually uninterrupted advance and with rumors circulating that an armistice had been declared, Billy and the other officers believed that the fighting would soon be over. On September 6, however, it became apparent that the stopover in Brussels had only been a temporary respite. The new orders for the battalion were to seize Bourg Léopold, the former training camp of the Belgian Army. The Germans demonstrated they were not going to give up without a fight, and the battalion was soon engaged in the worst fighting of the entire campaign.

On the morning of September 8 Billy's company set off to capture the village of Beverlo, held firmly by the Germans. It was raining heavily that day, with the first evidence of autumnal chill. Although the battalion made steady progress along the road, inflicting heavy losses, the Germans were fighting fanatically. By evening Billy's company had lost a quarter of its men. That night Billy and John Knatchbull shared a drink together after what they both regarded as one of the worst days in the war. Both had gone into battle frightened, not so much by the stiff opposition or the possibility of being killed as by the sudden realization that they might have to endure these harsh conditions month after month before the war would be over.

At midnight Cowley observed a German scout car driving through the wood about three hundred yards away from the company position. The Germans obviously now knew where the British were for the night and would have a chance to reinforce their defenses. Cowley thought that they'd better be prepared for heavy fighting the following morning.

No. 3 Company's objective on September 9 was to capture the east end of the village of Heppen and there to join up with No. 2 Company, which would be approaching from the west. The weather had cleared, and the morning was bright and sunny; nevertheless, Billy was wearing his white mackintosh. Knatch-bull thought this an odd and even dangerous choice because it made Billy such an obvious target. Only British officers were al-lowed to wear clothing other than battle dress. The Germans, who were looking to kill officers, knew how to pick them out by their badges of rank or, more recently, after weeks in battle, by their makeshift, nonregulation clothing. As Cowley had pre-dicted, the Germans were prepared to put up such a fight that they had placed their stretcher bearers in the front line.

After the company began to move forward, Billy, carrying a huge pair of wire cutters, approached Sergeant-Major Cowley. "Sergeant-Major," he called out, "go on with company head-quarters. I'm going this way, and I'll catch up with you later." He pointed to the western flank of the company's position, where Cowley assumed that he was going to look for No. 2 Company with the idea of "marrying up" that company with his own. Ac-companied by Ingles, Billy headed some five hundred yards to the left on the outskirts of the village. Moments later Ingles came running back to company headquarters with terrible news. Billy had been shot dead by a German sniper.

After losing every other officer the men of No. 3 Company were demoralized by their company commander's death. Realiz-ing that it was his duty as senior officer to set an example by carrying on, Sergeant-Major Cowley shook himself out of his own fear and told his men, "Stay here a minute. I'll go forward." In the midst of heavy fire Cowley ran into town and climbed up the spire of a church to check the position of the Germans. When he saw the Germans lined up for a counterattack, he radioed his men to warn them.

At the end of the battle only forty of the Guardsmen of No. 3 Company were left unwounded; Cowley had to employ German stretcher bearers, taken as prisoners, to carry off the dead and wounded. Only when they were finally relieved by the Belgian Army, did No. 3 Company withdraw. Cowley and his men all had been trained that under no circumstances does a Coldstream Guardsman ever retreat.

In taking stock of the day's casualties Cowley learned that Lord Hartington had been shot in the heart, the bullet piercing the steel of his pocket mirror. Billy was buried where he had fallen in a makeshift grave until his family could be notified.

On September 16 Kathleen was in New York with her family. She had gone off by herself to shop at Bonwit Teller that morning. The Fifth Avenue stores seemed as well stocked as ever —an odd sight to Kathleen or any visitor from England when most storefronts in London and even the shelves themselves were barren. With the severe clothing shortages and ban on imports some among Kathleen's aristocratic circle had resorted to furtive arrangements to get hold of American goods; Lady Astor had recently been fined for asking a friend from America who would be crossing the Atlantic to buy silk stockings, evening shoes, and a fur jacket for her.

On Fifth Avenue that day only a close look at the mannikins in the store windows would have revealed that the elegant *haute couture* being shown was American made, since clothes could not be imported from Paris. Although fabric-conserving regulations restricted the size of skirts, hems, pockets, and ruffles, and styles were Spartan, "American ingenuity," as *Vogue* had written, "makes of a shortage not makeshift but new worlds."

Back at the Waldorf, Mr. Kennedy, agitated, emerged from his suite and asked Eunice to find Kathleen. "I've got a telegram here," he said soberly.

"Is it about Billy?" Eunice asked.

"Yes, he's been killed."

Eunice located Kathleen on the second floor of Bonwit's and chatted with her for several minutes, admiring her purchases. Their plan had been to meet for lunch. Attempting to betray nothing by the tone of her voice, Eunice remarked lightly, "Before we go, I think you ought to go back and talk to Daddy."

"Something's happened," Kathleen declared suspiciously.

"Why don't you go talk to Daddy?" Eunice repeated.

They were silent all along the dozen blocks to the Waldorf. Fifth Avenue was bustling, as it had always been with noontime shoppers and diners. Apart from the presence of uniforms and the absence of water and butter in the restaurants, there was no evidence that a war was going on. Kathleen and Eunice passed Fifty-second Street, where she and Jack and Joe had frequented all the little basement swing clubs, and then Rockefeller Center, where at the Rainbow Room, "Sixty-five Stories above the Stars," she had gone to hear Ray Noble, an English bandleader. If she closed her eyes, it would be easy to pretend that Joe was still alive and that the three of them would be meeting up in New York later and that she didn't have to make this journey back to the Waldorf to hear the news she knew her father had to deliver.

Joseph Kennedy was waiting for them at the door to his suite. He ushered Kathleen in alone, then closed the door behind them and told her that Billy was gone.

Kathleen did not emerge from her room until dinner time, her eyes red and swollen. The meal was awkward and strained. Everyone tried to be solicitous of Kathleen yet diligently avoided any mention of Billy. Even Eunice, her closest sister, avoided talking with Kathleen, she was so uncharacteristically sad. At the end of the evening Mr. Kennedy finally thought to ask her if she wanted anyone with her. Without hesitation Kathleen asked for Patsy Field. Kennedy disapproved of Patsy as much as he did of her brother, assuming both had been a bad influence on Kathleen, but he was desperate to ease his daughter's pain. At midnight he placed a call to Patsy. "I hate your guts, as you well know, but I have to ask a favor of you," he began bluntly. "Will you come and stay with Kathleen?"

Patsy flew up to La Guardia Airport the following morning, where she was met by one of Kennedy's employees. Before being taken to the Plaza, where Mrs. Kennedy was staying, as usual, with the children, she was driven to see Mr. Kennedy at his separate suite at the Waldorf. He thanked her for coming and then, as though not knowing how else to show his appreciation, clumsily offered her some nylons.

When she was alone with Kick, Patsy asked her, "What have you been doing since you received the news?"

"Mostly going to Mass," Kick replied. She admitted that she was going for her mother's sake rather than her own. Mrs. Kennedy believed that Kathleen would benefit from making peace with God over the marriage at this time. Kathleen felt very sorry for all her recent suffering. There had been Joe's death, Rosemary's regression, and her own marriage, and she hated to add to this burden. Patsy was touched that Kathleen would worry about her mother at a time like this.

"Have you been able to sleep?" Patsy asked. When Kathleen shook her head, Patsy reached into her purse and fished out some sleeping pills. *Sometimes God needs augmentation,* she thought.

That evening Joe Kennedy insisted that the entire family dine out together at Le Boisson, a small French restaurant in the Helmsley building. During the meal he offered to get tickets to any show on Broadway and looked surprised when there were no takers. Patsy felt she was witnessing a chilling performance. She was disturbed by the family's frenetic need to carry on as though nothing had happened. Once Kathleen had told Patsy she'd been taught that Kennedys didn't cry. There she sat now, numbly trying her best to participate, Patsy thought, all the while choking on her pain and outrage and incomprehensible sense of loss.

For the next two days the family swarmed around Kathleen, attempting to engage her in activity, Mrs. Kennedy prodding her to come to Mass or go shopping. It angered Patsy that the Kennedys, for all their good intentions, would not leave her and Kathleen alone. One morning the two of them were finally able to get away for a few hours, and as they walked up Fifth Avenue, Kathleen began pouring out her feelings. She had carried Billy's photograph with her the past few days, and Patsy had often found her staring at it in disbelief, as if trying to comprehend how it could be that the gentle, sweet-faced youth in the photograph, dressed so incongruously in the drab uniform, could now be lying dead. Kathleen had had five weeks with the person in that photograph, and now she was his widow. Her entire marriage had consisted of a few awkward evenings in the cramped room of a country pub, with the unsettling presence of a uniform in the wardrobe. Right after Billy was killed, Charlotte McDonnell Harris had had a baby. Nancy Tenney, for all her terrible suffering, at least had her daughter, Tangley. All she had left of Billy was the photograph.

On September 30, 1944, with only Kathleen and Billy's immediate family in attendance, a simple memorial service was held for Billy Hartington in the little church in Edensor, the village near Chatsworth. Since the fourteenth century many of Billy's ancestors had been laid to rest in the tiny plot behind the church. But with Andrew still fighting abroad and the war still on, the Duke and Duchess of Devonshire had decided that Billy should be given a military funeral in Belgium and permanently buried beside his comrades. Sergeant-Major Cowley had been dispatched back to Heppen from the front line to identify his remains.

Eleven

Billy was the second heir to a dukedom to be killed thus far by the war. In English newspapers friends and fellow soldiers lauded him for his outstanding bravery in battle. One fellow Guardsman wrote that after D-Day, Billy had yearned to fight in the front line but instead had been ordered to stay behind and command the reinforcements.

Though bitterly disappointed, he put all his energies into keeping some 200 equally disappointed men up to scratch.

Then in Normandy I can still see his dismay when told that his company had done enough and must hand over the lead to another. Billy had the truest form of courage, he could steady and inspire his men in a remarkable way. During three critical days he was the senior officer left and commanded the battalion with skill and gallantry in a difficult situation. Great gifts were his. I saw how experience and battle were enriching them.

The articles about Billy also made much of Kathleen's misfortune in losing both a favorite brother and a new husband within a matter of weeks. For a time a rumor circulated that she had been pregnant when Billy died and that the shock of the news had brought on a miscarriage. People had been too horrified by this latest news to inquire whether or not it was true.

The story may have resulted from a misreading of an *Evening Standard* article announcing that Lord Andrew Cavendish, Billy's younger brother, would be heir to the dukedom unless Kathleen were to give birth to a boy. Without a male heir she would lose all claim to Chatsworth or to any portion of the Devonshire estate. Billy's will provided Kathleen with five thousand pounds (the equivalent of twenty-five thousand American dollars) but left the bulk of his estate to his first or only son, or, failing one, to the eldest son of his brother. If Billy had been survived by a male heir, Kathleen might have been given a role in the running of the family estate (Billy's grandmother on the Cavendish side, for example, was mistress of Hardwick Hall). As a childless widow, however, she lost all the benefits of her position except her title.

For months Kathleen couldn't bear to sleep in a room by herself. She stayed with her in-laws for a time, then moved in with Billy's aunt Anne Hunloke in Westminster. In each case she insisted that someone share a bedroom with her. At home, when she had first heard of Joe's and Billy's deaths, she had cried very little; now, for days on end, she wept in her room. With the duke and duchess so obviously devastated by the loss of their son, she felt comfortable grieving in front of them. She often confided in Billy's eldest sister, Elizabeth, who most resembled him among his siblings and had probably been his favorite.

Now that she was widowed, Kathleen understood that there was no longer an impediment to her return to the Church. As Father D'Arcy and her Farm Street advisors explained it, she would have to confess her sin and make the required act of contrition, but thereafter she would be able to receive Communion. She was grateful for her acceptance back into the Church, but she didn't see any need to atone for her actions. Why should she repent for having married Billy? She was only sorry that he was dead. How ironic that the Church would absolve her sin only after her husband had been killed. "I guess God has taken care of the matter in His own way," she remarked wryly, "hasn't He."

Among Kathleen's Anglican circle it was rumored that Mrs. Kennedy believed not only that there was a causal relationship between Kathleen's sacrilege and Billy's death but that God in His wrath had struck down both Joe and Billy, for plotting the unholy marriage together. By killing Billy, God, in effect, was giving Kick another chance.

In October, when Jakey Astor married Chiquita Carcano in a Catholic ceremony, Kathleen was one of the first to send the bride a congratulatory note, "welcoming" her to the "club." She seemed to feel a need to affirm that she herself had made the right decision by seeking out other Catholic women with mixed marriages. In Chiquita, who was obviously destined to suffer the disapproval of her in-laws, she saw a potential confidante. Jakey's decision to marry a Catholic according to the stipulations of her Church had so enraged his mother, Nancy Astor, that she refused to attend the wedding. Unfortunately Chiquita, whose English was poor, found Kathleen's note disconcerting. She misinterpreted its breezy language as an insinuation that she was being welcomed into an elite circle of young Catholic women who had managed to snare a peer of the realm—which was exactly how her mother-in-law viewed the situation.

As the months passed, Kathleen had no ostensible reason to stay on in England. Despite the wartime travel ban Mr. Kennedy could have arranged for her to return to the States at any time. But the prospect of going home wasn't really comforting. The Church had forgiven her, but she wasn't sure that her mother had. Grateful for some reminder of their son, the Duke and Duchess of Devonshire were encouraging her to stay. And they were giving her the emotional support she knew she wouldn't find at home.

That fall Kathleen decided to return to the Red Cross as a volunteer. She accepted an assignment as a staff assistant at the Charles Street Club. This time the work seemed vital. She was no longer the frivolous girl on the bicycle. The war had taken her husband and her brother and profoundly altered the course of her life. She now felt compelled to help work toward victory.

For Joseph Kennedy only public recognition of Joe's bravery and distinction offered the slightest consolation for the loss of his eldest son. Joe was posthumously awarded the Navy Cross and— probably at the urging of Naval Secretary James Forrestal, one of the ambassador's old friends—a new destroyer was christened the *Joseph P. Kennedy, Jr.* Kennedy's need to honor his son seemed insatiable. In HyannisPort he built a new altar dedicated to Joe in the family's parish. In honor of Rosemary he also wished to set up a Joseph P. Kennedy, Jr., Foundation to work with the retarded. In an attempt to comfort his grief-stricken father Jack Kennedy began to work that fall on a tribute to Joe. He gathered individual essays from his friends and family for what was to be a privately published volume called *As We Remember Joe,* thus setting the precedent for the future laudatory books which would be written upon the deaths of other family members.

In the introduction Jack wrote:

Joe did many things well, but I have always felt that he achieved his greatest success as the oldest brother. Very early in life he acquired a sense of responsibility towards his brothers and sisters, and I do not think that he ever forgot it. Towards me, who was nearly his own age, this responsibility consisted in setting a standard that was uniformly high. . . . I think that if the Kennedy children amount to anything now, or ever amount to anything, it will be due more to Joe's behavior and his constant example than to any other factor. He made the task of bringing up a large family immeasurably easier for my father and mother, for what they taught him he passed on to us, and their teachings were not diluted through him, but rather strengthened.

Kathleen merited her own entry, for, as Jack noted, she had been increasingly drawn together with Joe in "that last crowded year in England." Kathleen also called her eldest brother the "foundation stone" of the family. His temper had often terrified her, and like her brothers and sisters she had looked upon him with a degree of awe. She recalled times when Joe had gone out of his way as her chaperon to put her in her "proper place" and when he'd lost his patience while they were playing gin rummy.

The only time he condescended (because that is exactly what he did) to be my bridge partner during that year was just before I got married and he was feeling particularly sentimental. Needless to say, I managed to lose five pounds for him.

But never did anyone have such a pillar of strength as I had in Joe in those difficult days before my marriage. From the beginning, he gave me wise, helpful advice. When he felt that I had made up my mind, he stood by me always. . . . Moral courage he had in abundance, and once he felt that a step was right for me, he never faltered, although he might be held largely responsible for my decision. He could not have been more helpful and in every way he was the perfect brother doing, according to his own light, the best for his sister with the hope that in the end it would be the best for the family. How right he was!

The war dragged on into early spring. Hitler clearly intended to fight to the death, even though there appeared to be no reasonable hope of a German victory. Finally, in late April, the German forces in Italy surrendered, and a week later Berlin fell. On May 7, 1945, as crowds gathered outside Buckingham Palace and Downing Street, Churchill announced that the war had ended and proclaimed May 8 as Victory in Europe Day, a phrase carefully chosen to emphasize that the war was not yet won against Japan. In fact, immediately upon the announcement of a victory in Europe one army training camp erected a sign: Don't lapse chaps: Japs.

Kathleen took part in the uproarious celebrations of V-E Day, but she had difficulty in looking upon peace as a triumph. "It seems hard to believe that the war is really going to be over soon," she had written Frank Waldrop, who had remained a steady correspondent after Billy's death. "I'm glad, thankful, but I don't think anyone here feels terribly joyful. Do you?"

In Britain, after the initial elation of victory, problems of sobering complexity loomed ahead in what commentators called the "postwar reconstruction." The deprivation that everyone had suffered during the war might go on indefinitely. Britain faced a terrible coal shortage, and certain foods were scarcer than ever; rationing threatened to continue for years. Kathleen and her aristocratic circle soon began to realize that the kind of life they had lived before the war might never be reconstructed. Even after the soldiers were evacuated from country houses, the grand scale of living they had formerly accommodated could not be so readily restored. The houses themselves would remain dingy until the government lifted its severe rationing of paint. The hedgerows and gardens trampled by marching soldiers would require decades to grow back. The great families would have to operate their estates with skeletal staffs of servants. Many former domestics who had been enlisted into war work were refusing to return to their old jobs after discovering that factory work offered better conditions and pay.

Perhaps most perplexing to the upper class was the ground swell of support among the working and middle classes for continuing and improving upon the socialist measures that had been adopted during the emergency. During the war the working classes had enjoyed full employment, a fair share of food and clothing, and equality with the upper class. According to the Bevin Boy scheme, a wartime measure to relieve the shortage of miners, one in ten conscripts had been drafted to the mines, regardless of background or education. Much of the British working-class population had been better looked after during the war than ever before. A family might have to wear Utility clothing, but they could take satisfaction in the thought that the aristocracy received no more coupons than they did, even if they were cashed in at Molyneux. The average British citizen had also grown accustomed to government catch words and slogans like "Don't take more than your share," which smacked of socialism. Almost immediately following V-E Day, Labour Party politicians and reformers were talking of the need to "build a new world." Commercial advertisements that had depicted country house scenes of dukes and duchesses now used as subjects the working-class tenants.

After being discharged from the Navy "by reason of physical disability," Jack had spent the first few months of 1945 recuperating at a hot springs resort in Arizona. Mr. Kennedy mailed his son frozen steaks and cartons of books on labor and made calls every day at exactly five P.M. to check on his uphill progress. Despite severe back pain, and recurrent bouts of malaria, Jack had wrestled that winter with the decision of whether or not to take up his dead brother's mantle and run for office. Joseph Kennedy had made it very clear that Jack now had a duty to go into politics in Joe Jr.'s place. Jack was beginning to feel as though it was the only way that he could truly make up for Joe's loss. Under enormous pressure from his father, Jack finally consented to run for Congress in the 1946 elections. Finding the notion of a political career humiliatingly self-aggrandizing, Jack had announced to his buddies that he had settled on a future in "public service." At a family dinner Honey Fitz had solemnly toasted him as "the first Catholic President of the United States."

Since Jack's campaign would not get underway until the fall, his father prompted him to work as a journalist that spring to keep his name before the public eye. Through his old friend William Randolph Hearst, Joe Kennedy wangled press credentials for Jack to cover the first United Nations conference in San Francisco as a correspondent for the Hearst newspaper chain. After filing a batch of stories filled with deep pessimism about the ability of the neophyte organization to maintain peace in postwar Europe, Jack set off for England to cover the elections. Churchill, who had set up a caretaker government following victory in Europe, needed a reaffirmation of public support for his leadership and had called an election for June 1945.

It was the first London Season since the war in Europe, and the pace of social life was hectic. Kathleen, Jack, and his traveling companion, Pat Lannon, a young businessman Jack had met in Arizona, attended wild parties in houses entirely bathed in light to celebrate the lifting of the blackout. At one, given at the country home of Douglas Fairbanks's ex-wife, they witnessed a high-stakes poker game in which one young peer gambled away some two hundred thousand pounds; with the country in such desperate economic straits this display of opulence embarrassed the hosts. One of the young women Jack took out that summer was Pat Wilson. In *As We Remember Joe* he had printed a group shot that included her without comment or explanation.

At a party given by the infamous socialite Lady Emerald Cunard, Kathleen found herself seated next to Evelyn Waugh. During the meal Waugh primly lectured Kathleen on Christian marriage law. Mistaking her amusement over his curmudgeonly pedantry for infatuation, he later told his wife, "The widow Hartington," as he referred to her, "is in love with me, I think."

The summer in England was to be a final fling for Jack Kennedy before the grueling business of electioneering. Every afternoon he and Pat Lannon, who were staying at Grosvenor House, invited a small group of young Englishmen over for refreshments and political chat. After all the sacrifices he had seen on the battlefield, Jack had been very disillusioned by the displays of national self-interest at the UN conference—in particular the unyielding demands of the Russians for territory in Eastern Europe. Unlike many of his contemporaries Jack suspected that America's noble ally during the war could not be trusted to keep its postwar promises. He and the others held heated discussions about the arms race, Russian aggression, the threat of a Communist takeover in bankrupt Europe, and the prospects of rebuilding the Continent.

All through June, Jack followed Churchill's campaign at racetracks and stadiums in the temperamental little car that Kick had managed to get hold of. He was rather shocked to see how the prime minister was booed and harassed during the campaign speeches that offered the prospect of further sacrifice to a population clearly fed up with the "toil and sweat" of the six years before. In stories filed to the States, Jack concluded that the Conservatives would just take the election, although he did concede that it was altogether possible that the once popular Churchill might lose. He was as stunned as everyone else when Churchill's government was soundly defeated by the Labour Party, which elected Clement Attlee as prime minister to handle the last stages of the South Pacific war.

Although the issues and the outcome of the June election were similar to those of Billy's campaign, Kathleen remained largely out of touch with the country's new political attitude. The politics she had adopted reflected the postwar conservative views of the class with which she now identified. She took an interest in Hugh Fraser's campaign for MP only because he was a close friend, and referred to him, in a letter to Frank Waldrop, as "one of the bright, young hopes of the Conservative Party." What mainly preoccupied Kathleen were her own future plans. She had no real reason to remain in England, now that the war was over and she was no longer the wife of a peer.

In July she spent a weekend at Hatley Park, the estate that Jakey and Chiquita Astor had recently purchased. Their other guest was William Douglas-Home, recently released from Wakefield Prison in Yorkshire. During his military service Douglas-Home had become increasingly horrified by the brutal exigencies of combat. Soon after he and his regiment had been shipped abroad for the invasion, he had refused to lead troops into a French town that had not been evacuated. As he had predicted when he refused his order, the battle resulted in the deaths of thousands of civilians. Douglas-Home's act of conscience had cost him twelve months in prison. During his incarceration Kathleen and Angela Laycock were the only friends who had come to see him. He had thought it rather daring for Angela to visit, when her husband was head of Special Operations, but he had been especially touched by the visits from Kick. Although she had been so recently widowed, she seemed not to resent his inability to espouse the kind of warfare that had killed her husband.

Still disoriented from his ordeal, he found Kathleen unusually sympathetic during his visit to Hatley. She even took turns riding on a donkey with him to try to snap him out of his withdrawn state, while it was obvious that she was barely able to conceal her own depression.

Lately her widowed state had begun to weigh on her more and more. She'd heard that the last of her single friends in America, including Betty Coxe and Chuck Spalding, had gotten married. Among her group in England, in the first lavish ceremony since before the war, Sally Norton had married Bill Astor, Jakey's older brother and the heir to the title.

Now that almost a year had passed since Billy's death, the Duke and Duchess of Devonshire had told her that the title would soon be passing on to Andrew. As the new heir Andrew would now be known as the Marquess of Hartington, and Debo would be the official marchioness. As the widow of the preceding marquis Kathleen would be known as Kathleen, Marchioness of Hartington, or Kathleen, Lady Hartington. Like that of most widows of peers her position in society would be the secure but rather superfluous one of a figurehead. The name that she would be taking on at twenty-five was usually reserved for middle-aged or elderly women. And even though the duke and duchess encouraged her to stay on with them, her new title was proof that she was no longer really part of the family.

Kathleen's one distraction from her troubles was her brother Jack. That summer he attended the Potsdam Conference, a last-ditch attempt by the United States and Great Britain to reach a compromise with Stalin over his postwar territorial demands. Plagued with a recurrence of malaria, Jack cut his trip short and flew home on August 6, the day before America dropped an atomic bomb on Hiroshima to end the Japanese war. Japan surrendered eight days later.

Jack's departure created a void in Kick's life. Now that the war was over, she began to think seriously about following him home.

In April she had written her father that she intended to return to the States in the summer; later that month Honey Fitz had informed the *Boston Traveler* that Kathleen was definitely expected back. Political considerations had probably prompted this announcement. With Jack preparing to run for office Joe Kennedy had already begun to set up an intensive public relations campaign. He had hired an ad agency to link the Kennedy name with the images of patriotism, heroism, philanthropy, and religious piety. The ambassador milked every newspaper and magazine contact he had to keep the two war heroes in his family before the public eye. He made large donations to religious organizations. Photographs appeared of him setting up the Joseph P. Kennedy, Jr., Scholarship Fund or on board the *Joseph P. Kennedy, Jr.* Jack made appearances before the Joseph P. Kennedy, Jr., chapter of the Veterans of Foreign Wars. Mr. Kennedy did everything he could to counter reports of an estrangement between Kathleen and the family; stories circulated of a supposed retreat she had taken in order to be accepted back into the Church. It was important to have physical evidence of the wayward daughter's return to the fold so that Jack would not have to explain to his Irish-Catholic constituency why his sister had married a Protestant.

After V-J Day, Kathleen resigned her Red Cross job and made plans to return home. She was still unsure how long she was going to stay. Although she missed her family and knew that her father in particular wanted her with them, she had begun to feel that her home was in England. Perhaps to strengthen her own position against the anticipated onslaught of the Kennedys, she delayed her trip by two months and then, before leaving, bought a house in London. It was a two-bedroom house in Smith Square, ten minutes from the House of Commons. Formerly owned by an MP, it contained a "division bell," which would ring when a parliamentary debate was about to begin. Arranging for Anne Hunloke to occupy the premises in her absence, Kick announced to British reporters that she was going home for a visit but that she clearly intended to return.

Joseph Kennedy met her at La Guardia Airport in New York. With his arm draped affectionately around her as they posed for news photographs, he announced that his beloved daughter had come home to stay.

So that Jack would not appear to be a carpetbagger, the Kennedy family had set up camp in Boston. During her first week there Kathleen met John White for lunch. He was in Boston, working for Polaroid. His engagement to Nancy Hoguet had continued uninterruptedly throughout the war. When actually faced with the imminent prospect of marriage on his return, however, he had promptly broken it off.

Although Kathleen was soon caught up in the familiar Kennedy activities, she realized quickly that her relations with her family were still strained. The football games and dinners and evenings at the theater could not bridge the gap between herself and her mother. She had assumed that her acceptance back into the Church would smooth over any past animosity, but she had obviously been wrong. It looked as though she might never be able to make up for what she had done, in her mother's eyes. She might have to resign herself to never being forgiven.

After living abroad for so long Kathleen was also finding it difficult to give up her freedom and fall back into the old family ways. Seeking privacy, she moved to a room in the Chatham Hotel, where she usually stayed in New York.

The mood in New York that winter was vibrant and hopeful. Kathleen's American contemporaries were giddily self-congratulatory as citizens of the nation that had provided the might and machinery to bail out the French, British, and Russian allies just in the nick of time. The Fifth Avenue stores were stocked with the first Paris imports in six years. "The New Look" of a new young designer named Christian Dior featured outrageously luxuriant, long swirling skirts that made the skimpy, less feminine fashions of the war obsolete. Food was plentiful, and gasoline rationing had been lifted right after V-J Day. After several years of economic plenty with American industry working to capacity for wartime production, everyone was confident that prosperity would continue. Opportunity abounded. Veterans had recovered their jobs, found new ones, or entered universities under the GI Bill of Rights. Americans who had accumulated disposable income during the boom war years now itched to spend it on new gadgets like television sets or cars.

Kathleen saw none of the kind of deprivation or want that was so pervasive in London; indeed, shortages of goods existed only because they couldn't be produced fast enough to accommodate the demand. Even after the unsettling resolution of the war with the dropping of the atomic bomb, an act which no one really understood, veterans had returned with a great sense of expectancy about the future. Columnists predicted an end to breadlines and disease, the dawning of an age of modular houses and disposable clothing. The fact that two nations as ideologically opposed as America and Russia had forged a military alliance was thought to signal a new era of global harmony and peace. The United States, the world's guardian and standard bearer, would solve any postwar problems that developed.

The thrust of Jack's campaign capitalized on this climate. Joseph Kennedy had already firmly established his son's reputation as a best-selling author, war hero, political correspondent, and member of an attractive, public-service–minded family. War veterans were held in the highest public esteem these days, and Jack's boyish, tousled-haired style seemed to embody the country's optimistic mood. Unlike the English, Americans were turning conservative. People distrusted Harry Truman, Roosevelt's successor after his death in the spring, and they were tired of the New Deal. They longed for new political directions. Jack's campaign slogan—"A New Generation Offers a Leader"—encapsulated the postwar yearnings of his peers.

In December, Kathleen's conspicuous absence at a major family event, the commissioning of the *Joseph P. Kennedy, Jr.* at the Charleston Naval Yard, was noted in the press. Although news stories reported that Kick remained in New York with her father, Joe Kennedy was in fact in Palm Beach with Jack; Kathleen was the only absent family member who could easily have attended.

In early spring, to downplay Jack's bachelorhood, the entire Kennedy family was recruited into the congressional campaign. Fourteen-year-old Teddy handed out leaflets; Rose Kennedy told stories of the London embassy days before female audiences; Eunice, Pat, and Jean hosted the Kennedy teas that were to become a trademark of Jack's campaigns.

Kathleen alone did not participate. The family had made much of the heroics of the dead older brother and campaigned before many war widows; they could have capitalized on Kathleen's loss as well. More socially adept than any other family member, including her father, Kathleen would have seemed a natural asset. Her pointed absence was partly her own choice. Although proud of Jack, she felt no real interest in the political process, and campaigning in Irish-Catholic ghettos was a little embarrassing for someone in her position. The truth was, however, that the family regarded her as a political liability. Jack was running a populist campaign in impoverished ethnic areas. It was difficult enough convincing voters in "three-deckered neighborhoods" that the rich Harvard graduate understood the working man without parading around his titled sister. The Boston Irish retained their traditional hatred and distrust of the British, particularly the peerage. For this constituency there really weren't any acceptable responses to questions as to why Kathleen had married the Marquess of Hartington.

While she was in New York Kathleen became reacquainted with Winston Frost, an ever-present member of café society whom she had met before the war. A lawyer ten years Kick's senior, Frost was tall, blond, and fine-featured, with a charming smile. The Frosts were an old Virginia family, distantly related to that of Page Huidekoper Dougherty. John White, who knew Winston from his college days, thought him a "fast tap dancer" and envied his easy success with sports and women. The Frosts had little money, but attendance at the right schools had given Winston entrée to the better families of the North. Throughout his career he had moved in moneyed circles. Winston Frost had a kind of elegance that appealed to women. He was a good dancer, loved the racing world, and knew the right after-dinner clubs. He had never married and was known as a notorious ladies' man. He was the first man Kathleen had felt attracted to since Billy's death. As their romance intensified she extended her stay.

One day in early spring Kathleen telephoned Charlotte McDonnell Harris, who was living with her husband in Rye, New York. She sounded very distraught: "Daddy says that Winston's involved with a woman," she told Charlotte. Evidently Mr.

Kennedy disapproved of Winston and had not refrained from saying so. He'd told Kathleen in no uncertain terms that Frost was no good and a playboy and had barraged her with phone calls and information that Kathleen refused to believe. "He isn't a playboy, I *know* he isn't," she insisted to Charlotte.

To substantiate his denunciation of Frost, Kennedy asked columnist Walter Winchell to provide him with specifics. He even produced a name and insinuated the woman was keeping Frost. Over the next weeks the ambassador hammered away at Kathleen until he succeeded in discrediting Winston and broke up the romance. She sounded heartbroken the next time she called Charlotte, but although hurt by her father's interference, she seemed oddly resigned. Once again she had come up against Joseph Kennedy, and the outcome had been predictable.

Shortly afterward Kathleen booked a return voyage to England. Her parents argued vehemently with her, insisting that she stay, but she refused. She had come to see how much emotional distance her marriage had placed between her and her mother. Now she needed actual distance.

Twelve

The small white Georgian townhouse at 4 Smith Square was the first place in which Kathleen had ever lived on her own. She hired a cook and a housekeeper and determinedly launched herself as a London hostess. The tiny rooms of the three-storied house had a special charm, brightened by the artful arrangements of flowers that Kick herself created. Finally one of her mother's lessons had taken.

Billy's parents loaned her eighteenth-century Hepplewhite chairs and other antique furniture from Chatsworth which had been in storage all through the war, when the estate had been occupied by the women's college. After the departure of the girls Chatsworth was in terrible disrepair, but the Duke and Duchess of Devonshire were still too disheartened by Billy's death to move back in and refurbish it. In the State Drawing Room, which had done service for five years as a dormitory, the breath of so many young sleepers had actually mildewed some of the Old Masters.

Kick began adding her own decorating touches to the Smith Square house with art and antiques picked up at auction. Her first significant purchase was a Chamberlain's Worcester porcelain tea and coffee set, for which she bid some eight hundred and fifty pounds at Christie's. She also had framed an eight-by-ten-inch photograph of her family—one of the well publicized shots of all eleven in a line—and displayed it on a table in the sitting room.

Amid the pervasive postwar drabness that had settled over England, everyone who knew Kathleen marveled at her dedication to rebuilding her life. Hugh Fraser would often point to her as a good role model for his sister Veronica, also a war widow, who was still listless and depressed.

Perhaps to help lay the memory of Billy to rest, Kathleen commissioned Oswald Birley, a well-known portraitist, to paint an oil of him in his uniform from an old snapshot. In the finished portrait Billy wore a wry half smile; he looked the perpetually expectant twenty-six-year-old heading off to war. Evelyn Waugh, still contemptuous of Kick's defection to the heathen, saw the painting after it was installed and pronounced the likeness of Kick's "Loved One" "most God awful."

Waugh was one of many among the burgeoning assortment of friends and acquaintances that Kathleen invited to her dinner parties. As though needing the assurance that she was still in the Church's good graces, she cultivated other noted Catholic intellectuals like Father D'Arcy. Janie Lindsay and David and Sissy Ormsby-Gore, who had recently returned to London, were frequent visitors at Smith Square, as were Hugh Fraser and Tony Rosslyn, who were all now MP's. These fledgling politicians would often drop in after a day at Parliament, which was just minutes away.

The 1946 Season, the first truly full-blown one since 1939, was being organized largely around charitable benefits for war veterans' associations and groups assisting the disabled or infirm. Fund-raisers and balls for the Royal National Lifeboat Institution and the British Limbless Ex-Servicemen's Association were held at the Dorchester or the Savoy, two elegant hotels that had survived the bombing. As a socially prominent war widow Kathleen received scores of invitations. At one of the first debutante parties given since V-J Day, she found herself as popular as ever, even with the younger men.

"It's absolutely maddening," one eighteen-year-old was heard to remark during the course of the evening. "Kick's taking all my dance partners."

"What do you expect?" her friend replied. "You're just a deb. She's an attractive *American* widow."

Although courted by many, Kathleen gravitated toward her old friend Richard Wood in the spring of 1946. She enjoyed his gentle, teasing sense of humor, which reminded her a little of Billy's. Wood had been fitted with artificial legs and had learned to walk awkwardly with the aid of a cane. He had reconciled himself to his disability and was determined not to let it become an obstacle to his political ambitions. The Halifax family, like the Devonshires, felt almost duty bound to enter politics. Richard, who intended to follow the path of his father, former Foreign Secretary Lord Halifax, considered running for MP in his district. Kathleen made numerous visits to the Halifax estate in Yorkshire. By summer she and Richard had begun discussing the possibility of becoming engaged.

Once again, however, she faced the prospect of a mixed marriage, although she found Richard much more understanding and generous than Billy had been. In preparation for a possible marriage he told her he wanted to learn whatever he could about her beliefs. When she produced a two-volume paperback by Archbishop M. Sheehan, forbiddingly entitled *Apologetics and Catholic Doctrine,* he accommodatingly read the entire text. Now and then Richard would ask Kathleen how she was able to subscribe to certain teachings that he found untenable, such as the doctrines of the Immaculate Conception and the infallibility of the pope. "But that's what I was *taught,*" she would answer stubbornly, as she had once answered John White. Richard suspected that despite Kathleen's protestations the grip of the Church on her thinking had weakened. She could not forget that in marrying Billy she had broken the rules. The fact that the Church had at one time excluded her perhaps made her more willing now to bend the rules to suit herself.

Together they read over the chapter on mixed marriage. Wood was shocked by the statements that warned of the dangers of marrying outside the faith. He felt he would never be able to convert but decided he would not object to his and Kathleen's children being raised as Catholics. He told her he would agree to take the promises and even to accompany her to Mass, that his only worry was that he might feel somewhat excluded.

In the end Kathleen decided not to marry him. The quiet respectability he offered her, which resembled the life she might have had with Billy, was not what she now sought. She also might not have felt emotionally strong enough to deal with Richard's disability, which would always remind her of the ravages of the war.

By the fall she had begun moving away from him. She was spending much of her time now with a new crowd that included Pat Wilson and Virginia Sykes and a rather raffish set of sophisticated married couples in their thirties. The friends she had made in her debutante days had all shared a strong sense of obligation to devote themselves to good works and enlightened leadership. Their parents, very much like the Kennedys, had impressed upon them that it would be wrong and wasteful to live idly on their wealth. For the most part Kathleen's latest acquaintances had no such compunction. Dedicated primarily to distracting themselves from the postwar pall, they traveled from fox hunt and grouse shoot to race meeting and continental resort.

Kathleen collected several beaux among this new crowd and soon paired off with Seymour Berry, the wealthy thirty-seven-year-old son of Lord Camrose. Seymour often surprised Kick with outlandish presents of diamond jewelry. After a time their friends simply expected as a matter of course that the two would eventually get married, until Kathleen discovered that Seymour was seeing another woman and was apparently still interested in playing the field. Thereafter she never took him seriously, even though he continued to pursue her. Most of Kathleen's acquaintances simply assumed that Seymour's other involvements had broken up the romance. But for all intents and purposes her relationship with Seymour—as well as with Richard Wood—was over the moment she met Peter Fitzwilliam.

Kathleen was first introduced to Earl Fitzwilliam in June, while she was still considering marrying Richard. She had chaired a committee of young women that had organized a ball in honor of the Commandos, a special operations unit that had been set up by Churchill in 1940. Because of his brilliant military career Fitzwilliam had been one of the stars of the occasion.

Evelyn Waugh, who had met Fitzwilliam in the Army, had once referred to him disparagingly as a "king dandy and scum," but even he had not been immune to Fitzwilliam's high spirits and Irish charm, especially after he had managed to procure for the writer a small box of excellent cigars during wartime.

Fitzwilliam had enjoyed himself immensely during the last years of the war. Bored as a captain in the Grenadier Guards and seeking fast, dangerous action, he had volunteered for the Commandos and was soon singled out for a tailor-made operation. The War Office had been in desperate need of a specialized ball bearing produced only in Sweden. To reach Sweden in order to obtain it, it would be necessary to break through the blockaded waters of the Skagerrak. Fitzwilliam had been assigned as defensive officer of the *Hopewell,* a small motor torpedo boat disguised as a merchant ship and outfitted with an antiaircraft weapon. Dodging enemy fire, the tiny *Hopewell* had scuttled back and forth between the northern British coast and Gothenburg and completed its mission successfully. Fitzwilliam's bravery had earned him the Distinguished Service Order, England's second highest military honor.

A gambler by nature, Fitzwilliam had found the same titillation in his Commando exploits that came from a toss of the dice. But his real passion involved horses. In 1942, when few people in Great Britain had enough disposable income to throw away on a bet, he had been one of the principal buyers of bloodstock. Right after the war, while it was still partially occupied by soldiers, he had purchased the Grange in Newmarket, one of the largest training stables in England, which he renamed after his ancestor, the Marquess of Rockingham, who had had a similar passion for horses. Peter's favorite painting, a three-by-six-foot canvas of Sampson, the largest racehorse ever bred, which Rockingham had commissioned from George Stubbs, hung in the enormous dining hall of Wentworth Woodhouse, the family seat in Rotherham, Yorkshire.

As many of Fitzwilliam's cash-poor contemporaries began dismantling their ancestral estates, he aggressively accumulated property to ensure that his hobby and passion would become a full-time pursuit. Handing over the vast family business concerns to a solicitor, his superior in his Commando days, Peter concentrated his energies on setting up the Rockingham Stud. By 1946 the Rockingham had grown to be one of the finest stud farms in England, with twenty-two horses in training, including Peter's favorites: Golden Girl, Air Raid, Peace Pact, and Light o' Love. Fitzwilliam had been voted president of the Racehorse Owners' Association and had been admitted into the highly exclusive Jockey Club. Among his intimates were the leading international racehorse owners, including the Aga Khan and Marcel Boussac.

With a net worth estimated at five million pounds the Fitzwilliam family fortune had been made in agriculture and coal mining. Peter's father, the seventh earl, had been considered in his day the richest man in England, with an income estimated at a thousand pounds per diem. Like the Cavendishes the Fitzwilliam family owned enormous estates scattered in various parts of England and Ireland, including Coollattin, their Irish castle, Milton in Peterborough, and Wentworth Woodhouse. Wentworth was every bit as grand as Chatsworth. Situated on twenty-two thousand acres of property, the Fitzwilliam estate was thought to be the largest house in England, with a thousand windows along a two-hundred-yard facade and a room for every day in the year. In the seventh earl's time guests dressing for dinner were given wafers to crumble and leave along the route to the dining room in order to find their way back at the end of the evening. A butler once reckoned that he had walked fifty miles through the halls and passageways in the course of serving during a four-day house party.

Peter's father had been famous for entertaining in grand Edwardian style. Guests were expected to appear in full evening dress for dinners that would be served on gold plates with gold cutlery. Like the Devonshires the Fitzwilliams had accumulated priceless collections of rare objects through the centuries: first edition Renaissance books, Greek and Etruscan vases, porcelains, and Roman coins. Wentworth's wine cellar was legendary.

Fitzwilliam's father had devoted most of his life to sport, holding political office for only a scant seven years. He had owned three packs of hounds, and it was not unusual for him to follow the hounds on his English estate and then travel to Ireland the following day to hunt with a different pack. He loved polo, horseracing, and big game safaris. The purchase of a four-thousand-ton liner provided him with a means of hunting for treasure in the South Pacific.

At the birth of his first and only son Earl Fitzwilliam had invited some thousand tenants and employees to an open house in Wentworth Park and had ordered vats of ale brewed that year to be set aside and opened on Peter's coming of age in 1931. Countess Fitzwilliam, Peter's mother, had markedly favored him over his four older sisters, possibly because sons were such a rarity in the Fitzwilliam family, historically a good producer of females. In the frequent battles that flared between father and son, Maud Fitzwilliam invariably took Peter's side. He had grown up with the assumption that there was nothing he wanted that he couldn't have. What Peter wanted most was speed—fast cars and horses. He was greedy for excitement and new experience, though little seemed to satisfy him.

It was said that Fitzwilliam could talk anybody into doing anything. Men as well as women found him irresistible. The night of the Commandos' Ball, Kathleen was the recipient of his lavish attention. She looked particularly lovely that evening in a pale-pink gown with aquamarine-and-diamond clips. Her honey-colored hair, still worn in a pageboy, had grown long, and she was thinner than she had ever been, which suited her. Fitzwilliam was markedly captivated.

His flirtation with Kathleen drew little comment that night, despite the fact that his wife, Olive, as president of the fund for the ball, was a conspicuous presence. Even as a university student Peter had had the reputation of a playboy who would flirt with any pretty woman who caught his eye. Over the years he had had a long succession of affairs—a tally he took no pains to conceal. In 1940 Jack Kennedy's law school friend Cam Newberry had met Peter and Olive Fitzwilliam during a vacation in Bermuda. Cam was astonished to observe Peter pursuing a young guest at the hotel while Olive attempted to look the other way.

Peter had met eighteen-year-old Olive Plunkett not long after his twenty-first birthday. Known to everyone as Obby, she had been blond, vivacious, excitable, and wild. As a small child Olive had loved to prance around like a horse. Her family nickname, Hobby Horse, shortened to Obby, had stuck. The daughter of an Irish Protestant minister, a member of the famous Guinness family, Obby had grown up in a modest household—until Bishop Plunkett had inherited his heirless relative's vast fortune. The Plunketts were at a loss as to how to handle that kind of money. The bishop moved his family into a mansion in Dublin and showered his children with presents. Like Peter, Obby had become restless and easily bored. She could be counted on to take up any dare. The terrible accident that occurred before her marriage was probably inevitable for a girl who did everything at breakneck speed. At a weekend house party during Royal Ascot, Obby, typically, was hours late in getting dressed. In her haste to catch up with the other guests, who had begun to leave, she ran down a passageway and crashed through a plate-glass door. Her face was badly cut. Even with subsequent plastic surgery the scars were still visible.

Before their marriage in 1933 Peter and Obby were known to many of their thrifty young married friends as an extravagant pair. Weekend guests at one of the Fitzwilliam estates would often find Obby pacing around in irritation. "Oh, what should we *do* this weekend," she would lament. "It's so *dull* just sitting here. What should we do? Let's go to Le Touquet." But if Obby and her friends did head off to France, she would soon tire of the jaunt and be anxious to return home before the end of the weekend.

Peter and Olive had viewed their marriage as simply another outrageous new adventure. In 1933 thousands of tenants from

Rotherham were transported to Dublin via two hired ships to attend the lavish wedding at St. Patrick's Cathedral. It was reported that Peter, ever the gay young bachelor, almost didn't show up. Dressed in a stunning gown of the palest ice blue, the bride was attended by six pairs of bridesmaids, dressed in gowns identical to hers but in progressively darker shades of the same color. On the way to the church the Irish guests were horrified when the wedding procession was held up by a funeral cortege. Superstition had it that meeting a funeral on one's wedding day forebode a doomed marriage.

The Fitzwilliams had skitted back and forth from the racetrack to the Caribbean for several years until a daughter was born. Peter felt too young to be a father, and Obby's novelty had worn thin. He began taking up with other women, and she began comforting herself with liquor. When invited to accompany Peter to Buckingham Palace, Obby drank to calm her nervous anticipation and ended up too inebriated to attend. On more than one social occasion Peter had had to blame his wife's absence on illness. In 1943, when Peter suddenly inherited the title, Obby was ill equipped to assume the responsibilities of a countess. Peter's absence during the war further strained their marriage. By the time he returned, Obby was a hopeless alcoholic. Maud Fitzwilliam blamed her daughter-in-law for the disastrous marriage.

After he met Kathleen, Peter began spending much more time at his London house in Grosvenor Square pursuing her. She was soon swept up in the heady excitement of the illicit romance. Their meetings had to be discreet. Despite the deterioration of Peter's marriage, even the more progressive circles in London thought it scandalous for a titled Catholic widow to be taking up with a married man, although it created less of a tumult than it might have before the war. To maintain appearances, they confined their rendezvous for the first few months to lunches at the Ritz or evenings at Smith Square or in the homes of close friends. Peter's friends were rather shocked by his new love interest. In the minds of this older crowd wholesome little Kick Hartington hardly fitted the image of the other woman.

Kick found Fitzwilliam's age, his experience, and his pleasure-seeking aimlessness refreshing. She enjoyed him as a raconteur who possessed her own family's brand of irreverent self-mocking wit. Some of Kathleen's titled English friends believed the pair shared what they viewed as a certain Irish "coarseness." Kathleen's earthiness occasionally surfaced in off-color jokes, and Peter brought that quality out in her. She was also impressed by his boldness and his business acumen. Fitzwilliam was one of the few among the aristocracy who had prospered from the war. He had purchased a nine-hundred-acre estate, one of the best-known properties in southern England. With the astute timing of a Joseph Kennedy, Peter had attempted to secure Coca-Cola franchises in northern England immediately following V-E Day, when GI customs were fresh in the English consciousness.

Partly because of Peter's tutelage Kathleen began to dress in a more sophisticated manner and to wear more jewelry. She was infuriated when a newspaper columnist referred to her as the "gum-chewing marchioness." Peter was also teaching her to follow his example in being much less guilty about having money or using it as insulation from the country's present austerity. As she became accustomed to Peter's bountiful spending habits Kathleen became less and less aware that her other friends might not be able to afford to indulge themselves as she did. The Duke and Duchess of Devonshire had given Kick carte blanche to entertain at Lismore, the breathtaking eleventh-century castle built on a magnificent bluff in Ireland by King John. For transportation around County Wicklow, Kathleen had arranged to import an American station wagon. Her English set considered the car an outrageous luxury, particularly with the United Kingdom facing a desperate fuel shortage.

Peter himself expressed concern about the impoverished state of the rest of the country only when it directly affected him. In the spring of 1946 Minister of Fuel and Power Emanuel Shinwell had passed a resolution making it legal to mine for coal on private property known to contain coal beds. Some of the last outcrops of unmined coal in the country—an estimated one hundred forty thousand tons—were known to lie in the thousands of acres of Wentworth Park. Fitzwilliam appealed to Prime Minister Attlee to prevent open-cast mining in the Wentworth gardens on the grounds that it would destroy a national landmark. Probably delighting in playing Robin Hood, Shinwell announced: "I may as well tell you I am not going to be stopped from getting it—whatever that may imply about aesthetic amenities."

In April 1946 German prisoners had been employed to remove fences, and bulldozers had crashed their way through two walls. Woodlands, avenues, hedges, and farmland were ravaged as bucket cranes excavated soil in preparation for the mining. Fitzwilliam watched in horror as the government tore up two thousand acres of park land that would require a generation to restore. After toying with the idea of donating Wentworth to the National Trust, he leased most of it to a physical education teachers' training college. He retained thirty rooms for his private use but resolved to make his home in Ireland and London.

Kathleen's new state of independence was periodically intruded upon by visits from her family. One afternoon that fall Kick called upon a new friend, Countess Birkenhead, and begged her to come to Smith Square the following evening. She explained that her mother, en route to the fashion salons of Paris, would be arriving in London for a fortnight. Kathleen intended to invite a large group of her friends over for the welcoming dinner. She sounded very agitated and nervous.

On Kathleen's instructions her housekeeper had embarked on a meticulously thorough cleaning of the house. Kathleen herself had checked and double-checked many details. Knowing that her mother liked a large bed, Kick planned to offer her her own bedroom and to sleep in the guest room. She had also taken great pains to arrange a full schedule of activities for her mother with a variety of people likely to amuse her. Only the most impressive among Kathleen's circle were to meet Mrs. Kennedy.

Kathleen was particularly eager for her to spend time with the Duchess of Devonshire.

Twenty-five-year-old Eunice was present at the dinner that evening, and Mrs. Kennedy announced proudly to the assembled guests that her younger daughter intended to become a nun. After dinner the women retired to the second-floor sitting room. Once safely out of earshot of the men Mrs. Kennedy whirled upon Kathleen. She wished to know what Kathleen was doing for the Church and for charity. Caught off guard by the question, Kathleen was flustered, and her friends felt embarrassed for her. She went to Mass every Sunday, but that apparently was not going to satisfy her mother. Mrs. Kennedy continued to probe with no response. "*Kaaath*leen," Mrs. Kennedy demanded in the same voice she had used when calling her daughter home to the house in HyannisPort, "what have you been doing for the Church?"

"Well," Kick replied finally, after groping wildly for an answer, "once a week I go to the Central Office."

The Central Office was the headquarters of the Conservative Party, but Mrs. Kennedy obviously took it to be a central charity organization, like the United Way. "Oh, well now," she replied, placated, "that's better."

In October an incident occurred that symbolized Kathleen's break with the past. There had been a rash of jewel heists, and Kathleen was numbered among the victims. Some forty thousand dollars' worth of jewels—including a set of Billy's cufflinks and a pair of Joe's navy wings, inscribed "To K from J"—were stolen. Kick publicly pleaded with the thieves to return the two sentimental items, to no avail.

Possibly because she suspected her housekeeper of collusion, Kathleen dismissed her and hired two portly Hungarian refugees as cook and housekeeper. The two sisters were to occupy the third-floor suite of rooms. Kathleen left them in care of the house as she set off for her customary winter visit to Palm Beach. She was eager to see Jack, who had just won his congressional election by a landslide.

Kathleen returned to London in the spring of 1947 to find everyone anxiously awaiting the Season. Some pomp and glitter had returned to Royal Ascot; men wore gray top hats and morning coats. Veterans were no longer being married in uniform. On the other hand fashion writers reviewing designer shows gushed over fabrics that appeared sturdy enough to last several years. Although the traditional rustling taffetas were advertised for Queen Charlotte's birthday ball, Molyneux's winter collection was made of genuine British velveteen, which, his customers were assured, looked and felt like the real thing. Upper-class women were being introduced to easy-care materials; Marshall & Snelgrove, a department store, advised, "A tailored shirt is a wise investment of *four* coupons, especially if it is in a washable material." If the queen and the princesses appeared especially well turned out, fashion writers were quick to assure their readers that their dresses had been worn before and that their majesties had not exceeded their coupon allotment.

Although the palace had not yet reinstituted court presentations, substituting presentation "parties," London was alight with festivity, in large part due to the excitement over the engagement of Princess Elizabeth to Philip Mountbatten. The theaters in the West End had reopened: Kathleen attended gala film premieres of *Nicholas Nickleby* and *The Best Years of Our Lives*. Swing had died with the tragic loss of Major Glenn Miller over the English Channel, but the younger generation was introducing new music; they formed conga lines and did the hokey-pokey and the palais glide at the Suffolk Hunt Ball. Society papers welcomed the June arrival of the American ambassador's wife, Mrs. Lewis Douglas, as the "first chatelaine" at Prince's Gate since Mrs. Kennedy. Before long the Douglases' eighteen-year-old daughter Sharman (or "Sas" to her intimates) had created a sensation in the press and at debutante balls. Kathleen was among the two thousand guests received by the Douglases at the traditional Independence Day garden party on the embassy lawns.

To that event and many others Kathleen went alone or relied upon one of her old escorts. As popular as she was at every festive occasion, her limited involvement in the Season clearly pointed up the social liability of her relationship with Peter. He was able to meet her only for lunch and furtive late-night rendezvous. At all the more important functions Obby was by his side. Kathleen trusted Peter when he assured her that he was working on obtaining a divorce, and she tried to content herself with his occasional presence. But the social life of the Fitzwilliams was well publicized. A large item appeared about the uproarious ball the Fitzwilliams gave at the Dorchester to celebrate the reopening of the Derby, and she couldn't possibly ignore the large spread in *The Tatler and Bystander* that featured a dashing Peter in his hunting pink coat and a very gay Obby performing a quick two-step at the Fitzwilliams' Hunt Ball in Coollattin. On other occasions, however, Peter wasn't above throwing Obby and Kathleen together. At the Yorkshire races the threesome was spotted dining together with some mutual friends at the same luncheon table.

Whatever the indignities of the situation Kathleen was deeply embroiled in her affair with Peter. Some time in 1947 her friends began to suspect that she had begun sleeping with him. She was blindly, recklessly in love, probably for the first time. She didn't seem to care anymore whether the affair was kept a secret or her reputation remained unsoiled. She had spent only a few weeks with a husband who, like her, probably had been a virgin on their wedding night. With Peter she was experiencing her first sexual passion. It almost seemed as though Kathleen wanted her friends to find out about the affair just so they would know how happy she was.

Kick's old prewar crowd worried about her as they came to understand the depth of her involvement. Her moral lapse was condoned as the result of loneliness, and her friends hoped she would find happiness after all she'd been through. But there was no getting around what many viewed as Peter's utter unsuitability for Kathleen. Besides the most obvious obstacle, his marital status, there was the fact that he had done very little of a worthwhile nature in all his thirty-seven years. When Kathleen first confided her hope of marrying him to Janie, Janie did not hesitate to tell Kathleen she considered Peter irresponsible and lacking in substance. "You don't know him, you don't know him," Kick protested. She argued that she had discovered qualities in Peter that were invisible to outsiders. Many of his best traits only needed to be cultivated.

David and Sissy Ormsby-Gore were even more disapproving, but they expressed their low opinion of Peter more tactfully. They wondered aloud to Kick if she wouldn't feel out of place in Fitzwilliam's world. Wouldn't she find his life irritating and tiresome after a time? David thought Peter the utter antithesis of everything Kathleen had been taught to value in terms of public service and sacrifice. As far as he could see, Peter had never made a sacrifice in his life. David also thought Peter extremely selfish to put Kathleen in her present position. In the most affectionate and teasing manner Sissy, who was still very religious, prodded Kick from time to time to stay on the right spiritual track. When Fitzwilliam came up in conversation, she reminded Kick what it would mean for her to marry outside the Church again.

Kathleen's in-laws knew of her relationship with Peter (whom Andrew, a racing enthusiast, greatly admired), but they avoided the subject. As Billy's family they considered it awkward to talk of her new romance, and they disliked butting into other people's affairs. Elizabeth Cavendish was the only one in the family whom Kick told about her marriage plans. She had grown close to Elizabeth in the months after Billy's death (Elizabeth had always thought Kick, with all her admirers, frightfully glamorous).

With other friends Kick refrained from discussing her involvement with Peter. She avoided mentioning him by name when she told Richard Wood she had fallen in love again. Some people doubted Peter would ever marry her—although it was common knowledge he wished to rid himself of Obby. Peter's own relatives doubted he was capable of being faithful to anyone, as much as he appeared infatuated with Kathleen at the moment. There was also some conjecture that Peter, with his lavish spending habits, might want to get his hands on some of the Kennedy money.

Whatever his motives Peter promised to marry Kathleen as soon as he could get free. Although he might have to work out a complicated settlement for Obby and his twelve-year-old daughter, Juliet, he was quite convinced that he could obtain a divorce. He suspected Obby of having her own affairs. Although he considered himself too much of a gentleman to institute divorce proceedings against his wife (which in England were almost always based on charges of adultery), he knew he could use her faithlessness to force her hand if he had to. Another woman would have to be named as the adulteress when and if Obby sued for divorce; probably Peter planned to arrange to name someone other than Kathleen in order to save her embarrassment. Maud Fitzwilliam was delighted when she heard the news of Peter's plans, as was an old Commando friend of his, Harry Sporborg. Sporborg had been impressed by Peter's bravery and leadership qualities during the war. He hoped Peter had finished sowing his wild oats. Perhaps a woman like Kathleen would help him to realize his considerable potential.

Regardless of what anyone thought, Kathleen was dead set on this second marriage, and her friends knew that once she had made up her mind, it would be impossible either to dissuade her or to make her understand the consequences of her decision. Kathleen desperately wanted the Church to accept the relationship. The likelihood that it would not disturbed her greatly. Again she consulted her Farm Street advisers, although she already knew their answer. Peter had stated emphatically that he would not convert or allow his heirs to be raised as Catholics. The Jesuits at Farm Street reiterated that the Church would never condone marriage to a divorced Protestant other than with its special stipulations. If Kathleen went ahead and married Peter outside the Church, not only would she be sinning, as she had been when she married Billy, but in the eyes of the Church she would be responsible for splitting up a marriage. She now faced the prospect of being ostracized all over again. Kathleen tried to rationalize these implications. If the Church had condemned her for marrying someone as obviously worthwhile as Billy, the

Church was clearly wrong, and she really had nothing left to lose.

All through that year Kathleen kept her relationship with Peter from her family. She mentioned nothing about it to her mother or to Pat, who came to visit her at Lismore. The first family member to hear of it was Jack, who stayed with her in Ireland during his first congressional junket. He appeared to be as supportive of Kathleen's wishes as Joe had been in the weeks before her marriage to Billy, although he warned her of the family's likely reaction. Possibly because Jack himself had become so firmly entrenched in carrying out his father's master plan, he even seemed a little envious of her boldness.

With winter approaching and her presence at Palm Beach expected, Kathleen knew that she could no longer put off informing her family of her intentions. She asked Elizabeth Cavendish to come with her to America. Elizabeth's presence was to be moral support as well as visible proof that Kathleen's in-laws were behind her. The night before they sailed, Kick had a long dinner with David and Sissy Ormsby-Gore. As she got up to go she broke down and wept. When she had married Billy, the wartime limitations on communications had shielded her from the interference of her parents, and she had carried out her decision as a *fait accompli*. Now she faced a direct confrontation with all the power her father had at his disposal to stop her.

Thirteen

As the weeks passed in Palm Beach, Kathleen seemed unable to bring herself to say anything about Fitzwilliam to her family. With Elizabeth Cavendish she idled away her time beside the great backyard pool behind the Spanish-tiled villa. "I'm lying here in the sun, thinking of you," she wrote on a postcard to her London housekeeper, Ilona Solymossy. That winter the English were coping with record-breaking cold, combined with a severe fuel shortage. Ilona had asked Kathleen to send her candles, since Londoners were forgoing electric light to conserve fuel for heat, and a candle shortage had also developed.

In early spring Kathleen left Palm Beach and headed north with Elizabeth still without disclosing her marriage plans. She stopped off in Washington to see Jack and Eunice but avoided a long stay, perhaps afraid she would be tempted to confide in her pious sister. Jack had bought a house in Georgetown, and Eunice, who was still contemplating a religious vocation, had moved in with him after securing a job as executive secretary for the Justice Department's Juvenile Delinquency Committee. She approached her work with characteristic zeal and busied herself setting up conferences and inspecting prisons. The Boston papers gave her a glowing press. She had also become a proselytizing member of the Christophers, an organization founded by Kick's old idol Father Keller and dedicated to inspiring lay citizens to work for political and social change. Taking the lead from his energetic sister, Jack had joined the Education and Labor Committee, which was currently dealing with crippling strikes, and he was making a reputation as a domestic red hunter. With some string pulling by his father he had been voted one of the Ten Outstanding Men of 1946 by the United States Junior Chamber of Commerce.

Jack and Eunice had begun cultivating a circle of friends among the ambitious young people who had flocked into Washington after V-J Day. They were known around town as a bright and committed twosome, whose small parties featured lively table conversation and after-dinner games such as charades and twenty questions. At these get-togethers Jack invariably launched into heated discussions of current affairs: the red menace abroad, the threat of Communist subversion at home, and the efficacy of the Marshall Plan in rebuilding Europe. One popular dinner guest from the congressional "class of 1946" was Senator Joseph R. McCarthy, whom both Eunice and Jack found amusing.

By the time Kathleen visited Washington, another popular guest, Robert Sargent Shriver, had become a prospective suitor of Eunice's. Kathleen, who had met Shriver before the war, had introduced him to her sister during one of her visits to the States. Curious as always about any of his daughters' boyfriends, Mr. Kennedy had invited him for breakfast, then offered him a job as his personal assistant in running the Merchandise Mart, a massive office complex in Chicago that Kennedy had bought in 1945. Soon after Eunice got her appointment in Washington, Kennedy transferred Shriver there. Born of a prominent Maryland family, the young man had all the proper matrimonial qualifications in the ambassador's eyes; he was Catholic, good-looking, easygoing, and willing to work for Joseph Kennedy, Sr. Eunice's friends suspected that Mr. Kennedy had planted Shriver in Washington to lure Eunice away from the convent into marriage, which would assure Kennedy of at least one business-minded family member.

Although Kathleen avoided discussing her love affair with Fitzwilliam with her devout sister, she did confide in some of her Catholic friends when she went to New York. Charlotte McDonnell Harris was stunned when she heard about Fitzwilliam, even though he sounded like the man she would have selected all along for Kick; Billy had always seemed a little tame to Charlotte. But it worried her to see Kick acting so recklessly. Kick had always been practical and even a little calculating about her romances. Now, however, despite all the trouble with her family she was about to face, Kick seemed to enjoy the doubly illicit nature of the romance. She even indicated to Charlotte that if Fitzwilliam could not get divorced—and he was apparently having some difficulty—she might consider running off with him. She appeared naïvely oblivious to the reverberations of causing a major scandal for one of the most prominent Catholic families in America. She also appeared utterly unconcerned with the practical problems entailed in running off with a married man.

When Charlotte asked where she and Fitzwilliam planned to live, Kathleen smiled as though she thought the question immaterial. "Why do you ask that?" she said.

Despite her bravado she still could not bring herself to inform the Kennedys. To Charlotte, Kathleen conveyed the impression that she was stalling by design. She had learned her lesson from the Winston Frost episode. This time she was not going to expose herself to either prolonged family discussions or any attempts by her father to break up the romance.

While in New York, Kathleen also stopped by to see her old childhood chum, Jackie Pierrepont, a member of an Episcopalian Social Register family, who had astonished his Catholic friends by converting to Catholicism during the war. While stationed in the South Pacific he had observed the profoundly uplifting effect that the Mass had upon the soldiers and had been impressed by the power and grandeur of the Latin ceremony, even in the most makeshift circumstances. When he returned home exhausted and despondent, Jackie had bought an ailing parish bookshop and reopened it as a general bookstore specializing in works by Catholics, particularly those by famous converts such as Waugh, G. K. Chesterton, and Hilaire Belloc, who had been behind the intellectual Catholic movement in England. The bookstore had become a hangout of sorts for Charlotte Harris and other old Irish-Catholic friends of Jackie's. Most of them found it difficult to understand why someone who hadn't inherited the burden of their religion would take it on so willingly.

One day during her New York visit Kathleen stopped in at Jackie's shop. "Hi, ducks," she said by way of greeting. Jackie noted that Kathleen seemed to be acquiring a bit of an English accent, which mixed queerly with the family's distinctive Bostonian drawl. To Jackie's surprise she had come to invite him to accompany her to the weekend celebration of the reopening of the Greenbrier Hotel in White Sulphur Springs, West Virginia, where her parents had honeymooned. The Kennedys were friendly with the owner, Robert Young, who had invited the entire family. Scores of celebrities were to be there for the reopening, including the still notorious Duke and Duchess of Windsor, who were very popular in New York society. It promised to be the social event of the spring. Robert Young had even arranged for a private train to transport the guests from various points along the East Coast.

It was to be Kathleen's final visit with her family before she and Elizabeth Cavendish set sail the following week. Rather than traveling with the rest of the Kennedys, however, she chose to take the train with Jackie. During the trip she turned to him and said suddenly, "I want to do something that is going to make everybody very mad at me."

"You're going to leave the Church?" Jackie asked.

"No, I'm very much in love with this married man." To make it clear that she was not breaking up a marriage, she added quickly that Fitzwilliam's wife was an alcoholic and his marriage a disaster. Her father would be furious, of course, but she thought—hoped—that she could handle him. It was the thought of hurting her mother all over again that she dreaded most. She asked Jackie to say nothing about her plans to anyone until Peter's divorce came through and it was possible to make an official announcement.

At the Greenbrier resort complex Kathleen and Jackie joined some two hundred guests. The main body of the hotel had been designed as an antebellum mansion. Negroes dressed as slaves served tea in the afternoon. The interior was elaborately designed in a pink and green color scheme. Jackie and Kick participated with the rest of the Kennedys in a crowded weekend of golf and dancing until midnight in the pink-festooned ballroom. The weekend had been widely publicized, and many journalists were present. Society writers had reported that Kathleen had been seen with the wealthiest man in Ireland, but she dismissed all rumors of a remarriage.

Kathleen waited until her last evening at Greenbrier to have the confrontation with her parents. On the train ride up north with Jackie the following day, she was still very shaken. She had been quite wrong in thinking she would mainly have to contend with her father's opposition. It was Mrs. Kennedy who had taken the unanticipated offensive. She had absolutely refused to consider the possibility of marriage to Fitzwilliam. Whatever else Earl Fitzwilliam was, he would be a divorced man. Her attitude toward such a sacrilegious union was unflinching. She threatened to disown Kathleen and refuse to ever see her again if she married Fitzwilliam. She would also insist on having Mr. Kennedy cut off Kathleen's allowance. And—Jackie was startled to learn from Kathleen—if Mr. Kennedy did not agree to these punitive measures, Mrs. Kennedy was prepared to leave him—or to publicly embarrass him by some other means. This last threat, as Jackie understood it, was Mrs. Kennedy's single trump card, and she evidently intended to play it if she had to, for the sake of her daughter's salvation.

As soon as Kathleen got off the train, she immediately went to see Patsy Field, the friend she had sought out when Billy was killed. But now Kathleen seemed in even greater turmoil. She was consumed with guilt over the effect her affair with Fitzwilliam was having on her mother. It hurt her terribly to think that if she went ahead with the marriage, her mother would regard her as dead. This upset her far more than the prospect of being disinherited or of making an irrevocable break with her Church.

Patsy had always found Kathleen staunchly protective of Mrs. Kennedy, even though she'd often giggled about her mother's idiosyncrasies: the lists Mrs. Kennedy pinned to her blouses, the determined daily walks, the "pasties" attached to her face all day long to avoid wrinkles, her incessant shopping. But Kathleen's laughter had always been affectionate rather than cruel. She sensed her mother's deep unhappiness. In Rose Kennedy, Kathleen saw a thwarted life that had once held so much promise. Like Kathleen she had been expensively educated and well traveled when she had fallen in love and married despite the disapproval of her father. Much of Mrs. Kennedy's potential had probably died with the first shocked discovery of her husband's blatant infidelity. But her religion had placed her in an even more painful position: She had been duty bound, regardless of her feelings about her husband's faithlessness, never to refuse his sexual advances or to prevent her almost annual pregnancies. As the years went on Rose Kennedy had retreated further and further into the Church and the details involving the well-being of her children. Duty had become the only evidence of her own existence. If her children strayed from the ever-narrowing path that she herself had chosen, Mrs. Kennedy had learned to rationalize their deviations. When Kathleen had disregarded her admonitions against smoking and drinking, it was because she wished to keep her figure and to ward off the ill effects of the damp English weather. It was only a lapse from the faith, such as the one Kathleen was currently contemplating, that Mrs. Kennedy could not rationalize away.

During the next few days Kathleen tried to distract herself from her troubles by making the rounds in Washington. John White had quit his job at Polaroid to return to the *Times-Herald* and his old habitat in the basement of Patsy's house. One afternoon, seated beside White on his bed in the "cave," where they had holed up in the old days, Kathleen told him that despite the objections of her family she intended to go ahead with her marriage. She reminded White of a little child in love. Cynical about the staying power of such passion, he privately thought that because she was at a very early stage of her affair, the intensity of her feeling made her overconfident that she would eventually overcome all obstacles. Love, she evidently believed, would conquer all. Ordinarily critical of other men and especially protective of little Kathleen, White nonetheless permitted himself to accept the uncritical portrait she drew of Fitzwilliam. He felt a twinge of jealousy, as he always did when one of his girls was getting away, but he approved of anyone who could make Kathleen so happy.

In the next few days he escorted Kathleen and Elizabeth Cavendish to the many parties given in their honor. He took an immediate liking to Elizabeth, who appeared relieved to be temporarily free of the position she had to uphold in England. Eunice was present at one party. Apparently she was shaken over the recent news about Fitzwilliam. As though searching desperately for an answer as to why Kathleen would contemplate committing a second sacrilege, Eunice cornered White at one point during the evening and pronounced accusingly, "*You* made Kathleen leave the Catholic Church."

On another occasion Kathleen was seated at a dinner table beside her old mentor, Frank Waldrop. Waldrop had always thought of her as a scrub-faced, skirt-and-sweater girl, but tonight he was impressed by the elegant self-assurance Kathleen had developed since he last saw her. They chatted about a new novel of Evelyn Waugh's and laughed about his priggish moralizing. At one point, though, Kathleen turned sober and talked bitterly of having felt cheated by the war. "You know, Frank, I had only five weeks with my husband and then he was gone," she said.

In all his letters to England, Frank had chided her about the infrequency of her visits to the States. Half teasingly he asked her when she would be coming home next.

Kathleen took his question seriously. "Frank," she replied, "I'm never coming home."

Kick spent her last night in Washington with Patsy. The two of them stayed up very late talking, seated side by side on Patsy's king-size bed. Fitzwilliam would just be returning from a trip to Africa when Kathleen arrived in Europe. She talked excitedly of the reunion weekend they had planned on the French Riviera over the Whitsuntide holiday weekend. Finally they would have some privacy and would not have to concern themselves with gossip. In discussing the trip Kathleen was careful to point out that they were to stay with mutual friends so that Patsy would not think they weren't being properly chaperoned.

They couldn't help laughing a little over Mr. Kennedy's suggested solution to the religious problem of a marriage to Peter. He had a scheme to convince Catholic Church officials that Fitzwilliam had never been baptized. Then Peter's first marriage would be considered null and void according to Catholic doctrine and Kathleen could marry him in the Church, providing Peter agreed to its stipulations. Patsy marveled at the notion that Kennedy would try to convince anyone that a peer of England had not been baptized—especially when Earl Fitzwilliam, like the Duke of Devonshire, was responsible for appointing a number of Anglican ministers. Everyone knew that the baptismal rite of an heir to a title was celebrated as elaborately as that of a prince.

Once their laughter over Mr. Kennedy's proposed solution had died down, Kathleen grew preoccupied with the possibility that she might never see her family again. For the first time Mrs. Kennedy had emerged as an awesome, terrifying force in the family. Kathleen had no idea how far her mother would go to prevent her marriage.

Patsy tried to be reassuring. In her opinion the entire clan would come around as soon as Kick was married. After all, she said, even Honey Fitz's daughter liked titles. Hadn't she secretly delighted in the notion of having a future Duke of Devonshire as a son-in-law?

Meanwhile, however, the family campaign against Fitzwilliam was fully underway. Kathleen had planned to fly to New York the day after seeing Patsy and to set sail shortly afterward for England. While she was at Patsy's, Kick was informed that Eunice had made an appointment for her in New York to see Monsignor Fulton Sheen, the Catholic bishop who had converted Clare Booth Luce. Sheen had obviously been chosen to act as a parental stand-in.

This particular strategy overwhelmed Kathleen. "I just don't want to do it," she repeated. "I don't want to see him."

"Then don't, honey," Patsy declared.

It was nearly two in the morning by that time, but at Patsy's urging Kathleen telephoned the Manhattan rectory and left a message canceling her appointment with the monsignor the following day.

Several days later Kathleen and Elizabeth Cavendish boarded the *Queen Elizabeth*. During the five days at sea Kathleen repeatedly tried to reach Peter by the trans-Atlantic telephone, despite the terrible connection.

Several weeks after Kathleen had returned to London, Mrs. Kennedy appeared at Smith Square, determined to have it out with her daughter alone. She insisted that Kathleen end her relationship with Peter, call off any marriage plans, and return home immediately. Evidently she associated London with all that had gone wrong with her daughter. After reminding Kathleen how God viewed divorce Mrs. Kennedy reiterated all her earlier threats about cutting Kathleen off, financially and otherwise. Kathleen wept helplessly, offering no resistance. Her tears left Mrs. Kennedy unmoved. This was the stance she had always maintained when prodding a recalcitrant child back into line. After four days they were still at an impasse when Mrs. Kennedy left.

Kathleen told her housekeeper she feared her mother would find a way to sabotage her plans.

"You are a twenty-eight-year-old married woman and a British resident," Ilona declared. "How could your mother possibly stop you from marrying?" She had taken a strong dislike to Mrs. Kennedy, whom she considered eerily removed from human concerns. In all her life Ilona had never seen an adult cower before a parent as Kathleen had before her mother.

Kathleen's worst fear was that her mother might turn her brothers and sisters against her. She couldn't bear the thought of never seeing them again. The fight with Mrs. Kennedy had made her realize she might not be able to go through with the marriage without the backing of at least one parent.

A few days later she decided to make a final appeal to her father, whatever the risks of causing a final break between her parents. After all, Mr. Kennedy had not actually forbidden her to marry Peter. His absurd suggestion about Peter's baptism had in fact demonstrated his support. Her father had been the one to send the loving telegram when she had married Billy. In the end he always stood by his children. If only he would agree to meet Peter, she knew he would give the union his blessing.

On the weekend she and Peter intended to spend in Cannes, Mr. Kennedy would be in Paris on a "fact-finding" tour for the Marshall Plan. If they met him there, they would be less likely to be spotted by reporters than in London. It would be easy enough to fly from Cannes to Paris.

Kathleen told Ilona she was going to call her father. Ilona never saw her more radiant than when she announced that he had agreed to the meeting she had suggested. On Saturday, May 15, she and Peter would join him for lunch at the Ritz Hotel.

To strengthen her case, Kathleen asked Janie and her new husband to come to the luncheon. Janie had recently divorced Peter Lindsay and married Max Aitken, an old Eton chum of Peter's. He was also the son of Lord Beaverbrook, one of the few peers who had been a friend of Kennedy's before the war. As a character reference for Peter, Aitken would impress her father.

Kathleen told very few others about her weekend plans. When she confided in Angela Laycock that she would be vacationing with Peter in France, she seemed embarrassed by the obvious implications. "Do you think me awful for going off with a married man?" she asked.

Peter was becoming much less cautious about appearing with Kathleen in public. Several days before their journey she accom-

panied him to the first of the Season's race meetings at Newmarket. That evening they drove to Milton, a Fitzwilliam estate
not far from Newmarket. Peter's cousin Tom occupied a wing of
the house, and Peter periodically dropped by there uninvited on
his way home from the races. When Tom answered the door,
Peter said, "Look, I've got Kick outside. May I bring her in?"

"For God's sake, do," Tom replied. Most of Peter's family
knew all about his wedding plans through Maud Fitzwilliam,
who did not conceal her delight at the prospect of a new wife for
her son.

"Oh, dear God!" Kathleen cried out in mock horror as she
stepped into the entrance hall of the mansion. "Not *another*
huge house!"

"Now, don't worry, Kick," Peter replied. "We'll be living in
Ireland."

During dinner he declared to his cousin, "We're going off to
try to persuade old Kennedy to agree to our getting married."
Then with a laugh he added, "If he objects, I'll go to see the
pope and offer to build him a church."

Fourteen

Peter Fitzwilliam always traveled light. When he arrived at Smith Square on the morning of May 13 to pick up Kathleen, he was amused to find that she had packed two large suitcases containing enough resort wear for at least two weeks and for any kind of weather, although they only expected to be gone for a long weekend.

Kathleen was wearing her going-away outfit—a smart little navy suit worn with pearls. Despite Peter's influence she was still a skirt-and-sweater girl at heart. Gone altogether, however, were the flannel nightgowns of her Washington days; her suitcases contained a blue silk negligee and filmy pink peignoir as well as embroidered camisoles and knickers and black lace garter belts. She had also packed a considerable amount of jewelry—much of it loaned to her by the Devonshires after the robbery. It was understood that she would return these heirlooms if she remarried.

Peter left with her for the airport in a great hurry. They were due to fly at ten thirty and were already behind schedule. "Wish me luck," Kick said to Ilona Solymossy, waving a white-gloved hand in farewell.

"Should I cross my fingers?" Ilona said.

"Yes, both hands," Kick replied.

"I will even cross my feet," the housekeeper said with a laugh.

They arrived a half hour late at Croydon, the airport out-side London where Peter had chartered a DeHavilland Dove twin-engine ten-seater. Arrangements had been made for the air-plane to land in Paris at noon, depart at twelve thirty, then ar-rive in Cannes at three thirty. After an hour stopover the pilot would head back to London.

Before takeoff the pilot, Peter Townshend, noted a squall over the Rhône Valley, an area en route to Cannes that was known for its often violent thunderstorms. Townshend planned to check conditions further during the stopover at Paris. Although bad storms all over the Continent were forecast, he had calculated that there would be enough time to get his passengers to their destination. If the weather worsened around Marseilles, in the south of France, he could always take a different route home. On a recent flight the airplane's undercarriage and two propellers had been damaged, but the repairs had been made and the plane tested to Townshend's satisfaction earlier that morning.

With the late start the Dove arrived at Le Bourget, the Paris airport, at twelve forty-five. After landing, Kathleen and Peter got out, informing Townshend that they would be gone about forty minutes. At the airport Peter decided to telephone some of his Parisian cronies. On impulse he invited them to lunch at the Café de Paris. He was known for orchestrating such im-promptu get-togethers. This time he was eager for Kathleen to meet some members of the French racing set. It would be a festive start to their first weekend alone. He ushered Kick into a taxi, and they set off for Paris without informing Townshend of their change of plans.

Shortly before two Townshend walked over to the meteoro-logical station to collect a weather update. He was handed a chart made up at nine that morning and was warned by the me-teorologists that conditions were worsening over the Rhône Val-ley. A massive thunderstorm with abnormally heavy rainfall was expected at about 5 P.M. Townshend glanced at his watch. They had already fallen an hour and a half behind. The flight from Paris to Cannes took three hours. To avoid the storm, they would have to leave immediately, but his two passengers had not yet returned.

Townshend had trained pilots and flown RAF Liberators during the war. He was accustomed to adhering to schedules planned to the last split second and hated the thought of making alterations in his meticulously worked-out flight plan. But now he realized that he and his radio pilot, Arthur Freeman, might very well get caught in the storm or be grounded in Cannes for the night. Restively he paced back and forth from his plane to the meteorological station. "I'm going to be late," he declared in French to the official on duty. "It's annoying."

For the next hour he kept revising his flight-plan departure time. Moments after he had moved the takeoff forward for the fourth time, Kathleen and Peter, accompanied by their luncheon guests, finally appeared. They were in a gay, carefree mood. Townshend was livid. Because they had been so late getting back, he informed them tersely, they would be flying over the Rhône Valley precisely at the time that a thunderstorm had been predicted. All commercial flights were being canceled. Although private planes could fly in any weather, the meteorological station had advised him not to take off. The flight was now too risky, and he intended to cancel it.

Highly annoyed, Peter began to argue with him. He considered it ludicrous to cancel all plans because of a little rain. Kick had looked forward to the trip so much. If they didn't fly that evening, they would have to call it off entirely. With the plan to meet Mr. Kennedy on Saturday there would be no point at all in leaving for Cannes the following morning. He himself was not at all afraid of a little turbulence. He was so insistent and so charmingly apologetic for having wrecked the schedule that Townshend found himself giving in. At three twenty he started the engines.

The Dove climbed to six thousand feet after takeoff, ascending to nine thousand five hundred feet, the cruising altitude, at Fountainbleau. Despite the altered time and weather conditions Townshend continued to adhere strictly to his original plan, with only two slight corrections to avoid turbulence.

At four fifty Arthur Freeman requested a forecast for Cannes at six thirty, when they expected to be landing. Impatient to make up for all the lost time, Townshend did not have him ask for an update of the conditions over the Ardèche Mountains, where the bad weather was expected.

"Rhône ahead," Freeman announced to the station at Lyons. After receiving the forecast for Cannes, Freeman lost contact with the ground. They were in the region of Vienne, at the edges of the thunderstorm, where atmospheric discharges prevented radio communication. Freeman switched his radio to various frequencies but could pick up nothing. Up until that time Townshend had known exactly where they were, but now without radio or good visibility he could only rely on instinct. Flying blindly through a cloud formation, a pilot could easily mistake a rapid bank sideways for a sudden pull-up, since the physical sensation produced by both—a flattening against the seat—was identical. To level the plane, a pilot in that situation was apt to react by pushing the stick forward, thus forcing an already descending airplane to assume an even sharper dive.

Townshend had remained at an altitude of ten thousand feet, even though, as an experienced pilot, he knew that a tiny craft could pass safely through a thunderstorm only at either a very low or a very high altitude. He may have been waiting for Freeman to manage to make radio contact again before changing his altitude; by law a pilot had to receive permission from ground control before doing so. In dangerous weather conditions, however, a pilot was allowed to change course on his own. From the difficulty Freeman was experiencing Townshend must have known that the thunderstorm was violent; after Valence he could actually see it ahead of him. Perhaps he was waiting to drop down until he had established his exact location. He was unaware that a southeasterly wind had blown the little Dove off course. By remaining at the prearranged altitude he was heading straight into the eye of the storm.

With bad visibility, no radio directions, and all his attention focused on steadying the craft in the turbulence, Townshend passed into the storm cloud. Suddenly the Dove began thrashing wildly. Alternate air currents tossed the little craft thousands of feet in different directions. For twenty minutes Peter and Kathleen endured a terrifying ride. One minute they were thrown against their seats, the next they were forced upward, gasping from the strangulating tug of their seatbelts. They couldn't even hold on to each other because they were at opposite ends of the passenger cabin. To distribute the weight evenly, Townshend had placed Peter in the forwardmost left seat and Kathleen in the last seat to the right.

Desperately Townshend and Freeman tried to regain control. The rain had obscured all visibility. Their instruments spun uselessly. Townshend had no idea whether they were climbing or descending until the plane shot out of the bottom of the cloud and he spotted a mountain ridge a thousand feet away. With the sudden sighting of ground he realized he was in a steep dive and that the plane would crash. Immediately he shoved his stick all the way back to pull out of the dive. The elevator tab that made the plane ascend was controlled by a foot pedal. Probably because it wasn't working properly Freeman abandoned the pedal and pulled directly on the elevator cable itself. Coupled with the stress of the turbulence the sudden change of direction was too much for the little Dove. As it thrust upward the starboard wing tore off. With the sudden loss of balance one engine tore loose, then the other, followed by the tail plane. The fuselage went into a flat spin and plummeted toward a ridge on top of a mountain peak. Townshend and Freeman stuffed handkerchiefs into their mouths, a standard procedure in a crash landing to avoid biting through the tongue. For about ten seconds Peter and Kathleen in their separate seats realized they were probably going to die.

In the midst of the violent storm a farmer named Paul Petit heard a loud racing of engines overhead followed by a sharp, high-speed whistle. As he ran out to investigate the noise he watched in dazed horror as an airplane emerging from a cloud disintegrated in midair. Petit lived alone with several fierce guard dogs in a nine-hundred-year-old red stone farmhouse near the peak of Le Coran, the highest of the Cevennes Mountains in the Ardèche. His father and brother were his only neighbors.

In the fearsome weather Petit and his father scrambled up a serpentine stone trail. On a ridge near the top of the mountain they found the body of the plane, nose down. They managed to pry open one of the doors. Even in the blinding rainstorm they could tell that none of the passengers had survived.

Petit began a slow descent to St. Bauzile, the nearest village. From a coin telephone outside the town bistro he placed a call to the *mairie* and the gendarmerie, telling them of the crash. An hour later several gendarmes, the mayor of the town, and a journalist followed Petit up the mountain to the wreckage. It took them two and a half hours to make the ascent. They looked inside the cabin to check the condition of the victims. The pilot and copilot lay crumpled against the cockpit, their earphones still on. The male passenger was crushed beneath his seat. The only accessible victim was the woman, still fastened by her seatbelt, who lay in a skewed position, her legs broken. In the woman's purse the police found her passport.

In Britain the first reports at 4:30 A.M. announced only that a private British plane had gone down, claiming between four and eight victims. An American passport bearing the name "Lady Hartington" had been found on the single female passenger. Perhaps because there were two Lady Hartingtons, Kathleen and her sister-in-law, Debo, newspapers and wireless broadcasts referred cautiously to the "Lady Hartington Passport Mystery" until a body could be positively identified. In America newsmen checked the passport number and identified Kathleen as the victim.

Eunice Kennedy answered the telephone in Georgetown when a call came after midnight on May 14, from a *Washington Post* reporter. "There's a story here that a Lady Hartington has been killed in an airplane crash. Is that your sister?"

"I'm not sure, I think there are two Lady Hartingtons," Eunice answered falteringly. *Please let it be Debo,* she thought, even if it was a terrible thing to wish.

The reporter said the victim's passport showed "Kathleen" as the Christian name.

"That does sound like my sister," Eunice replied agitatedly. She demanded to know how the reporter had learned about the name on the passport. When she hung up and told Jack of the call, she retained only the faintest hope that there had been some mistake.

Jack immediately got on the phone to Ted Reardon, his executive assistant. Reardon had been Joe's roommate at Harvard and had remained devoted to the family after Joe was killed. He promised to telephone some of his news contacts and check out the story. An hour later Ted called Jack to confirm that his sister was dead.

"Fine, Ted," Jack replied, sounding suddenly exhausted. "Will you come over in the morning and make arrangements for the family?"

Reardon's wife awoke shortly afterward and found her husband staring at an open page of *As We Remember Joe.* He pointed to the photograph at the bottom of Kathleen's entry. It was the single, well-publicized photograph of her wedding. A grinning Joe peered behind Billy in his Coldstream Guards uniform and Kathleen in her makeshift wartime bridal costume. "Imagine," Reardon said, "first Joe, then Billy, then Kathleen. It happened so fast to all three of them."

Joseph Kennedy was asleep at the George Cinq Hotel in Paris when a call came through from America at 6:30 A.M. Kennedy's old friend Joseph Timilty, who was traveling with him, took the call. A reporter from *The Boston Globe,* who had been trying to get through for two hours, notified him of the crash.

Timilty told the reporter to hold on while he woke Kennedy and broke the news. He returned to the telephone a few moments later. Kennedy had been too shocked to speak when told of his daughter's death. Timilty rushed away from the phone to be with him.

Later that morning in St. Bauzile gendarmes extracted the bodies and laid them on makeshift stretchers. The authorities removed all valuables, including Kathleen's pearls and wedding ring; when they could find only one pearl earring, they looked accusingly at M. Petit. A doctor from a nearby village arrived to perform an external examination of the victims. All four had died on impact after suffering massive cuts and bruises to the head. Fitzwilliam was terribly disfigured and one leg was crushed. Freeman's hand was burned and badly cut, with one finger nearly torn off—the result of his last-ditch attempt to pull the elevator cable. As the passenger in the rear Kathleen had suffered the fewest injuries. The right side of her face had a long gash. Along with her legs, her jaw and her pelvis had been crushed when the plane hit the ground.

Petit's hundred-year-old oxcarts lurched down the mountain, carrying the bodies to St. Bauzile. In the *mairie* the bodies were laid in makeshift coffins, then transported that evening to Privas, the largest town in the Ardèche. There they would remain until the nearest of kin could come and identify them. Harry Sporborg was the first among Peter's associates and relatives to be notified of the tragedy. After dispatching Peter's trainer to Privas, Sporborg was faced with the painful task of informing Maud Fitzwilliam that her son and sole heir was dead.

Joseph Kennedy, who told reporters he hoped there had been a mistake in his daughter's identity, spent much of that day traveling to Lyons and down the Rhône River to Privas. When he arrived, the gendarmes escorted him to the *mairie*. Flowers covered the four lead-lined coffins. An official opened one for him. Kennedy gasped and stared unbelievingly at the body inside.

When he called home that evening, he said nothing about Kick's disfiguring wounds. He told the family crowded around the telephone how "beautiful" she had looked. She had been found on her back, as though "asleep," with her shoes gone. Wasn't that just like Kick, who always went around barefoot?

"Kathleen is dead," John White wrote in mournful disbelief in his diary the day the story came over the wire at the *Times-*

Herald office. "It's like a toothache. You forget it for a while." All Kick's friends, on both sides of the Atlantic, were stunned by the horror of the double tragedy. *Oh, dear God,* Patsy had thought while reading a newspaper account of the crash, *that was the trip!* In England, David Ormsby-Gore sped home after hearing a bulletin on his car radio so that he could break the news to Sissy before she heard it on her own. Janie Aiken had been readying herself to leave for Paris.

In Washington it was Reardon who arranged to get Jack and Eunice up to HyannisPort. Overcome with grief, Jack had closeted himself in a back room, admitting only servants delivering trays of food. By evening, when Lady Astor's niece Dinah Brand Fox went over to the Georgetown house, she found Eunice and Jack waiting to fly to Boston. They kept pacing in a tense, scattered way, as though suddenly endowed with a senseless, unchanneled energy.

Glowing eulogies of Kathleen appeared in British newspapers. "No American, man or woman, who has ever settled in England was so much loved as she; and no American ever loved England more," wrote one admirer. ". . . Strangely enough it was those in London who are most disenchanted with this day and age who perhaps derived the greatest comfort and delight from her enchanting personality."

In America, John White was moved to write a special tribute, using the title of Kick's old column, "Did You Happen to See . . . KATHLEEN?"

It is a strange, hard thing to sit at this desk, to tap at this typewriter (your old desk, your old typewriter), to tap out the cold and final word—good-by.

Good-by little Kathleen.

The wires have at last stopped rattling out the details of what happened in France, Thursday, late . . . in the storm. . . .

Kathleen. Little "Kick." Where have you gone? . . .

It seems such a short time ago that you came to the

Times-Herald. Bright, pretty, quick. Vivid. Filled with over-
bubbling enthusiasm, eager, eager to learn everything. The
friendliest little creature in the world, with that compelling
gaiety, that merriment.

Who can weigh or measure the blessing of a high heart?

And you went away to England and married Billy, Marquess of Hartington, and four months later he was killed in
France. And your brother Joe was killed and brother Jack
nearly died in the Pacific.

Do you go agrieving, by the week and by the month?

Nope.

You did not.

When you came through here the other day you were
merrier than even you had ever been.

"Hello-o-oo. It's Kick. What's the sto-o-ory?"

Telephones jangled and there was commotion in the city
room and in the city.

So now a plane goes down.

*Lady Hartington was found stretched on her back and ap-
peared to have been asleep. . . .*

Kathleen, Kathleen. . . .

The column was typeset but finally judged to be too personal
and killed before the evening edition went to press.

After the initial shock wore off, Kathleen's friends were a little
embarrassed for her. How awful that in dying she had been
caught sneaking away for that one weekend with Fitzwilliam. It
seemed so unfair that after so much suffering she could not have
had even that little bit of happiness. British and American newspapers had exercised remarkable restraint in the matter-of-fact
first reports of the crash. They avoided speculation as to why
two unrelated titled citizens were traveling alone together, but
all of London knew to read between the lines.

Her body lay in state for several days in St. Philippe du
Roule, a Catholic church in Paris, after being transported from

Privas. A nun of the Order of the Sisters of Hope watched over the bier, which was covered in purple brocade and banked with red, white, and pink roses. Mr. Kennedy stayed in Paris with the coffin until arrangements could be made for the funeral. Whenever questioned by the press about his daughter's burial, Mr. Kennedy replied dazedly, "I have no plans, no plans." For days Kathleen's final resting place remained undecided. The Devonshires finally pointed out that even though Kathleen had been planning to marry someone else, she had died, after all, as Billy's widow. Since she had so loved England, she herself would probably have chosen to be buried in the family plot near Chatsworth. They left the decision up to Mr. Kennedy. To their surprise the ambassador acceded without argument.

The death of the eighth Earl Fitzwilliam was a terrible blow to Rotherham, particularly since he had left no heir. On May 19 the casket was slowly driven along the straight gravel stone path from Wentworth to the twelfth-century church, built in memory of one of Peter's ancestors. Peter's body was laid beside the tomb of his father, who had died just four years earlier. It was Maud Fitzwilliam, not Obby, who made the funeral arrangements.

On May 20 Protestant nobility and important members of the British government crowded into the high Jesuit Mass sung for Kathleen at Farm Street. The only Kennedy present was her father. The rest of the family had stayed in HyannisPort, holding a small memorial to which only a few close friends were invited. After the Mass in London some two hundred of Kathleen's friends crowded into a special train and accompanied the coffin to Derbyshire. Employees and tenants of the estate lined the streets as the procession made its way through a private entrance of Chatsworth to the quiet graveyard behind the Edensor church, where the Bishop of Nottingham conducted a short service.

Mr. Kennedy looked on as the Catholic priest prayed for his daughter in the burial grounds of a notoriously anti-Catholic family. He appeared awkward in the company of his daughter's friends—the grown children of many of those who had ostracized him ten years earlier. Among the wreaths that covered the casket was one with a handwritten note from his old enemy, Winston Churchill.

As the coffin was lowered into the ground Kennedy, standing by the foot of the grave, put his arms around Ilona Solymossy and her sister. Afterward, without so much as a nod of acknowledgment toward the Duke and Duchess of Devonshire or the priest, he turned away from the grave site, leading the two sisters toward his car. As they walked he enlisted their help in determining which of the possessions in Smith Square were to be returned to Billy's family.

Kathleen's father had left all the details of the funeral to the Duke and Duchess of Devonshire. He'd even neglected to pay the priest who served the Mass. It was the duchess who finally thought up the epitaph for Kathleen's tombstone:

JOY SHE GAVE   JOY SHE HAS FOUND

Kennedy sailed home the following day, remaining in his cabin for most of the voyage. When the ship docked in New York, Joseph Dineen, one of Kennedy's cortege of friendly reporters, accompanied him for a stroll around the deck. Dineen tried to divert him from his brooding silence. "What do you think of the Marshall Plan now that you've looked over the ground? Have you changed your mind?"

Mr. Kennedy didn't even seem to hear him. "It's no use, Joe," he said finally. "Nothing means anything anymore."

But something did still matter a great deal to Joe Kennedy: the public image of the family now that Jack was moving forward with his political plans. The rude facts of the airplane crash did not square at all with the image Mr. Kennedy had been shaping over the years; a God-fearing convent-school girl did not fly off alone with a married man to the French Riviera.

Before he left Privas, he had been given Kathleen's luggage. In among her effects were a family photograph album, a set of rosary beads, and a douche.

After holding off for a few days the American press finally

began asking questions about why Kathleen and Fitzwilliam had been together. Instinctively employees of the Kennedys and the Fitzwilliams had entered into a conspiracy of silence. To protect the memory of her beloved young mistress, Ilona Solymossy, whose telephone rang incessantly with calls from reporters, finally came up with the story that Kathleen had been headed on a trip to meet her father when her old "friend" Earl Fitzwilliam had offered to give her a lift. Although she did not go into the nature of the "friendship" between Lady Hartington and Lord Fitzwilliam, she told herself that she wasn't really lying because no one ever specifically asked. Members of both families adopted Ilona's initial premise and elaborated on it.

The first story broke in the New York *Daily News,* which was published by Kennedy's old crony, Joseph Patterson, who had been the one to suggest that Mrs. Kennedy be hospitalized to avoid having to answer the press's questions about Kathleen's marriage. It was headlined "Chance Invite Sends Kennedy Girl to Death." According to this account Kathleen, who had just returned from America two days before, had planned to meet her father in the south of France but had been unable to get a seat aboard a train or airline on such short notice. In the Ritz Hotel in London, the story went on, she "casually encountered" Lord and Lady Fitzwilliam. Hearing of her plans, Fitzwilliam had offered her a seat in the private plane he had chartered to visit "racehorse breeders in France." Fitzwilliam's secretary was quoted as saying that "Lady Hartington was an old friend of both Lady and Lord Fitzwilliam's. She had been delighted with the offer of a lift."

The *Daily News* story was widely reprinted. No reporter ever investigated why Kick was traveling to the south of France to meet her father, who was in Paris, or whether or not Fitzwilliam actually had stables near the Riviera (he didn't). If any reporters did make inquiries, their findings never made it into print. The "chance meeting" at the Ritz became the official explanation for Kathleen's flight to Cannes with a married man.

Subsequent features on the crash embroidered on the fiction. In describing Kathleen's place of death one story noted that she had studied at the convent school in Neuilly ("She knew and loved well the French countryside where she met death"), giving her final destination religious overtones. Several reports placed the entire family at the Derbyshire burial, while another had Mr. Kennedy implying that he had seen Kathleen in Paris before her death.

The purpose of the trip continued to puzzle many people. Those few who knew that the couple were meeting up with Mr. Kennedy wondered whether they had headed for Cannes in the storm after frantically looking for him in Paris without success. Some had heard they had been en route to Italy to request a special dispensation from the pope. That rumor probably started from a news report maintaining that Kennedy had come to Paris from Rome, where he had had a papal audience. Lady Astor was convinced that the crash had been engineered by Vatican agents, who were trying to prevent another sacrilegious union.

Catholics finally came to accept a romantic version—that Kathleen and Peter were rushing off to elope on a passionate and doomed impulse. Some even believed that that kind of unspeakable act could bring about a sudden violent death. Poetic as the image might have been, that version didn't really make sense. Lovers running off to marry might act recklessly. But even the most reckless lovers wouldn't head off in a tiny twin-engine ten-seat airplane into a raging thunderstorm, fully knowing that bad weather had swept the Continent and that all other flights had been canceled.

Some of Kick's friends who had disapproved of Peter decided that she would have come to her senses when actually confronted with the prospect of marrying him. Charlotte Harris thought it was probably better that Kick had died with Fitzwilliam rather than living the rest of her life in terrible guilt over breaking with the Church and her family. When one of Peter's friends bemoaned the gruesome senselessness of the tragedy, a companion replied, "I think that's an awful lot of nonsense. They were very much in love with each other, and they were both killed together. I think that's a very good way to die."

Evelyn Waugh blamed himself for Kathleen's death because of

certain advice he had given her one evening over dinner. Years
later, in delivering an unsolicited sermon to the Catholic Clarissa
Churchill for marrying Anthony Eden outside the Church, he
would use Kathleen's story as an object lesson:

> An American Catholic girl married outside the Church
> because she was in love with a man under orders for the
> front. It caused great scandal. . . . Then she was widowed,
> repented & was received back. She asked me what she
> should have done and I said: 'If you want to commit adul-
> tery or fornication & can't resist, do it, but realize what you
> are doing, and dont give the final insult of apostasy'. Well
> the girl followed my advice next time & was killed eloping.
> So my advice isn't, wasn't much help.

Rose Kennedy made just one connection—between the presence of the married man in the airplane and the state of Kathleen's soul. Right after the funeral Mrs. Kennedy mailed out to
Kick's British and American friends a small printed Mass card
with the last studio portrait of Kathleen and a prayer. The
prayer was supposed to be a plenary indulgence, applicable to
souls in purgatory, if said before a crucifix after Holy Communion. Many English Protestant friends of Kick's were stunned by
what they viewed as the bad taste of the gesture. Even the most
bigoted among them considered Kick an exemplary Irish Catholic. It was preposterous to think that someone like her would
need years of prayer to escape damnation. After reading the card
one old acquaintance ripped it up in a fit of rage.

The summer of the year that Kathleen died, Jack Kennedy
went to England. During his stay he stopped in to see Ilona
Solymossy, whom he had met in 1947. He tried to draw out of
her every last recollection of his sister. At the end of the visit,
as though he'd just divulged his darkest secret, he announced
with finality, "We will not mention her again." Twenty-three-
year-old Bobby Kennedy, who came to see Ilona a month later,
similarly asked about his sister and made the same declaration
before he left.

As the years went on the rest of the Kennedy family rarely spoke of Kick in public or made any gestures toward keeping alive her memory. There was no privately printed commemorative book written for her, as there would be in turn for every male in the family who died. Mr. and Mrs. Kennedy erected no buildings and set up no foundations or scholarships in her honor, as they would for their three dead sons. In 1952 the family donated three hundred thousand dollars toward the building of a gymnasium in Kathleen's name at Manhattanville College in Purchase, New York. It was the Catholic college attended by Mrs. Kennedy and her younger girls. At Manhattanville, Ethel Skakel and Joan Bennett would meet Pat and Jean Kennedy, by whom they would be introduced to their future husbands, Bobby and Teddy. Kathleen had never gone to Manhattanville, or any other Catholic college for that matter.

When Bobby Kennedy's eldest daughter was born in 1951, he decided to name her Kathleen Hartington Kennedy. The family had only one stipulation: that she never be referred to as "Kick."

The Duke of Devonshire had died two years after Kathleen's death while engaged in one of his favorite pastimes, chopping wood. A decade later, when Jack Kennedy was elected President, he invited Andrew and Debo, the new Duke and Duchess of Devonshire, to attend his inauguration. On a trip to Ireland during his presidency he took a detour to Kathleen's grave in Edensor. After leaving the cemetery Jack paid his respects to Ilona, who was employed at Chatsworth. True to his vow of a decade and a half earlier, he did not bring up his sister's name.

Once Jack had achieved the presidency, the official Kennedy literature designated Kathleen only as "the sister who died in a plane crash." Her marriage outside the Church was always played down or included with an explanation of the pressures of wartime. Occasionally the family implied that Billy and Kathleen had not settled on the religion in which they would bring up their children. Because of her involvement with the Red Cross it came to be assumed that Kathleen, like her husband, had died during the war. To one newsman, a friend of the family's, Rose Kennedy once matter-of-factly characterized Kathleen as the only one of her nine children eager to leave home.

After Jack and Bobby were assassinated, Kathleen was simply listed as one of the four children lost by the tragedy-prone family. (The tragedy of Kathleen's death seemed to pale beside the violent deaths of the two younger brothers and what turned out to be the senseless heroism of Joe Jr. when it was discovered years later that the launching site he was to blow up had been abandoned months before his fatal mission.) The "chance meeting" story remained unchallenged and made its way into biography after biography, along with information about Kathleen's "gift of faith" and the lengthy "retreat" she made after Billy's death. In her autobiography, *Times to Remember,* Rose Kennedy reversed her daughter's destination and wrote that Kick and a "few friends," returning from a holiday on the Riviera, were en route to meet Mr. Kennedy in Paris when their plane crashed.

Those few who had known about Peter Fitzwilliam wondered over the years what effect Kathleen's death had had on the relationship between her parents and whether they carried any guilt over it. But it was understood that Kathleen was to remain a closed subject in the Kennedy household. Charlotte and many of the old circle particularly knew not to talk about Kick in front of her mother.

But on one occasion a year or so after Kathleen died, Mrs. Kennedy herself brought up her daughter's name. Dinah Fox had come to visit the family in Palm Beach. All the young Kennedys were out, and Dinah had found herself alone with Mrs. Kennedy for the evening. Dinah's presence evidently stirred up memories for Mrs. Kennedy—memories of Kick and those extravagant days they had all shared long ago in Prince's Gate before the war. Once she had begun talking about her daughter, she seemed unable to stop. "You know, I really *adored* Kathleen," she declared a number of times. "Where did her life go?" she asked in pained bewilderment at one point in the evening.

Dinah thought it was as though Mrs. Kennedy needed to know not simply why Kick's life had ended so senselessly but why she had lost her, years before she died.

Y
—